GW00633899

DENTIST IMPERIAL

by

MARY BAKER

Copyright © Mary Baker 2011

Dentist Imperial

ISBN: 978-0-9554618-3-5

The right of Mary Baker to be identified as the author of this work has been asserted by her in accordance with the Copyright, Designs and Patents Act 1988.
All rights reserved

No part of this publication may be reproduced, stored in a retrieval system, or transmitted in any form or by any means, without the prior permission in writing of the publisher, nor be otherwise circulated in any form of binding or cover other than that in which it is published and without a similar condition, including this
condition, being imposed on the subsequent purchaser.

A CIP catalogue record of this book can be obtained from the British Library

Published in Great Britain by
Cam Publications

Printed in England by Witley Press Limited

Cover design by Anthony Thompson

Dedicated to the memory of Dr Thomas W Evans 1823—1897 who would have disapproved of this book, especially as the two volumes of his memoirs *Recollections of the Second French Empire* were the primary source of information.

Also by Mary Baker

1

It was lucky that Dr Brewster — the celebrated Dr Cyrus S Brewster — had written to warn Evans, his new assistant, of the primitive conditions still existing in Europe, despite the scientific advances in that most scientifically advanced of centuries, the nineteenth. However, the American pioneering spirit cannot be daunted, even by Paris.

"Well, Thomas, it's no Philadelphia," said Mrs Evans, as they were jolted over rough roads and down muddy lanes in a cab whose driver and horse believed in ambling rather than trotting briskly through the city. "We'll just have to make the best of it."

"I fully intend to," declared Evans, ready to tackle any challenge Europe could hurl at him.

For thirty years, Dr Brewster had staunchly flown the flag for America: on a pole below a second-floor window of his house. The Stars and Stripes fluttered in the breeze, flapped in the wind and dripped rain onto the heads of patients when they apprehensively approached the building for their appointments. In that dark narrow street of dark narrow houses, Dr Brewster had gone from middle-aged adventurer to elderly cynic, as he attempted to force the civilized benefits of New World skill and technology onto the backward wilds of Europe.

It was the mid-nineteenth century when Dr Thomas W Evans arrived to carry on the Brewster mission. Filthy slums, labyrinthine streets, stinking alleys, decayed tenements, and a distressing lack of plumbing: that was Paris. The French seemed not to have heard of the advantages to be gained from the great American invention of town planning, and had just let the place grow anyhow for centuries, without the slightest effort at efficiency. And what was worse, they apparently liked their city in all its squalor. They seemed not to notice that it was squalid.

"Boil the water," Brewster decreed. "It comes straight from the Seine, and what goes into the Seine, I refuse to discuss in mixed company and before a meal." Brewster was over seventy, but years of confronting and outmanoeuvring unco-operative patients had kept him lithe and vigorous. If the French had been unable to defeat him, even at his age, they stood no chance at all against the young Thomas Wiltberger Evans.

The year was 1848, and the French had decided to follow the splendid American lead, organize a revolution, and get rid of a king. Again. According to Evans, they ought to have been more strong-minded first time around, but the French dithered so. They had allowed their noble Republic to degenerate into an empire under Napoleon, and the moment things got a little awkward, it was back to the Bourbons and Louis XVIII. That experience should have taught everyone a lesson, but no; along came Charles X, to make Louis look fairly moderate. A revolution solved the problem of King Charles, but then the French went into another dither. Freedom or subservience? The Republican Party demanded an elected head of state, while the Monarchists held out for a crown. A compromise ended the stalemate; the French elected a king, and congratulated themselves on their reasoning. However, it quickly became obvious, even to them, that Louis-Philippe was impossible. From the very first state occasion, the citizen-royal had insisted on carrying an umbrella, and despite ministerial advice, despite cartoons in the foreign press, the man clung to his brolly. The French would argue to their last breath in defence of an individual's right to personal freedom, and indeed many of the populace freely admitted to owning an umbrella, but the day that Louis-

Philippe appeared in public with a red umbrella whilst wearing a blue coat, the nation could take no more. There was, of course, an immediate revolution, a new republic formed, and that great democrat, Louis-Napoleon Bonaparte, nephew of the Emperor Napoleon, was elected President of the Second Republic. Things were looking up, in Evans's opinion. There was hope, even for Europeans, when they had the sense to be guided by America.

"I won't retire until you've settled in, Evans," said Brewster.

"I'm ready to start work straight away," Evans declared eagerly. He was twenty-four, inclined to plumpness, which made him seem shorter than he actually was, and nobody looking at the brown-haired, plain-faced Evans could have realized that they saw a man whose name would live on for centuries. Even his own father, a retired clerk of moderate means and large family, had not understood the destiny that called to his youngest son.

"But what's wrong with being a lawyer?" Evans *père* demanded in exasperation. "All right, so they're swindling vultures, and I'd make sure that your grandmother's silver spoons were locked away before I let a lawyer anywhere near the house, but at least they know how to get their hands on some cash."

"Man doesn't live by bread alone," decreed Evans *fils*, "which is just as well, as biting on a hard crust can have disastrous consequences for the teeth." All great men have overcome opposition, and Evans did it by ignoring his father's advice entirely. Besides, no part of the Constitution forbad dentists from making a dollar or two along the way, so in vain was Tom urged to apprentice himself to a merchant, if the law held no attraction. Thomas W Evans had higher ideals, and the strength of mind to live up to them.

"There's plenty of work to be done here in Paris," Brewster

3

informed Evans. "The American Legation relies on me, and they wouldn't have a tooth left between them, if I'd abandoned them to French dentists. Diplomacy would be at a standstill."

"It's that bad?" said Evans, in astonishment.

"The Dark Ages of dentistry," replied Brewster. "A pair of pliers in one hand, a bucket for the blood in the other, and a Frenchman calls himself a dentist."

"Appalling!"

If Evans thought that he had never heard anything so terrible, worse was about to be revealed to him, as Brewster continued, "And should you have to make a house call on a French patient, don't be surprised to find yourself sent around to the tradesman's entrance and expected to use the back stairs."

"Like a grocer or a tailor?" demanded Evans. "I'm a professional man, a graduate of Jefferson College, and as an American, I'd give my life in defence of equality, equality for all. The holder of a Jefferson College Dental Diploma is the equal of anybody who goes through a front door. I'm not a knife grinder or a delivery boy."

"This is France, Evans."

"I don't care if it's benighted Britain. Nobody tells me to go to a side door. I scorn dictatorship and tyranny. Have the French never heard of liberty?"

It was all very well for Dr Brewster to talk about following French customs; the French would have to learn some new customs, should they want the services of Dr Thomas Wiltberger Evans because he was a democrat, without the slightest prejudice against anybody. Duke, lord or king, he was determined to treat them as equals, and for such a lofty principle, there are times in life when you have to take a stand against injustice, exactly as Evans's grandfather had

4

done when he faced the British at Mullin's Pond. Not perhaps the most celebrated American victory in the War of Independence, but every little helps, and the spirit of Mullin's Pond lived on in Thomas W Evans. He was as sympathetic to the plight of suffering humanity as the next dentist, but there could only be one possible response for a democratic republican when ordered by a servant to go around to the tradesman's entrance.

"—and you can tell your master from me that he'll remain in agony, as far as I'm concerned," Evans shouted, while the front door closed in his face. "Jefferson College alumni don't go around to a tradesman's entrance, like pedlars."

Anyone would have thought that American dentists were in the habit of murdering their wives and burying them in coal cellars, fumed Evans as he stamped angrily down the road. If the French wanted painless — well, comparatively painless — dentistry and the very latest scientific knowledge, they had to treat an American dentist as he had the right to be treated. With respect. With deference. With esteem. To be precise, with equality. No welcoming front door, and even the siren-song of a gumboil could not entice Evans to enter the premises, so strong was his resolve. All freedom fighters must make sacrifices for their cause, and Evans was not the dentist to flinch from his duty.

Those early days, living among the unenlightened French, brought Evans close to despair because Europeans treated their teeth so casually, only prepared to acknowledge that they had some when things went wrong. Regular check-ups were unknown, toothbrushes neglected and dental hygiene considered obsessive behaviour. The whole-hearted American devotion to teeth was simply not there, and when a Gallic mouth opened, Evans prepared to shudder at the sight within

5

"The French don't deserve to have any teeth," Evans declared bitterly. "You won't believe this, Agnes, but I actually saw a man in a restaurant shoveling dates into his mouth, literally cramming them in, without first checking carefully to make sure all the stones had been removed. I expected to see his teeth shatter to bits before my very eyes after such foolhardiness."

"Most irresponsible." However, pretty fair-haired Agnes Doyle Evans, with the straight American teeth that had captivated her husband, was less troubled by the wild conduct of the reckless French. Unlike Thomas, she adapted to situations, rather than expecting them to adapt to her. Back home in Philadelphia, Agnes's mother always said that Aggie was born sensible, and only once in her life had Aggie been temporarily sidetracked from that usual good sense. At eighteen, she began calling herself Clarissa, and fell in love at first glance with the devastatingly handsome Ezekiel Mortimer Qualthrop, a kind and generous young man, who unfortunately remained unaware of the existence of either Aggie or Clarissa. She knew that he, a son of the celebrated Qualthrop's Pickled Limes empire, was almost certain to marry one of the richer Philadelphia heiresses, but that knowledge could not lessen the blow when he did. Agnes was in her early twenties by then, and sound commonsense, left simmering on a backburner for three years, boiled over into her life. She was getting no younger and no prettier. Did she want to remain the unmarried daughter at home, helping out in the family store and devoting her days to parents who regarded the single state as dismal failure, or should she marry the plain and stout Thomas Wiltberger Evans, a newly qualified dentist, short on stature and money, but big on ambition? Marriage to Evans would mean the end of all her secret hopes, but even if Ezekiel Mortimer Qualthrop's

6

wealthy bride did perish in a tragic coaching accident or a tragic shipwreck or a tragic anything, he was unlikely to turn to the Doyle family in search of the second Mrs Qualthrop. Agnes married Evans. As her mother said, Aggie was born sensible.

"You can't blame the French for their lack of knowledge," Agnes said charitably. "They haven't had our advantages, Thomas, our liberty and progress; not to mention the Founding Fathers, the Constitution, and Wells Fargo."

"That's no excuse for wantonly risking teeth," declared Evans. "If the American Legation staff weren't in such dire need of me, I'd pack up and go home tomorrow. Today, if I didn't have that ulcerated tongue to look at."

But destiny had other plans for Thomas W Evans.

Dr Brewster thankfully said goodbye to his French problems, and returned to that happy land of freedom and front doors. The Paris house he left behind him was dark, with small rooms and narrow passageways that stubbornly refused to look like an American home, despite the honour of having a Stars and Stripes draped proudly over every fireplace. Mrs Evans did her best, but the house stayed defiantly continental, and even a picture of the patriarch of modern American dentistry, Dr Romulus J Hinkle, suffered the indignity of being mistaken for a portrait of the Emperor Napoleon in one of his more belligerent moods, while a drawing of the Liberty Bell, intended to inspire the Legation staff with patriotic fervour while they waited, made them think of Notre Dame instead, and all Paris knew that Victor Hugo had been forced to cut the chapter about Quasimodo's sadistic dentist, after the printer fainted clean away while setting up the type. As for the sketch of the signing of the Declaration of Independence, everybody assumed it was something to do with one of the many Treaties of Amiens.

Coming to France would have seemed a terrible mistake to Evans, were it not for the fact that he never made mistakes. From earliest boyhood, he had always been right, and had no intention of doubting himself, merely because an entire country was out of step with him. He knew his duty to those American Legation mouths, and was confident that he could find plenty of work inside them, even if French front doors obstinately refused to admit him. No other dentist in France was better qualified; in fact, no other dentist in France was qualified at all, according to Evans, as only the Jefferson Medical College could turn out the correct product, complete with that crucial Dental Diploma. It did not matter how scurrilously the French treated him, he had determination enough for twenty Jefferson-trained dentists, and when opportunity finally knocked with some urgency on the door, Thomas W Evans was ready to take his place in history.

****

Gustave Farjon had only started his new job the previous week, and it was his first important assignment. Under normal circumstances, he was everything that could be required of a young clerk, with his sleek black hair and sleek black clothes, but that day he was breathless, hat awry, coat unbuttoned and gloves forgotten. Emergency, thought Evans with his usual astuteness.

"Dr Brewster must come to the Elysée at once, this very minute, this very second —"

"The Elysée!" exclaimed Evans. But perhaps the man just meant a house in the Elysée Palace area. All the same, it was a cut above the usual addresses.

"It's an emergency. Get Dr Brewster immediately."

"He isn't here. Dr Brewster retired weeks ago, and went back home to the States."

8

"He can't have!" gasped Farjon, looking desperate. His very first mission, and he had failed to secure its objective, failed miserably. "The President himself told me that I had to get the American dentist."

At destiny's call, Evans was ready. "I'm an American dentist. I'll see President Bonaparte."

"But he said that it had to be Dr Brewster," Farjon protested.

"Well, it's Dr Thomas W Evans or nobody, if he wants an American dentist. That, or catch the next boat for New York." In the States, the situation would be called a seller's market.

As a civil servant, Farjon disliked being forced to use his initiative, but surely the wrong American dentist was better than no American dentist at all. Farjon wavered, knowing that he did not have time to debate the question fully with himself. "Oh — all right. But hurry! President Bonaparte's in agony, absolute agony."

"There's one thing that the President has to understand though," Evans said firmly. "I go through the front door of the Palace."

"The front —?" Farjon looked blank. He was a very junior bureaucrat, who had as yet received no training on the subject of front doors and so remained unaware of the vital significance of their rôle in life.

"Yes, the front door. The first sign of any tradesman's entrance and the deal's off. And should I have to go up any stairs, they must be the front stairs. If not, the President stays in agony. Take it or leave it."

Farjon took it. He also had to take a detailed lecture on the history and status of Jefferson College, but Evans went triumphantly through the front door of the Elysée Palace. It was a proud and historic moment in the fight for equality, justice and dentistry. It was also, when storming French front

9

doors, an excellent one to begin with.

Louis-Napoleon Bonaparte, nephew of a famous uncle, had made two less successful attempts to storm that very same front door, via the long-established European custom of *coup d'état*. Impatient to bridge the gap that lay between him and the Elysée Palace, Louis-Napoleon had tried, in both Strasbourg and Boulogne, to rally the local Army garrisons behind him by announcing that he was ready and eager to take over the country, but on both occasions he had been thwarted by the apathy of an ungrateful French populace, who neglected to start an immediate revolution that would sweep him into absolute power. Despite his Bonaparte surname, Louis-Napoleon was then forced to acknowledge the democratic process, and he grudgingly condescended to be a Presidential candidate in the newly-founded Republic's election. Louis-Napoleon owed his victory to French nostalgia for departed days that few of them could remember with much accuracy, and to being someone's nephew. He had been someone's son as well, but nobody seemed to notice, with Uncle Napoleon permanently blocking out the sunshine and blighting Louis-Napoleon's whole existence. Any man with an uncle who had conquered Europe faced problems beyond those of the common run of nephews, for such a nephew could hardly drift into accountancy or manufacturing, when the family business was quite clearly pillage and plunder; but after Uncle Napoleon failed his relatives at Waterloo, there was nothing for a conscientious nephew to do except wait in the wings until a suitable moment arrived when he could stride out into the political limelight and assume his rightful rôle as autocratic ruler of the French. Of course, to be elected a mere President was practically an insult to a member of a family unaccustomed to limitations on power, and nobody could describe a President's restricted term in office as any sort of job security, but Louis-Napoleon graciously consented to lower his standards and start his career on the bottom rung of the Head of State ladder. It went annoyingly against the Bonaparte tradition to compromise, a pastime reserved for lesser men, and he was already sensitive about the fact that he did not in the least resemble his uncle. There was no brooding Corsican intensity in Louis-Napoleon. He looked French, with his plain face, dark hair and small, waxed moustache: a noticeably apprehensive Frenchman, as Evans was announced.

"I don't need a dentist," President Bonaparte declared, as he headed towards his office's open door and safety. "The pain's completely vanished. Sorry to have troubled you, but I'm much too busy to see anyone today. I haven't a moment to spare."

Five years of dentistry had taught Evans to be quick on his feet, and the door was closed before the President could make his escape. "Of course you're busy, sir, but an examination won't take a minute," Evans said so confidently that it almost sounded as though he were telling the truth.

"Less than a minute?" The President hesitated.

"I know that even a minute lost is a minute owed to France," conceded Evans. "But think how much more time will be lost, unless your agony is relieved by the very latest scientific knowledge, direct from Philadelphia, the home of Jefferson College, that citadel of progressive thinking and excellence in dentistry."

"I've heard dentists in America have special instruments that don't hurt," said Bonaparte, with the true politician's reluctance to commit himself to a definite course of action.

"Dentistry's an extremely advanced science in my country," remarked Evans, employing the very finest Jefferson College evasiveness technique, acquired only after

11

many semesters of diligent study.

"Well —all right —as long as you're sure it won't hurt."

"Mr President," said Evans, lifting his large black case onto Bonaparte's desk, "with my American skill, I can guarantee that, when I start work, you won't even be aware you've got teeth."

It was no exaggeration. One look at the rows of gleaming instruments inside the black case, and President Bonaparte had collapsed in a heap on the floor. An unconscious patient was always preferable in Evans's experience, as his job became so much more enjoyable without any of that hysterical struggling, wildly aimed blows and screaming. An insensible Bonaparte meant that all was speed and efficiency; the problem detected and solved in seconds with a nimble-fingered wielding of pliers, while Evans hummed a snatch of *The Star-Spangled Banner*.

It was the start of a relationship destined to last for over twenty years. Evans thought of it more as a friendship; Bonaparte did not.

2

After the Elysée's palatial splendour, the return to everyday life, particularly in the cramped gloominess of the ex-Brewster residence, was a decided anti-climax. Instinctively, Evans knew he belonged in that other world, where men of achievement, men of power, men like him, took decisions that could affect people for the rest of their lives. He had always known that he was preordained to become a leader of his profession, and leaders were required to support each other.

"When I revived him, the President didn't remember a thing," Evans told his wife, as they ate dinner. Agnes had already heard the minutiae of his story, but Evans was determined not to deprive her of a second opportunity to appreciate every detail. "And I assured Bonaparte that the swelling would go down. Given time."

"If he stands with the light behind him, nobody will notice a thing," said Mrs Evans, always prompt with level-headed advice. "And I'm sure it'll be possible for him to avoid portrait painters meanwhile."

"When I left the Palace, I went out by the front door," Evans added proudly. "I chanced to mention front doors to the President, and he told me to leave any way I liked. 'Just go' were his exact words. A true democrat. Practically American. Although he'd never get himself elected in the States with those teeth. They've been totally misunderstood by all the so-called dentists he's ever had the misfortune to consult. You wouldn't want to see the devastation wrought inside that mouth."

"I'm unlikely to get the opportunity," commented Mrs Evans, bearing her deprivation with fortitude.

"A man shouldering President Bonaparte's responsibilities

must have teeth that he can rely on," declared Evans. "Look at his uncle's downfall. Entirely caused by untrustworthy teeth."

"I thought the Emperor Napoleon simply lost a battle."

"But why did he lose that battle?" demanded Evens, his answer ready. "Because on the morning of Waterloo, that very morning, the Emperor Napoleon was in such agonies of toothache, he couldn't even sit on a horse to survey the battlefield. Of course, his Generals had to invent an excuse for the apparent neglect of duty, but Jefferson College's Faculty saw through the ruse. The total course of European history was decided by inadequate French dentistry."

"Well, teeth won't be the cause of President Bonaparte's Waterloo: not with you around, Thomas."

"No," agreed Evans. "I shall insist on regular appointments, daily if necessary, for the sake of Europe. He's very self-sacrificing though. When I told the President that I'd see him first thing tomorrow, Bonaparte said no, I'd be sent for should he ever need my services again. And when I informed him that with those teeth, there was no 'should' about it, he said he was too busy to discuss the matter. Such a sense of duty. Even his teeth come second to France."

"No wonder," remarked Mrs Evans. "There's an election in a couple of months."

****

That same election, with its threat of misguided voters evicting him from the Elysée Palace, had been much on President Bonaparte's mind. With an uncle renowned for conquering Europe and a father who had been King of Holland, albeit in a temporary capacity, it was hard for Louis-Napoleon to content himself with a mere fleeting glimpse of power. Democracy was all very well, but it did rather limit a

Bonaparte's horizon.

"Just anybody could be voted in at the next election," said the President, slumping over his office desk in despair. "He might be totally incompetent or a ruthless dictator, and what will happen to France when this incompetent dictator ruthlessly stages a *coup d'état* and grabs absolute power, I shudder to think."

"We're all shuddering right there with you." A born-again republican, the new Minister of War was a sympathetic listener to any Presidential problem, but especially to those problems that seemed to requite a martial answer. General Saint-Arnaud was an enthusiastic warrior, proud of having kept his youthful looks and figure, although he did not blame the President in the least for being short and stout, the unfortunate side of a Bonaparte inheritance, but the General could not help reflecting that the Saint-Arnaud shape was in every way superior, particularly when accompanied by an air of aristocratic grace, despite the democratic times forced onto France. "We'll probably end up with some unknown civilian as the next President, a panic-stricken nonentity who won't take a proper interest in the war."

"What war?" asked Bonaparte. "Nobody told me we were at war."

"Well, technically, we're not fighting anybody at this precise second, but hostilities are bound to start somewhere sooner or later, because they always do. As a matter of fact, you could declare war today, if you felt like it. A President only has to decide that the Republic's in mortal danger, and he can order the Army to commence shooting the enemy without further ado."

"That sounds reasonable enough," said Bonaparte. "And the Republic *is* in mortal danger."

"Terrific!" exclaimed Saint-Arnaud, a General who enjoyed

great job satisfaction. "Who's the enemy? Prussia? England? Austria? We're ready, sir, whichever foe you care to choose."

"I'm glad you agree with me on this point," said Louis-Napoleon, beginning to realize the advantages of having an army at his beck and call. "It's such a comfort to know that I can ask you and your men to stand with me in the defence of our beleaguered Republic."

"Oh, you don't have to ask the men a thing, sir. We never do. We simply shoot them if they don't obey our orders."

"That would certainly speed up a lot of Government business," admitted Bonaparte. "Military rule is so efficient. If I wanted to shoot somebody at the moment, I'd be forced to appoint a committee to look into the matter, and then wait five or six years for the paperwork to be completed. All the fun would have gone out of it by that time."

"Your Uncle Napoleon never bothered with committees."

"But he was an emperor, and an emperor can have committees guillotined when they won't agree with him; a simple, yet effective, way of cutting down on bureaucracy. Oh, if only France could be an empire again." Bonaparte paused to sigh wistfully, glancing at Saint-Arnaud to gauge his reaction.

A successful General becomes even more successful by spotting which way the wind is blowing, and making sure that he leans in the appropriate direction. Saint-Arnaud spoke slowly, but his thoughts were gathering speed. "Because of the danger to the Republic — because of that dictator ruthlessly determined to seize absolute power after the next election —"

"You think a new emperor is essential? To protect the Republic?"

"Definitely," replied Saint-Arnaud, delighted to reveal himself as a team player. "We need an emperor to safeguard our liberty, our equality, and our what-not."

"As Minister of War, that's how you perceive the situation?"

"Categorically perceived."

"Then I have no choice," declared the President. "It's clearly my duty to remain in office permanently. For the sake of the Republic."

"Absolutely. Long live the Republic! Long live the Emperor! Long live our new Napoleon! This'll show Europe that France is back in business again."

"But some of the Deputies are so resistant to progress. They might make trouble."

"They can't, if they're all in jail on treason charges. Leave everything to me. I'm ready and eager — and especially eager to get that Finance Minister under lock and key. The clerks in his department write the most impertinent letters, and he won't do a thing to stop them. A man's financial affairs are his own business; I don't care what anyone says."

"I can think of a few journalists who richly deserve a treason charge as well," said Bonaparte, feeling suddenly hopeful for the future of his country. "Describing me as portly! Portly! My figure's a lot trimmer than Queen Victoria's, and the Russian Czar positively waddles. Why do those treacherous hacks pick on me?"

"It's the Army's job to support you by fighting all such traitors," declared Saint-Arnaud. "And we've an equal duty to occupy the printers' offices, so that we can make sure nothing else detrimental to the state gets published."

"You must guard all the official buildings too, particularly after I've announced my decision to give the Deputies a short holiday until further notice. We don't want any troublemakers sneaking inside the Chamber, trying to deliver speeches or start debates."

"What's there to debate? Besides, they won't feel like making speeches: not with the Army camped on their doorstep. In my experience, civilians seem to find the sight of a fixed bayonet pointing at them quite intimidating."

"I swore an oath to be faithful to the Republic, and this crisis won't find me forgetting my duty to the French people." Louis-Napoleon did not resemble a Bonaparte, but he could sound like one, especially with an army to back him up. Reorganizing a republic was not a task that a man could accomplish without a little help, and President Bonaparte had no false pride forcing him to refuse that assistance. After all, Uncle Napoleon had permitted the French Army to take part in every single one of his battles, and a nephew could be no less magnanimous.

"With a five o'clock start, we should have everybody rounded up before six-thirty." Saint-Arnaud's imagination saw glorious visions of a new Napoleonic era of campaigns and conquests, with himself artistically placed on horseback at the head of the troops. As Minister of War, he was only too willing to live up to his job title. "By eight, we'll be able to sit down to a leisurely second breakfast, every task completed. The military way is so labour-saving, you'll find, sir. When matters are left to civilians, entire weeks can be wasted on a single election."

"I've always been very outspoken on the subject of Government waste," recalled Bonaparte: "waste of both time and money. I must remember to point out how much the average French tax-payer will save, now that I've devised an economically advantageous method of eliminating the expense of Presidential vote-counting."

"The nation will rejoice to hear the news," predicted Saint-Arnaud.

****

Even though it was December, Saint-Arnaud hardly noticed the darkness or the chill of the night air as there is nothing like the sound of marching boots at five-thirty in the morning to put a bounce in a General's step, and make him nostalgic for the good old days of invading Algeria. He prided himself on his strategy, and it was flawless that day. While Saint-Arnaud reflected complacently on his skills, other groups of soldiers were also on the march, preparing to take up their positions with fixed bayonets at the more strategic points of the city, and the General was proud to think that Paris had no chance against the might of the French Army. Anyone tempted to riot and throw up a barricade could forget the idea, because the city was secure, and everybody knew that the rest of France always followed meekly in the Parisian wake.

A few crisp orders, and the Finance Minister's house had been surrounded by troops. It was a large and elaborate building, almost a mansion, Saint-Arnaud observed grimly; a *banlieue* palace, doubtless paid for by victims of the devious taxation schemes that Minister Passy himself plotted, in his blatant attempt to bankrupt honest Generals. Rarely had duty and pleasure mingled in a more delightful fashion for Saint-Arnaud than during that particular defence of freedom.

"He's still in bed?" repeated the General scornfully, as a startled maid-servant found herself showing a squad of armed soldiers into the drawing-room. "With the afternoon practically upon us? Typical of the man! Kindly inform your master that the Minister of War is here on state business."

Hélène Marin had had no idea that life as the lowliest maid in the house could suddenly become so enthralling. She was fifteen, still pretty despite the long hours of hard work, and a horde of soldiers, mostly young soldiers, all in colourful

19

uniform had livened up her dull routine considerably. Even more intriguing was her master's dramatic emergence in nightclothes from his bedroom.

"General, I told you," declared Passy, "taxes have to be paid. Everyone pays them. Even I have to pay them. There's nothing anybody can do. You'll just have to accept the situation." He was never at his intellectual best, Passy felt, at such an unearthly hour, but perhaps he should have listened to his wife, and dressed before confronting Saint-Arnaud. Although proud of his glossy hair and the features he thought of as rugged, Passy knew that he was not the most slender of politicians, and the voluminous nightshirt did nothing to disguise the generous undulations of his stomach.

"Arrest the Minister," Saint-Arnaud ordered his men airily.

"Arrest me!" exclaimed Passy in astonishment. "Why should I be arrested? You're the one who won't pay up."

"But, as it turns out, I don't have to take any notice of your extortionate and unreasonable monetary demands."

"That's ridiculous!" Passy declared. "I personally went over the figures on Monday morning, General, and you owe the Republic precisely five thou—"

"Nonsense. The Emperor himself told me that I don't owe a thing."

"Emperor? What Emperor?"

"You refuse to acknowledge France's Head of State? That's treason, as far as I'm concerned. Men, take the ex-Minister to the Mazas prison at once." Saint-Arnaud had always enjoyed barking out orders, but never more so than at that moment.

"You're paying the money. General," shouted Passy, as half a dozen bayonets were pointed in the direction of his nightshirt. "You can threaten me all you like, but you're coughing up. This isn't a military dictatorship."

"Well, it's not a republic," remarked Saint-Arnaud.

****

By eight o'clock, all the other troublemakers had been safely rounded up and were keeping the ex-Finance Minister company inside the Mazas prison. As Parisians left their homes that day, they were greeted by the sight of marching soldiers in the main streets, military guards outside government buildings, and posters announcing a State of Emergency. Accustomed to a change of régime every few years, the French took the news in their stride, but the American dentist in their midst was astounded.

"I can't believe it," declared Evans. "I just can't believe it."

"It says so on all the public notices. Parliament dissolved, Republic re-organized, and President ruling by emergency decree," his wife pointed out. Agnes Evans had digested the news with her breakfast, and by lunchtime she was ready to get on with normal life again: as normal as life could ever be among capricious foreigners. "I know it's not our sort of Government change-over, Thomas, but it definitely happened."

"But I still can't believe it," protested Evans. "A man, with as many dental problems as President Bonaparte, taking on countless extra responsibilities, clearly determined that his people shouldn't suffer as he does. Such self-sacrifice! Such patriotism! This is no ordinary man."

"You're right. Ordinary men don't usually get the chance to run a military dictatorship, especially when they aren't even soldiers themselves."

"To think that there were all those traitors around him," marvelled Evans. "And every last one of them plotting to overthrow the Republic, as if the President didn't have enough worries. A lesser man would be overwhelmed by

21

those teeth."

"He should be able to concentrate on them now, with most of his former Cabinet locked up."

"At least he does have one loyal Republican with him."

"And so handy that it should turn out to be the Minister of War," commented Mrs Evans. "Most convenient, to have the Army with you, when you're staging a *coup d'état*."

"To take firm control of a lawless situation isn't a *coup d'état*," Evans explained, tolerant of Agnes's limited grasp of politics. "A *coup d'état* is what would have happened if President Bonaparte hadn't taken charge so altruistically."

"He shows no sign of relaxing his altruism."

"None," said Evans with a sigh of admiration. "In fact, there's a rumour that the President is even prepared to take on the burden of an imperial rôle, so dire does he consider the situation to be."

"Yes, it's a pretty dire state of affairs to have an imperial republic."

"Precisely," agreed Evans, pleased to have clarified matters. "And I fully intend to support his Majesty by lifting the responsibility of those gums from his shoulders."

However, the new Emperor Napoleon was so busy selflessly dictating for the benefit of his subjects that, in those troubled times, his devotion to duty came before his Imperial teeth, and he would never have kept another dental appointment, had not Dr Evans been equally determined, and ready to storm the Emperor's office as unperturbedly as though its occupant were still a mere President.

"It's essential that I examine your Majesty's teeth. We owe it to France, sire. We owe it to history."

The entire French nation under his thumb, Napoleon reflected gloomily, and he had to be tormented by an independent American dentist. "Evans, if I told you to leave, as a favour to me, would you just go away?"

"Go away?" repeated Evans in astonishment, before realizing that there could only be one possible explanation for Napoleon's resolve to take such a risk with his teeth. "You want me to go on a special mission for you, sire?"

"A special mission? You?" The Emperor looked surprised for a few seconds, possibly at Evans's quick understanding of the situation, and then Napoleon said eagerly, "Yes. That's it. That's it exactly. A special mission. If I asked you to go away on a long journey, a very long journey, would you consider it?"

"I'd leave at once, sire."

"Really? You would? You'd actually go away? Oh, why didn't I think of this before?"

"Simply name my destination, your Majesty."

Napoleon thought, not something he cared to do on a regular basis but this was an emergency. "Karlsruhe," he said at last. "Go to Karlsruhe."

"Karlsruhe," agreed Evans. "I'm practically on my way there."

"Now that I'm the Emperor Napoleon III of France, it's my duty to marry."

"And duty must be done, sire, no matter how unpleasant."

"Exactly. Yet I can't marry just anyone."

"Of course not, your Majesty."

"It's a great responsibility to found a dynasty."

"None greater."

"And any future emperor must be given a sporting chance of inheriting sound teeth."

"The best start in life that there is."

"No son of mine is going to be known as Napoleon the Toothless. Forty years of agony, I've endured, absolute agony, excruciating agony —"

23

"And then I became your Majesty's dentist," Evans said proudly.

"Yes." Napoleon looked distinctly underwhelmed by the thought, but continued doggedly, "Well, anyway, there's a Princess Carolina at Karlsruhe, and I want you to go and examine her teeth. She's the granddaughter of the Swedish king, and related to half Europe — the aristocratic half of Europe I mean, naturally."

"Naturally," echoed Evans.

"But I'm not interested in her family background, just those teeth."

"You're as democratic as an American, sire."

"We're all equal at the dentist's," said Napoleon, feeling that he would arrange matters better, given a chance to seize power from the deity. "Leave immediately, Evans, at once, if not sooner. Cancel all my appointments. However, there's no need to rush the journey. Why not do a little sightseeing when you're in Karlsruhe? There's bound to be something there, an opera house or a museum, an art gallery perhaps. Whatever it is, visit it."

"I wouldn't dream of depriving your Majesty of my support a moment longer than necessary," declared Evans. "You can count on my loyalty. I'll be in and out of Karlsruhe like lightning, and race back to Paris before you know I've gone. Just one question, before I dash off —"

"Yes?" Napoleon asked warily.

"Where is Karlsruhe?"

****

"Your Majesty." Evans sprinted breathlessly into the Imperial office, before the guard at the door had a chance to stop him.

Napoleon hastily pushed a bag of bonbons into his desk

drawer, and tried not to look guilty. "I thought you'd be away much longer, Evans."

"I knew speed was essential."

"Well, not all that essential —"

"The Karlsruhe Court plainly considered it a very delicate compliment that your Majesty should send the Imperial Dentist to them, yet so concerned were they for the welfare of your teeth, sire, that they urged me not to linger in their midst. I offered to make an appointment for the Austrian Emperor on the way home, but unfortunately he was too busy to see me, and so were his courtiers, but Princess Carolina —"

"You can give me the details later," said Napoleon, reaching out for some official papers to shuffle. "Next week, perhaps. Or better still, next month. Yes, next month, Evans. I'm so busy at the moment, as you can see, that I can't possibly —"

"The princess is charming, accomplished, refined, and quite attractive in the right light, but her teeth —" Evans grimaced at the traumatic memory, and shook his head sadly. "Oh dear, those teeth! A more distressing sight I've rarely seen. Her so-called dentist should be charged with grievous bodily harm."

"Then Princess Carolina is out," decreed Napoleon. "Sound teeth are a necessity in this matter, and I don't care how much of a huff the Swedish king gets himself into. The marriage is off."

"Perhaps it's for the best," conceded Evans. "Princess Carolina seemed to be a little nervous in character, particularly when I suggested that we try out my new foot-pump dental drill."

"The Empress, mother of a future Imperial dynasty, must have courage and dignity," stated Napoleon. "If a lady has these qualities in the dentist's chair, what greater test is there in life?"

"She'd be worthy of an Imperial family, sire, especially if her teeth were just as worthy."

"There's obviously been too much aristocratic inbreeding over the generations," said Napoleon, superior in the knowledge that his relatives were upstarts. "Even that good French Bernadotte blood doesn't appear to have helped Sweden much, by the sound of it. These old royalist families have had their day."

"This is the age of the self-made man," Evans pointed out, with equal complacency.

"Exactly. I'm a self-made Emperor, and I'll rely on my destiny to bring me an Empress with the right teeth."

"Actually, your Majesty, while we're on the subject of exquisite teeth —"

"Yes?" Napoleon asked cagily, backing towards the door.

"Among my patients, there's a young lady, a young aristocratic lady admittedly, but despite that handicap —"

Dr Evans's practice included the late Count di Montijo's two daughters. They were related to the Spanish royal family, and their British mother could claim kinship with many of the inhabitants of the House of Lords; yet Evans, that grandson of the American Revolution, was determined not to be prejudiced against anyone, not even the British nobility, in his mission to find the Emperor's bride, and the di Montijo daughter, Eugenia —

"She's remarkable, your Majesty, remarkable. Young and pretty and —"

"Young and pretty?" Napoleon was already interested, and he had still to hear the crucially important bit of Evans's description.

"She's got the most perfect teeth I've ever seen: outside the States, that is, of course. Straight, firm and perfectly proportioned, those teeth should last her a lifetime, if she follows my guidance. You wouldn't scratch at precious jewels with a metal spike, I told her, and no jewel is more beautiful than the pearls that are your teeth, so avoid toothpicks. Regular check-ups are essential, I added, and forget all about candy —"

"Yes, yes, yes, but tell me more about her appearance," demanded Napoleon, with a quick glance at his desk drawer to confirm that it was properly closed on his secret stash of bonbons.

"Beautiful is the only word for those teeth."

"Yes, but what about the rest of her?" Napoleon asked impatiently. "What about her figure?"

"Oh, very nice, and she's got such a caring disposition. Why, last year, she voluntarily gave up her own appointment to somebody in pain, and rushed out of my waiting-room before she could be thanked. And, indeed, even before her next appointment could be arranged."

"That's what I call presence of mind," commented Napoleon.

"Only last week, she asked another patient if he'd like to take her appointment, as well as his own, so that he could have double the time with me," recalled Evans, still hardly able to credit the generosity he had witnessed. "When he refused, she insisted that he had the extra hour."

"Good thinking, Eugenia!" remarked Napoleon in awe. "And you say she's young and pretty?"

"Those teeth of hers might be American." There could be no higher compliment.

"I'll invite the family to the Palace," Napoleon decided.

****

In preparation for his forthcoming marriage to whoever

27

turned out to be the lucky possessor of imperially perfect teeth, Napoleon had moved into the Tuileries Palace. The Elysée was adequate for a President, of course, but an emperor could never really feel at home in such ex-republican surroundings, and if the Tuileries Palace had been good enough for Uncle Napoleon, it was good enough for Nephew Napoleon and his future dynasty. The sole missing item chanced to be the future dynasty's mother.

It was the first French Imperial grand ball for nearly forty years, and only the new Emperor's Uncle Jérôme could remember the last one in detail enough to criticize the present decorations, and say how much better parties were in his young days. Evans, whose access to aristocratic gatherings had previously been somewhat limited, could discern no fault with any of the arrangements, when he called to examine Napoleon's teeth before the party. His mind at ease about the ability of the Imperial mouth to cope with such a momentous occasion, Evans took a detour on his return journey to the Palace's front door.

With plaster swirls on its walls like icing on a wedding cake and polished mahogany floor reflecting the many lights of the crystal chandeliers, the ballroom appeared to be the most beautiful scene in the world, from the balcony where Evans stood looking down on the arrivals, every single one of them a potential patient for the Imperial Court Dentist. Despite the overwhelming scent of hot-house flowers and beeswax, he lingered, fascinated by the pageant below him. The bright colours of crinolined ballgowns contrasted agreeably with the sober black of male evening attire, and as the musicians began to play Dupont's superior non-Austrian non-Strauss *Imperial Valse,* the guests rushed to claim partners, eager for the dancing to start.

"Is she here yet?" demanded Napoleon, hurrying onto the

balcony to prepare for a later Grand Entrance in his new Commander-in-Chief's uniform. For once, he was prepared to approach Evans voluntarily, confident that even an American dentist would be unlikely to insist on a second check-up in the middle of a ball. "Which one is she?"

Evans pointed. "In the pale green dress."

The beautiful Eugenia di Montijo wore a noticeably low-cut gown, and was laughing in the midst of a group of attentive men. She seemed to be protesting that already her dance card was so filled with names, no more could possibly be added to it, but to compensate the disappointed suitors, she promptly danced a few steps with each of them, pirouetting from partner to partner in a swirl of skirts. The jewels in her golden-chestnut hair and around that extremely low neckline flashed as they caught the light, but it was her smile that dazzled Evans. He had once thought his wife's teeth fine-looking, but Eugenia's were in a mesmerizing class of their own, and Evans suddenly regretted having married young, before he had had a chance to see what the world could offer.

"Remarkable," he sighed.

"I'll say!" agreed Napoleon, his eyes on the low neckline.

"Just wait until your Majesty sees them close up. Astonishing! Astounding!"

"You're telling me!"

"You won't see better in Europe, sire."

"Too right!"

"Teeth worthy of France, worthy of an Empire."

"Teeth?" repeated Napoleon absently. "Oh, yes, she's got teeth as well, you say."

****

The Emperor's engagement was swiftly followed by the

Emperor's wedding at the end of January 1853. The bride looked strikingly beautiful; all the newspapers were unanimous on the point. Napoleon had very sensibly decided that, to safeguard national unity, editors disagreeing with any aspect of the Imperial régime would be hauled before the courts, and either fined or imprisoned or have their papers closed down, preferably all three. Such a rigorous approach to patriotism meant it was unlikely that the new Empress Eugénie would be described as anything but beautiful, whatever her appearance. However, Napoleon's determination to prevent the press from making an error of judgment seemed unnecessary for once because his bride really was eye-catchingly attractive.

Evans, the first American dentist to stand outside Notre Dame Cathedral and cheer at a French Imperial wedding, felt pride in a mission successfully accomplished. One Empress, complete with sound teeth as ordered, supplied to the nation, and now any future heir had a fifty-fifty chance of inheriting a mouthful of the best teeth in Europe. The Emperor's confidential dentist had completed his first historic task, and by coincidence, Eugenia di Montijo was another person with a destiny.

"When I was a little girl, a gypsy predicted that I'd be a queen one day," she told Evans.

"That's uncanny!"

"I don't suppose she knew the difference between an empress and a queen," Eugénie said charitably.

"Your Majesty will show the world the difference," Evans promised.

"Anyway, it's a bit late to ask the gypsy for my money back."

"Your Majesty is so very practical."

"Whenever anyone says 'Your Majesty,' I look around to

see who's come into the room. I keep forgetting it's me."

"A mistake nobody else's going to make."

"Being an empress is a great responsibility," remarked Eugenie.

"The greater the responsibility, the greater the glory," proclaimed Evans.

"I can't possibly be seen twice in the same dress. Jewels are less of a problem, of course, because nowadays it's quite acceptable to wear diamonds a second time. But when it comes to hats —! A nightmare!"

"Your Majesty won't fail when it comes to duty, and nor will I. As Imperial Court Dentist, I must insist on regular check-ups, and a new toothbrush every week."

"Yes, so important. I'll make an appointment with you as soon as possible, Dr Evans. Next week. Better still, next month."

Eugenia, renamed Eugénie in an attempt to disguise the dearth of Gallic ancestry, was ambitious enough to ignore her family's protests about marrying a man of doubtful background, and yet more doubtful means of acquiring power. But even without the gypsy's encouragement, Eugénie would have been quite prepared to accept the first king or emperor who came along, however the title was manufactured. This enterprising spirit, so American-like, enchanted Evans, almost as much as the beauty of her teeth. He considered Eugénie so perfectly matched to Napoleon that the twenty year age difference went unnoticed: by Evans, at any rate.

With an empress in the Tuileries Palace, the Imperial Court became the centre of Parisian social life. There were dinner-parties each evening, during which the Emperor led the conversation, and so fascinating a speaker was he, that any discussion rapidly turned into a monologue. No matter how often they had heard Napoleon's reminiscences, or how long he spoke, his listeners would sit, as if stunned, until the moment they left. And they always left early, doubtless to hurry home and ponder the Emperor's words at leisure because a little imperial philosophy, like furniture wax, goes a long way.

Napoleon's gift as a raconteur was too great to be denied the rest of the nation. Without anybody at all urging him to do so, the Emperor generously decided to devote whole minutes of his valuable time to dictating his thoughts. The French newspapers eagerly printed each instalment, whenever they were ordered to do so, along with editorials assuring Napoleon that his style was better than Victor Hugo's; an appraisal that sent the grouchy Hugo stamping off for a seventeen year exile in the Channel Islands. He simply could not deal with the competition.

Examples of the Emperor's brilliant wit were also widely reported, and not only in those loyal newspapers.

"It looks like rain," Eugénie had commented one day.

Without even a second's pause for thought, Napoleon replied, "That's because it is raining."

All the courtiers around him at once fell about with laughter, wiping away tears of merriment. Evans, who was lucky enough to be present, entertained the American Legation staff for months with this fine example of scintillating repartee, and it never failed to awe his patients into rigid silence as they sat in the dentist's chair, which gave Evans the opportunity to expand on his theme.

"It's just like a fairy-tale," he would declare enthusiastically to whomever the chair's unresponsive occupant happened to be. "The Palace, the parties, the beautiful Empress, the gallant Emperor; yes, everything's exactly like the end of a Hans Christian Andersen story, minus any of the usual bother with wicked stepmothers, drowning mermaids and freezing to death in the snow."

The Empress would have agreed with Evans, up to a point. Eugénie, in the widest crinolines and lowest necklines, concentrated on the great social occasions. Ambassadors, statesmen, high-ranking soldiers, aristocrats, men of wealth - —Eugénie invited them all to the Tuileries Palace, and sometimes she invited their wives as well. Even artists and musicians found themselves welcomed from time to time, provided they dressed fashionably, of course, and their works were popular. It was all so very democratic that Evans wholeheartedly agreed with the faithful French newspapers when they described the Empress as the most stylish and captivating woman in Europe, a description that chanced to coincide with Eugénie's own opinion of the new Empress, and as every visitor to the Tuileries brought her a present, life was like a continual birthday. It would have been the perfect fairy-tale described by Evans, but *roses have thorns and silver fountains mud*. There was one snag: the Emperor.

"I got soaked when the cavalry rode by," Napoleon complained one evening, as he strode into the imperial drawing-room. "If they'd had the slightest consideration for me, they'd have slowed to a walk, but no, not them. They had to cut a dash, whatever happened to their Emperor, and I was forced to stand in the wake, and salute as though nothing had happened. I'll be doubled up with rheumatism if this goes on."

"The rain's just as wet when it falls on me," Eugénie declared absently, trying on a hat in front of the mirror. "I would have been drenched, absolutely drenched, if I'd left the carriage when I visited that orphanage. You should have seen the poor little orphans bringing their posies out to me. Drowned rats weren't in it, and my heart ached for them, as I

33

told all the journalists there."

"Why do so many ceremonies have to be out of doors?" demanded Napoleon.

"If you're proposing to inspect the cavalry indoors, the servants will leave; I warn you now."

"And this evening I'll get soaked again," Napoleon said in exasperation. "I've got to switch on the gas supply for the lights in the new boulevards."

"Well, I'm not going, and that's that."

"Nobody will notice. *I'll* be there."

"What a treat for everybody," muttered Eugénie.

"Haussmann's promised me that he's made the boulevards so wide, no one will ever be able to build barricades across them," said Napoleon, and the memory of that promise brought sudden contentment with it. "Mobs will have to study mechanical engineering before they can revolt now."

"I suppose you think you've outwitted them."

"I flatter myself, I —"

"Yes, you do," agreed Eugénie.

"I'm rebuilding Paris," Napoleon pointed out. "That's more than my uncle ever did. He just went around bombarding Europe until it was one gigantic heap of rubble. I'm much more constructive than that."

"Only because you can't get taxes out of rubble."

"Precisely," said Napoleon.

The dark little shops and filthy lanes, that had so depressed Dr and Mrs Evans on their arrival in France, were demolished to make way for the wide boulevards, with their mansions and great public buildings. Slums were cleared from the centre of Paris, along with the poor, who had no need of a central address anyhow. A dozen new bridges spanned the Seine; the Bois de Boulogne was landscaped, while fountains and statues appeared in the better quarters of the city. Most importantly of all, in Evans's opinion, a system of sewers was designed, so modern that it became the envy of Europe.

The glamour of newly-built Paris left Evans feeling wistfully dissatisfied with his lot, and it became essential that the Imperial Dentist move from the less than fashionable quarter that had been adequate for Dr Brewster's more mundane practice. Evans was determined never to forget his duty to the American Legation staff, but equality demanded that he had as good an address as any other Courtier, and so a fine house was selected, which by happy chance, was in the Avenue de l'Impératrice. Not that Evans, a rational man of science, believed in omens, but it seemed a delicate compliment to the Empress that he should live in the very avenue named for her. The new house, *Bella Rosa*, was as spacious as an American one, with a large garden, and stables too, because gone were the days when Evans walked or took cabs. A landau was acquired, and even more impressively, a coachman to go with it, although Célestin did double as the gardener, but appearances had to be maintained, with the Evans practice more and more drawn from Imperial Court circles and the Diplomatic Corps, grand patients who were treated at a grand office in the Rue de la Paix because, both professionally and residentially, he was a dentist on the up.

Keen to have a witness from Philadelphia who could confirm that letters home did not exaggerate his success, Evans invited the youngest of the clan, with her husband and baby, to come to Paris for the summer of 1854. His sister Julia fulfilled her obligations by marvelling at the house, the garden, the landau, the city and the social circles in which Evans's patients moved. Impressed, the visitors extended their stay, and left reluctantly before autumn storms made the Atlantic crossing unpleasant. They travelled to Liverpool, and sailed for New York on September 20th aboard the *SS Arctic*.

Tragedy should have had no place in that enchanted year, but off Newfoundland, the *Artic* collided in fog with the *Vesta*, a French steamer, and out of two hundred and eighty-one passengers, only twenty-three survived. Julia, her husband and baby were not among them.

Work and more work helped Evans to cope with his grief, resulting in one very wealthy dentist, and he was not the only person prospering in Napoleon III's Paris, as the rich grew richer and the poor were tidily hidden out of sight. Also out of sight was any opposition to Bonaparte rule. Charitably, the Emperor allowed Republicans complete freedom of movement and speech, whenever they chose to live in exile abroad; his secret police did not pursue them, from the moment troublemakers left French territory, and sometimes the dissenters were even escorted to the border, at no cost whatsoever to themselves. This humane, yet effective, method of freeing the country from tiresome political squabbles had a simplicity that filled Evans with admiration, because it was positively heart-warming to live in so harmonious a nation, where happiness was as universal as the Emperor's popularity.

3

Evans dashed unannounced into Napoleon's office, pushing aside the guard at the door. "Your Majesty! Are you hurt?"

"He fired the revolver right in my face," Napoleon said indignantly. "Twice!"

"A rotten shot! Thank God!"

"Students! I don't know what they're teaching them in the university these days, but I fully intend to find out and put a stop to it at once. There I was, minding my own business, just about to cut a ribbon and declare the bridge open to traffic, when suddenly, I find a revolver virtually pressed to my forehead."

Evans gasped in horror. "A miracle that you've been spared to us, sire."

"That idea of copying the Prussians, with their compulsory military service, is out. Imagine, Evans, thousands of trained marksmen loose on the streets. I wonder the Prussian king can sleep at night."

"The Prussian king!" As a democrat, Evans scorned all kings, and his tone was curt. "Insomnia is certain to be Friedrich Wilhelm's lot. He doesn't have the loyalty of his subjects, unlike your Majesty."

Yet, for some reason, Napoleon did not seem reassured by Evans's words that day. "I must see that high railings are put around the Tuileries."

"Only a great mind could think of such practicalities at a time like this," declared Evans.

"My mother always said I was clever. What do tutors know?" demanded Napoleon, adding grimly, "I'll double the guards, and make sure nobody with evil intent gets anywhere near me. And while we're on the subject, what are you doing here, Evans? I cancelled my appointment. I'm far too busy cracking down on treason and the causes of treason to see you today."

"And then the Emperor insisted I leave," Evans reported to his wife when he returned home. "Of course, I told him I could wait until his Majesty had a free moment or two, but he refused to listen to me, and said my patients must not be deprived. No other ruler would be so considerate, only minutes after being practically gunned down in cold blood."

"That's the trouble with students; everything's so slapdash," said Mrs Evans. "My brothers were exactly the same. They'd simply blunder ahead, not even attempting to work out a detailed plan; yet you can't just get up one morning and think, 'Today I'll scribble off that essay, when I get a few seconds,' or 'Today I'll assassinate an emperor, if I can spare the time.' These things take preparation and careful groundwork."

"But how much more everybody's going to value Napoleon, after such a narrow escape," declared Evans. "Europe can breathe freely again, now that the Emperor's been spared. In fact, the whole world will rejoice at the sight of him still in our midst."

****

The whole world with but one exception. The Empress Eugénie, sitting opposite Napoleon in the Imperial carriage on their way to the opera, stared fixedly at her husband's head and did not rejoice.

"I see that you've noticed my new hat," the Emperor said proudly.

"I haven't been able to avoid doing so," replied his Empress. An elaborately ornamented copy of the bicorne, so often to be spotted in portraits of the first Napoleon

Bonaparte, did not seem to Eugénie the ideal accompaniment to formal evening wear, especially when perched above her husband's plain face, beady eyes and waxed moustache. "Your hat's not the most conventional of headgear."

"It is rather dashing," admitted Napoleon, with a modest simper. "Not many men could get away with it."

"I agree."

"But I never shirk my duty as Emperor."

"It's your duty to be seen wearing *that* in public?"

"I must be the first in fashion."

"Well. I'm sure no second man will be sporting one like it at the opera."

"And tomorrow, the whole of Paris is going to be talking about this hat."

"It wouldn't surprise me in the least," agreed Eugénie.

"Of course, the Czar will be wearing an exact copy before the week's out,"

"Why ever would he do that?"

"Because he couldn't start a fashion like this to save his life."

"But would he want to?" asked Eugénie.

"I predict that the newspapers will be full of my hat tomorrow morning," said Napoleon, as the carriage slowed on its approach to the opera house. The Emperor made a few last-minute adjustments in an attempt to find a jauntier angle for the hat on its world debut, and he smiled in anticipation of the admiring uproar that would greet him the moment his feet hit the pavement. "In fact, the editors are going to be pushed to find adjectives enough to describe the full impact of —"

The bomb, thrown from the crowd, struck the side of the carriage, landed in the road, and then exploded.

Evans sat in his drawing-room, absorbed in the very latest copy of *Progressive Dentistry*, a magazine that had come all the way from New York, and yet was only twelve days beyond its publication date; such were the amazing velocities achieved by the nineteenth century's most modern steamers as they sped across the Atlantic. Evans was so spellbound by an article entitled *Restraining Patients —The Humane Way*, that he failed to look up when his wife hurried breathlessly into the room.

"Thomas! I've just heard! The Emperor and Empress! They're both dead! It's a revolution!"

"No, no," Evans said absently. "I was with them only an hour ago."

"But —!"

"I called to examine the Emperor's teeth before he went to the opera. Unfortunately, he was too pressed for time."

"But it happened outside the opera house Cook just told me. Someone threw a bomb at the carriage."

"A bomb!" *Progressive Dentistry*, along with its humane advice, landed unceremoniously on the carpet in a flurry of pages. "It can't be true!"

"According to the greengrocer's boy, it is. And you know how reliable a greengrocer we have: the freshest fruit and vegetables, whatever the weather."

"This is a calamity!" gasped Evans, stunned.

"I don't know what we'll do, if there's a revolution. We're supposed to be dining out this evening with the Hendersons. Do you think we should go?"

"Dinner will have to wait." At destiny's call, Evans stood up and strode purposefully towards the door. "I have to go to the Tuileries at once. The Imperial baby's in great danger. I must rescue him."

"But there might be riots or —"

"No matter," declared Evans. "The Prince Imperial's my patient: or will be, when he gets some teeth, and I have a sacred duty of care. I'll take him to the American Legation for safety."

"But mobs could be storming the Palace at this very minute!"

"Then I've no time to lose," announced Evans.

****

Célestin, the coachman-gardener, was ploddingly calm, accustomed to Dr Evans and his frantic emergencies. The horses were harnessed and the landau on the road, while Célestin tolerantly ignored the demands for haste and more haste. He was forty, small, dark and unimpressed by his close connection to the Imperial teeth, and although circumstances might be dire, no horse was ever hurried when in Célestin's care.

The gas-lit streets seemed as calm and orderly as usual, yet Evans sat on the very edge of the seat, trying to will the horses to go faster, despite Célestin. But for the dignity of his position as Imperial Court Dentist, Evans would have seized the reins himself, and risked a gendarme's caution for reckless driving, because at any moment he expected to encounter riot and revolution. However, to his immense relief, the area around the Tuileries was still peaceful, almost torpid considering the appalling events of that fateful night. Napoleon's sensible high railings were firmly in place, as was the guard, and Evans jumped out of the carriage before it stopped in his rush to get to the gate. The front gate, of course. Even in a grim emergency, democracy was second-nature to a Jefferson College graduate.

41

"I've heard terrible news!" Evans cried, running up to the guard. "Is it true?"

Alphonse Voruz was pleased to have some company on that cold January evening. Sentry duty was all very well, but it played havoc with a tall and handsome young man's social life. He certainly saw people, but diplomats and Imperial party guests were not inclined to stop and chat to a guard. "Yes, it's true," he replied with a welcoming smile. (Better teeth than Evans would have expected to see, given the usual standard of French Army dentistry.) "Quite true, I'm afraid."

"This is dreadful!" Evans was almost overcome by the thought of the Emperor in bits, and the Empress's perfect teeth lost to the world forever. But grief would have to wait when destiny had entrusted Thomas W Evans with a mission. "Where's the Imperial baby?"

"The baby?" repeated Voruz in surprise. "In his cot, I suppose."

"You suppose!" snapped Evans. "Shouldn't you know?"

"Me?" Voruz looked blank.

"Yes, you!"

"But why me?"

"Because he's your sovereign, now that the Emperor's dead," Evans said furiously. "Do your duty, man!"

"But the Emperor's not dead, Dr Evans."

"He lives!"

"Oh yes, he's absolutely in the land of the living." Yet, despite the glorious news he had just related, Voruz did not sound overly enthusiastic.

"Oh, thank God! Thank God! And the Empress?" demanded Evans, hardly daring to hope for a second miracle. "Is she alive?"

"Probably. I don't suppose that the Emperor would have bothered to stay and hear the opera, if she hadn't been there to make him."

Evans leaned back against the high railings in relief. "Then it was merely a wild rumour I heard? Something about a bomb —"

"Oh, no, that's true enough," Voruz assured him. "A bomb was thrown at them, but missed its target."

No wonder that the Emperor disapproved of the English fad for school sports, Evans thought with admiration. In his wisdom, Napoleon had obviously foreseen the dangers of a generation expert in aiming javelins and putting the shot. "I must go into the Palace at once. Congratulate them on a miraculous escape."

"But they're not back from the opera yet." Voruz stood at ease, glad of a chance to prolong the chat. "There are three long acts, with a ballet right in the middle as well. Donizetti does go on a bit at times, if you ask me. Though to be fair, it's a complicated libretto, and takes a lot of explaining."

"They're prepared to listen to an opera, right to the bitter end, after an assassination attempt?" Evans demanded incredulously. "What a sense of duty!"

"Well, they were practically outside when the bomb exploded, so I imagine it seemed a pity to waste the whole evening. You know the Emperor; he hates plans to be altered, whatever happens to other people."

But Evans had no interest in other people either. If the Emperor and Empress were safe, that was all he needed to know, and he hurried into the Palace to await their return, while Voruz, deprived of company with his story only half told, gloomily resumed his duties.

****

"Your Majesties!"

"Evans!" Blown sky-high without a moment's notice and

43

then, on an emperor's return home, it was to find a dentist lurking in the entrance hall. No wonder Napoleon felt decidedly put out by the evening's events. "I can't possibly have made an appointment with you for this hour of the night. I refuse to believe it."

"I didn't make an appointment either," Eugénie added with equal firmness.

"I'm so thankful to see both your Majesties safe," declared Evans. "All France will rejoice. This is a glorious deliverance, a glorious night."

"Glorious! What do you mean, glorious? Just look at my hat!" cried Napoleon in fury, thrusting the late masterpiece at Evans. "Ruined! A piece of shrapnel went clean through, knocked it right off my head."

"Dreadful!" Evans examined the relic, and saw that the Emperor's judgment was right as usual; the hat had indeed been mangled beyond hope of recovery.

"Those English!" fumed Napoleon. "It turns out that the bomb was made in London."

"They can't forget how the French showed them up in the Crimea, and still resent their Lady with the Lamp being put in the shade by the Mademoiselle with the Macédoine," declared Evans, the battle of Mullin's Pond still rankling. "Typical of the British. We've had trouble with them in my country too."

"I'll never be able to wear this hat again," the bereft Emperor lamented.

"There's always some light, even in the most Stygian of darkness," muttered Eugénie.

"At least there weren't any casualties," said Evans, attempting Imperial comfort.

"Oh, but there were," Eugénie informed him. "Ten dead, I believe, and over two hundred injured. It quite spoilt the opera for me, every time I remembered what had happened."

"Your Majesty is all compassion."

"I'm known for my thoughtful nature, Dr Evans. There was a really touching tribute to my benevolence and kind-heartedness in *Le Figaro* only last week. I was close to tears, reading it."

"As were we all."

"The first time I'd worn it too," said Napoleon, gazing wistfully at his assassinated hat.

"The British will pay for it!" declared Evans. He was wrong.

****

The British Government claimed that if Italian anarchists decided to make a bomb or two in London, to throw at French Emperors in Paris, English law had no objection whatsoever. A completely different matter had Napoleon travelled to London for the bomb-throwing, the Emperor was informed; the police would then have leapt into action, arresting everybody in sight, and should Napoleon happen to be assassinated in London one day, the conspirators would be hanged for sure. However, the assassination attempt chanced to take place in Paris, and that minor geographical fact quite altered the situation for the British. Awfully sorry and all that, but foreigners in England were perfectly free to plot against other foreigners, as long as they had the courtesy to do the actual murdering abroad. Heaps of apologies, of course, but not a thing the British Government could do about it. They even refused to pay for a new hat.

The bomber turned out to be one Felice Orsini, an ardent ex-citizen of Rome in his late thirties, determined to drive the occupying Austrian forces from the Italian States. Why he thought that assassinating the French Emperor in Paris would help achieve his ambition was not quite clear, but

Orsini had always been stronger on patriotism than reasoning. From exile in London, he had travelled to France under the name of Oswald Allsop, which was a positive insult to his Italianate good looks, passionate nature and musical accent, but Orsini was prepared to make any sacrifice for the cause.

He was defended at his trial by Jules Favre, an emotional man, a very emotional man, as Latin in appearance and temperament as his client, and a soft touch for every charity collector in the city. Favre had worked days on what he hoped would be a really effective defence: a defence that glossed over the unfortunate incident with the bomb, but was chock-full of heartrending pathos about Orsini's forlorn childhood, details obligingly supplied by the accused himself.

Heroic father in the Italian Resistance shot dead by cold-blooded Austrian soldiers, as he tried to prevent them bayoneting a baby — no, several babies actually, with a few toddlers thrown in for good measure. Equally heroic mother, grief-stricken, expiring in a fever only days later. Two desolate orphans left to face the world entirely alone.

Orsini noted with approval the way Favre's voice faltered, almost as though he were too moved to go on, as indeed he should be with such a tragic story to relate, and Orsini determined to sound just as moved, when his own chance to speak came. No point in having endured a wretched childhood, if it could not be used to one's advantage later on, especially when Napoleon's blinkered newspapers seemed to regard the guillotining of Orsini as a *fait accompli*.

"Two desolate orphans, without protection, without support. All they had in the world was each other, only each other, nobody else to care whether they lived or died, nobody else on the face of the earth. Then one day, one dreadful day, one appalling day, the elder boy — the elder boy —"

46

Favre's voice again shook with emotion, and what exactly happened on that dreadful day to the elder boy remained a mystery, as Favre, overwhelmed by the catalogue of tragedy, broke down in a flood of tears. So wonderfully touching was the speech intended to make the court overlook the little matter of a bomb, that Favre found himself totally unable to deliver it, and every attempt he made to enlighten his audience as to the ghastly fate of the elder boy resulted in even more bitter sobbing.

Orsini, eager to be the noble and sensitive martyr for the cause of Italian freedom, grew impatient. Nobody paid the slightest attention to him, as court officials hurried about, offering his so-called defender drinks of water, while the prosecution advocated deep breathing, and there was even some judicial advice concerning the efficacy of herbal tea on the nerves. Orsini, who had looked forward to presenting the French with a piece of his mind on the subject of Emperors who were allowed to seize power and then retain it, was decidedly put out when proceedings were abandoned for the day to give Favre a chance to recover. Favre recover! Orsini was the one with the traumatic childhood. Favre had not even been there, for all his showy display of grief, as if nobody else had any sensitivity worth mentioning. It was Felice Orsini's place to be the one overcome with memories of past sorrow: Felice Orsini's right. Favre recover, indeed!

However, the next day went no better for Orsini, as Favre made a second brave, but tremulous, attempt at the fate of the two desolate orphans.

"Alone in the world to fend for themselves, without friends or protectors, just each other, nobody else for comfort and support, nobody else to care, nobody but each other, until one terrible day when, horrible to relate, the elder boy — the elder boy —" But the thought of that elder boy was still too

47

much. Favre choked with emotion, and the tears began to flow once more.

It was typical, Orsini thought with considerable resentment, just typical. Lawyers not only helped themselves to a man's life-savings, they swindled him out of his childhood as well. Orsini had gone to all the trouble and inconvenience of a terrible infancy, before he selflessly flung a bomb or two around to demonstrate his deep-rooted sympathy for those forced to suffer under a dictatorship, and a lawyer shanghaied the publicity. The newspapers reported Favre's distress with a welter of adjectives, but printed barely a word on the topic of the man who had gone out of his way to give Favre some thoroughly undeserved fame. Orsini would have been entirely disillusioned, had he not already grasped that the French papers were prejudiced against him. Nobody could deny that creating a country was a full-time job, yet in order to give France a helping hand on the way back to democracy, Orsini had taken whole weeks out of his campaign to liberate and unify the Italian States, and no one seemed to appreciate his generous altruism. The newspapers had, instead, chosen to go on and on about the people killed by the bomb, calling it premeditated murder, when Orsini never had the slightest intention of murdering anybody except Louis-Napoleon Bonaparte, and he was still very much alive unfortunately. The people caught between the self-styled emperor and the bomb had merely been unlucky, because should they not have chanced to walk by, just at the very second when Orsini happened to lob a bomb in the direction of the Imperial carriage, every single one of them would have been alive to that very day, and Orsini could not be blamed if people deliberately selected such an ill-starred moment to take an evening stroll. It was impossible to plan for every eventuality, and nobody felt sorrier than

Orsini that Parisians were not more fleet of foot. There was no reason for the French press to get hysterical about foreign assassins; a home-grown assassin would have run into exactly the same problem Orsini had, that night outside the opera house.

It was a stitch-up, Orsini realized, an absolute conspiracy against him. And to make matters totally exasperating, Favre, not content with bungling the entire defence, determined to distract the reporters at the very instant when they should have been noting the calm bravery displayed by his client, while the death sentence was announced. However, instead of journalists busily writing that Orsini stood upright, proud and unflinching, as the unjust verdict of the corrupt judicial process was read out, everyone in court was transfixed by the sight of Favre, who slumped to the floor in a headline-grabbing faint, and nobody even thought to ask Orsini's opinion of the death penalty, in the general rush to revive Favre.

And still not satisfied, despite whole columns of newsprint describing his sensitive nature, Favre decided to ruin, absolutely ruin, Orsini's last chance to show the world how a courageous Italian patriot faced death with laughter on his lips —well, if not laughter exactly, at least the hint of a sardonic smile. But Orsini was destined to be thwarted yet again, for the treacherous Favre insisted on visiting his victim at the very hour set for the execution. In vain did Orsini protest that he preferred to be alone, that he was far too busy to see anyone, that he had some really memorable last words to compose; already it was too late. The selflessness of the ex-desolate orphan, trying to spare another man the distress of that final visit, had Favre in paroxysms of grief as Orsini tried to push him out of the cell. So violent was the sobbing, that Favre accompanied it with an equally violent nose bleed, and Orsini was forced to waste some of the last minutes of his life hovering over a prostrate lawyer, applying the cold water compresses supplied by worried guards, who obviously feared that the wrong man was about to die on them.

To leave the weeping and gory Favre, still prone on the cell floor, was a positive relief, but that relief turned to fury when Orsini noticed that he was splattered with his incompetent defender's blood. He knew, he just knew, that the crowd around the guillotine would assume he had tried to cut his throat, to cheat them out of their morning's entertainment, and it would be in all the newspapers that Felice Orsini lacked nerve enough to face a public execution for his enslaved homeland. He made a hasty attempt to shout "Long Live A Unified And Liberated Italy!" but it sounded half-hearted, even to him. Some days, nothing goes right.

****

Napoleon's composure, despite Italian bombers and British obstinacy, gave outsiders the impression of a self-absorbed man, with little feeling and no empathy, but Thomas W Evans knew the real Emperor. After all, the excuses Napoleon made for cancelling his dental appointments often revealed great imagination, and his ability to see everything from his own point of view meant that no time was wasted on lesser people's problems. That single-mindedness was evident in all matters Imperial, whether domestic or foreign.

"I'll have to cancel the appointment today, Evans. I can't think how the two engagements came to be confused but, by an unfortunate coincidence, the Russian Czar's arriving at any second. In fact, I can hear Alexander's carriage this very minute." Napoleon glanced out of his office window to confirm his deliverance, and then let slip a cry of anguish. "My hat!"

"Your hat, sire?" Evans said blankly.

"Yes, my hat! It's my hat! Alexander's copied my hat, the one I had specially designed to wear to the opera. It's the same, Evans, exactly the same in every detail. Those Russians have spies everywhere."

"They were probably making detailed sketches of it at the very moment when the bomb blast sent your Majesty flying through the air."

"And I know that the Czar's going to claim it's his own design, I just know he is," declared Napoleon in fury.

"Retribution's sure to follow such a despicable act," said Evans, always confident that providence would not let him down, although the punctuality of the Czar's day of reckoning was to come as a surprise even to him. "I've heard that Alexander's teeth are not his greatest asset. Entirely due to infrequent check-ups."

"Coward!" Napoleon commented scornfully. "Afraid of a little discomfort, the cry-baby."

"Put it this way, we certainly won't be hearing him whistle."

"I suppose the Czar wants to get a look at my new coat; that's why he angled for an invite here."

"He might be able to copy the design, but not your Majesty's panache when wearing it."

"Just wait until Alexander claps eyes on my get-up at the review. That'll make him think."

A military review was to be held at Longchamps in honour of the unprincipled Czar. It had been planned as a day to forgive and forget, despite the number of times Alexander harped on about 1812, and to show him that French soldiers had more stylish uniforms than those drab Russian ones. In fact, Napoleon was so determined to be magnanimous that he even allowed the Czar plus hat to share the Imperial carriage, while they watched the cavalry parade by in dignified French fashion without the jumping, stamping and kicking that Cossacks seemed to regard as so necessary on every occasion. Napoleon was just about to comment on the simplicity of the plumes in the cavalry hats, when the band began to play Mikhailevitch's *March Specially Composed For The Most illustrious And Munificent Czar,* which had been chosen to show that there were no hard feelings about the Crimea. The fact that the French had won the war so gloriously was barely to be mentioned at all, and nor was the fact that France had much better composers than the toadying Mikhailevitch.

The band members had thought that nothing could save them from the intricacies of 13/14 time, when Fryderyk Berezowski, a wild-haired Polish music student, could take no more. Maddened, he charged up to the Imperial carriage, and fired a gun in what he optimistically hoped was the direction of the Czar. In one smoothly agile movement, Napoleon was crouched on the floor of the brougham, but the less gymnastic Czar jerked his head around in astonishment, dislodging the contentious hat. Napoleon had grown up on stories about the Bonaparte luck, but never had it been more strikingly demonstrated to him, and an uncle could not have seized the moment more decisively than did a nephew seize the hat.

Berezowski was less of a strategist than either of the Napoleons, but even his passionate Slavonic nature had to accept that a parade ground filled with armed soldiers was not, perhaps, the most sensible place for an assassination attempt, and he found himself overpowered, just as the Emperor finished work on the hat.

"That madman nearly killed me!" Alexander declared indignantly. "I felt the bullet go by."

Napoleon arose from the carriage floor with a coolness that entirely failed the Czar. "Did I ever show you my hat?" he inquired, picking up the now lifeless headwear, and handing it courteously to the Czar. "The one the British blew up, I mean."

"My hat!" gasped Alexander, snatching it from the Emperor's hand. "It's ruined! Ruined!"

"Yes," agreed Napoleon. "I noticed."

"It was an original design too: quite unique."

"Not all that unique," retorted Napoleon. "I refer you to the photographic proof."

"Everybody knows that photographs can be faked." It was an unfortunate episode in diplomatic relations, but the Czar simply did not have the Bonaparte presence of mind under fire. The autocratic ruler of all the Russias expected a significant death, a conspiracy of boyars at the very least, not some half-witted student, who was not even Russian. What sort of death would that have been for the history books? And at a race course as well, nowhere near a decent palace or battlefield. To make matters worse, it turned out that Berezowski was a gatecrasher, as much without a ticket as a title; yet he had had the audacity to try and assassinate a Czar, when nobody beneath the rank of Grand Duke should even think of taking a pot shot at one. There is such a thing as etiquette.

"That Pole was clearly no more than a hired gun," declared Alexander, in a pathetic attempt to save face. "I expect my son's impatient to inherit. I know he's only twelve, but so advanced for his age."

"The whole English nation conspired with every Italian State there is, in a desperate bid to assassinate me," Napoleon remarked with the proud hauteur of one who knows his value. "And I won't be a bit surprised if it turns out that the Austrians were involved as well, to say nothing of the Hungarians. In fact, it was an international conspiracy, not some lone music critic."

"That's not what it'll say in the Russian newspapers," declared Alexander, who was in no mood for casual chit-chat. And Mikhailevitch's attempt to curry favour with his *March Specially Composed For The Most Illustrious And Munificent Czar* failed dismally, because Alexander decided that he hated the piece, and Mikhailevitch was sent to Siberia for five years, although not because of his music. At least, not primarily.

4

"It's another miracle that the Emperor survived the cowardly attack on him," said Evans, when reporting the incident to his wife.

"The Emperor? I thought the Czar was the target?"

"That's what Alexander wants you to think, Agnes, because the man's full of deceit. It starts with a stolen hat, and you think he can't stoop any lower, but before you know it, he's ignoring treaties and declaring war."

"Why would a Polish music student want to kill the French Emperor?"

"Who can read the mind of a madman? Napoleon was lucky not to have faced one of our more skilled American gunmen. Europeans rely too much on rank and influence, instead of solid hard work and target practice."

"There isn't the same efficiency and enterprise here in Europe," conceded Mrs Evans. "An American assassin would have been much more thorough, and saved time and effort by shooting both Napoleon and Alexander in one go."

"That's why the Emperor so admires the American character: the famous Yankee know-how."

"Yet I've heard that he's more friendly to the South. They say Jefferson Davis sent a secret envoy to negotiate with him."

"Gossip. It's the Emperor's sympathetic nature. He instinctively champions the underdog, and everybody knows the Confederacy will lose the war. It's only chivalry that makes him appear to favour the Southern States."

"According to the English papers, if France recognizes the Confederacy, Britain will too," said Mrs Evans, who did not have the benefit of daily contact with the Imperial Court, and was inclined to read the newspapers for information, even though her husband related Napoleon's views to her at every meal. "The mills in the north of England are being forced to close, because they haven't been able to get any supplies of cotton since the blockade began. It seems that the British blame the Federal Government for stopping the trade and causing such hardship among the mill workers. At least, that's what was in the London *Times*."

"Propaganda," declared Evans. "It makes no difference what a few journalists scribble about the temporary unemployment of a handful of people."

"But if Britain recognizes the Confederacy —"

"The British will do what the Emperor does. Even they know he's the leader of Europe. Why else would they encourage Italian conspiracies to blow up his hat?"

"But the Emperor's never spoken out against slavery, and if he does acknowledge the Confederacy, he might even agree to support the South financially."

"It won't happen. The Emperor doesn't need to talk about slavery. Everybody knows that he believes in justice and liberty for all. It's why he was forced to seize power, remember, to protect his country from extremists. Abraham Lincoln vowed to do exactly the same thing when he was elected President; the only difference is that he'll abandon his office after a few years, while the Emperor's quite prepared to devote his whole life to the service of France."

"But if the Emperor's so anti-slavery, why hasn't he said outright that he supports the Federal Government?"

"Politics," explained Evans. "It's obvious that he supports the North. That's why he's done nothing whatsoever to help the Federal cause."

Mrs Evans looked baffled, undoubtedly aware that Napoleon's strategic brilliance was beyond her grasp: a problem she shared with many others, in both Old and New

56

Worlds. "Well, if you're certain, Thomas —"

"I am," declared Evans.

Yet, despite his absolute confidence in the Emperor, Evans found himself worrying. Wily Southerners, resident in Paris, were continually trying to bribe Imperial Court officials with huge amounts of cotton. It had not been a very successful manoeuvre up to then, as the French were more accustomed to receiving their bribes in hard cash, but Evans was concerned enough to bombard Napoleon with articles from the New York papers, and as much information as could be gleaned from the American Legation, to counteract the pernicious Southern influence. Luckily, Evans had many unusual opportunities, denied lesser men, to defend the Federal cause at the Imperial Court, and he was not restrained by a fear of being intrusive, chiefly because the thought never occurred to him. There were corrupt French officials, up to their ears in cotton, to contend with, to say nothing of the scheming British; but Evans's great advantage stemmed from the fact that Napoleon was always a captive audience, whenever his dentist spoke to him about the American Civil War.

"Mouth open a little wider please, your Majesty. Thank you, sire. This won't hurt." Evans had learnt, early in his career, to ignore all extraneous cries of pain. They were such a distraction from the matter at hand. "Don't believe anything you read in the British newspapers, sire. It simply isn't true that the Federal Government hasn't guns enough for all our soldiers, especially now, because I got together with some fellow Northerners, also living in Paris, and we chartered a ship to take— Head a little more to this side, your Majesty, please."

Napoleon tried to resist the attempt to separate his neck from his shoulders, and discovered that his skull seemed to be held in some sort of vice. He struggled to screech out a protest, but found that he could not even swallow.

"We were able to buy all the guns and ammunition we wanted, right here in France, without any trouble at all: enough to fill the whole ship, in fact. And we dealt only with the French armaments industry, because no Northerner would even look at a Prussian gun, while he can get such superior ones in France."

To learn that his dentist went in for gun-running, and apparently had access to a vast arsenal of firearms, was unlikely to count among the more pleasant surprises in Napoleon's life. An armed dentist was not a thought he cared to dwell on at the best of times, and that particular moment, flat on his back with a metallic mouthful of dental instruments, came close to being one of the worst.

"I had a telegram from Mr Tollemache this morning," Evans continued. "He's a British Member of Parliament, but a fairly good man all the same. Pity about his teeth. He consulted me, when he was on holiday here last year, and I did what I could, but once a British dentist has been let loose in a mouth, there's never much hope. He tells me that Mr Roebuck is to make a statement in the House of Commons later today, about a conversation he claims to have had with your Majesty."

Damn Roebuck! The squealer would be unable to keep a secret if he were gagged. Napoleon made a reckless effort to speak, and promptly choked on the half-dozen instruments that slid down his throat. He gasped for air, and then choked again.

"I agree," Evans said warmly. "But Mr Roebuck will allege that your Majesty told him France is going to recognize the Southern Confederacy."

And so that was Roebuck's idea of confidential

negotiations: blab everything to the entire world. Quite obviously no fervent American Federalist had access to the back-stabber's teeth. Napoleon thrashed his arms about in an endeavour to end the appointment there and then with imperial resolve, but the dentist was fifteen years younger than the Emperor, and armed with that scraping thing.

"I knew it was all lies," declared Evans. "I've already drafted a telegram to Mr Tollemache, denying Mr Roebuck's foul slanders. All your Majesty has to do is agree, and I'll send it off at once."

At once! To be rid of Evans immediately, Napoleon was prepared to agree to anything. Besides, the thought of being treated in future by a dentist with a grudge against Bonaparte foreign policy was somewhat alarming. From start to finish, teeth were simply not worth the trouble they caused.

"Thank you, your Majesty. The telegram will be on its way to London the very second I'm finished here. No, sire, I wouldn't dream of deserting you right in the middle of so vital an appointment. Anyhow, Mr Roebuck never manages to get himself to the House of Commons much before evening, and as soon as he tries to speak, Mr Tollemache will leap to his feet and produce your Majesty's telegram, only too pleased to oblige by contradicting Mr Roebuck's wild claims. As it happens, they belong to different parties, but the truth, and nothing but the truth, is Mr Tollemache's sole motivation. And this won't hurt either, your Majesty."

Napoleon cried out, but not in assent.

"I'll be glad to foil a British plot," said Evans. "I won't forget the way they conspired with Italian anarchists, in that cowardly fashion, to blow up your Majesty's hat. Mouth a little wider, sire, please."

Evans felt so sorry for the Emperor in those days; people thrusting advice and opinions at his Imperial head, no matter how inconvenient the circumstances, but Napoleon could always count on one loyal friend, prepared to stay faithfully at his side.

"I think I must increase my visits here, your Majesty," said Evans, as a wheezing Napoleon, with clothes crumpled and hair awry, was finally released. "Constant vigilance is the secret of preserving teeth, and if I have to come to the Palace twice a day, three times a day, then so be it. I'll devote my life, if necessary, to each remaining tooth, because I look on it as a sacred charge that only death can end. Together, sire, through the years, we'll drill and fill and scrape and —"

"Evans," Napoleon said wearily, "have you ever thought of going back home to America?"

"America?" repeated Evans in surprise.

"Yes. America."

"Does your Majesty want me to gather first-hand information about the political and military circumstances to guide Imperial policy on the Civil War?"

"Yes, yes, Evans, that's it! That's it exactly," said Napoleon, as ready to grasp opportunity as if it had been presented to him on the Czar's hat. "Why didn't I think of it before? You can visit your friends, assuming you have any, and all your relatives as well. Go now, and stay as long as you like."

"I'll take the very next boat for New York to get the information your Majesty needs," announced Evans.

"Excellent!"

Napoleon looked as though a great burden had been lifted from his shoulders, Evans noted with sympathy. The Emperor had clearly been more worried by the American situation than anybody realized, and he was courageously determined to deny himself the personal attention of his Imperial Dentist for an unknown number of weeks in the cause of truth and justice. Such self-sacrifice left Evans in awe of Napoleon's altruistic sense of duty, and he hastened to assure the Emperor, "I won't be away a minute longer than necessary, your Majesty, not a second longer."

"Oh, take your time," Napoleon said cheerfully. "And should you decide to stay over there indefinitely, that'll be fine. No need to rush back."

But rush would have been Evans's middle name had he not already been blessed with Wiltberger. A steamer across the ocean to New York, and Evans was on the road to Washington DC where, as the French Emperor's Confidential Dentist, he worked his way swiftly through the ranks of Government right up to Secretary of State Seward, one of President Lincoln's chief advisers. The more narrow-minded European politicians had been somewhat surprised that an emperor should dispatch his dentist, rather than an ambassador, on a diplomatic mission, but to the Americans, who value their teeth above all other earthly possessions, the Emperor Napoleon was obviously a man with his priorities in the right order.

"Seward's sending a dentist to see me," President Lincoln remarked to his wife, at breakfast in the White house.

"Why?" demanded Mrs Lincoln. "What's wrong with our dentist?"

"Nothing, I guess, but this one comes from France."

"I've always had my doubts about Seward. I suppose plain American dentists aren't good enough for him. He has to import a fancy Frenchman."

"No, he's actually American, this Frenchman, and Seward says he thinks it's important that I see the dentist, for some reason or other."

"Nonsense. It's only neuralgia; I've told you," declared Mrs Lincoln, with all the firmness required in dealing with a

President who lacked the good sense to follow her advice at all times. Abraham was too tall, too thin, too untidy, and too inclined to look vague whenever she spoke. To a small, brisk, neatly dressed, determined woman with unbounded ambition, who knew that she would have made a better President than her husband any day of the week, he could be infuriatingly slow. "And you need a haircut," she added.

"I had one," said Lincoln, without interest.

"Three months ago. Seward will be sending you a barber next. This isn't the way to get re-elected, you know."

"If I'm re-elected, it'll be because of what happens in the war, not my hair," said Lincoln.

"You never did understand politics," retorted Mrs Lincoln, as her husband strolled out of the room.

First the front door of the Elysée, then the front door of the Tuileries, and finally the front door of the White House; equality certainly knew how to distinguish the extraordinary dentist from the run of the mill majority. Other visitors to the Presidential mansion might have been awed by their surroundings, but Evans, who regarded the Tuileries Palace as his second home, could not be impressed by a building that called itself a mere house. Conscious of the historic importance of his mission, he felt no surprise to find himself about to speak to the President of the united bit of the States, because it seemed natural to Evans to be among men of authority, few of whom could ever hope to wield the sort of terrifying power that a nineteenth century dentist had over his patients.

"Mr President, I'm Dr Thomas W Evans, and I'm here to assure you that the Emperor Napoleon III of France won't ever recognize the Confederacy," declared Evans, the moment that Lincoln appeared. "Not for one minute would his Majesty consider supporting the South, not for one second.

He'll never give his backing to the Confederacy, never!"

"Glad to hear it," said Lincoln, placing a desk between himself and the enthusiastic visitor. "My wife says it's only neuralgia, and she's usually right."

"There's no question whatsoever of French recognition for the South, and as the Emperor leads European opinion, no other country there will support the Confederacy either. The entire Old World is with you, Mr President. You have my word on that."

"Good," said Lincoln, trying not to look as much at a loss as he felt. "You're a dentist, Seward tells me," he added, as Evans seemed to expect rather more of a response.

"I'm the Imperial Court Dentist, trained at Jefferson College itself," Evans declared with pride. "Personal dentist to his Majesty the Emperor Napoleon III of France. That's why I can speak so confidently about French foreign policy."

"I see," said Lincoln, blankly. "Well, thank you for your visit. I'm sure the neuralgia will soon be gone."

"There's just one other thing —"

"Yes?" Lincoln asked warily.

"The Emperor will want to be certain that he's backed the winning side. Not that it makes the slightest difference to him, of course, because as I've already explained in detail to his Majesty, this is a war for equality, for justice, for the right of all men to be free; and, by an odd coincidence, those are the very reasons that forced the Emperor to seize absolute power in the first place. But, even so, I'd like to be able to assure him that the Federal Government's going to come out on top."

"I guess we'll pull through," said Lincoln, who appeared surprisingly indifferent to the prospect of not having the French Emperor's approval. "We should be all right, in the end at any rate. General Grant seems fairly confident."

"General Grant! You're right! He's the one I should speak to next. Are there any messages you'd like me to give to him? Don't hesitate to ask, Mr President. No task is too burdensome in the service of our great country, no duty too onerous."

Lincoln thought. "You could give Grant my regards," he said at last.

"Consider it done, sir, and the moment I'm able to sum up the complete military and political situation, I'll be on the next boat back to Europe. Are there any messages you'd like me to deliver in person to the Emperor Napoleon, as your special envoy? Speak freely, sir."

"You could give him my regards as well," suggested Lincoln.

"And how pleased his Majesty will be to receive those regards, Mr President, because you and he have so much in common. Of course, you're not the son of a king, but neither was he for long. The moment his uncle got defeated at Waterloo, the Bonapartes were kicked out of Holland without even a word of thanks for taking on the responsibility of absolute power. The Dutch simply didn't see the bigger picture. But I expect you had similar difficulties in Kentucky."

"Not that I can recall," Lincoln admitted.

****

Fortress Monroe, Virginia, sounded as impressive an address as any centuries-old European castle. However, instead of aloofly residing in a tapestry-walled map-room overlooking a moat, General Grant was perched on a camp chair outside a tent, in the middle of a busy military town of larger tents, while his men ran up and down and shouted over the monotonous clang of a blacksmith's hammer. A civilian was a novelty, and Grant looked up with interest as a small and stout man strode purposefully towards him.

"General Grant? I'm Dr Thomas W Evans, and President Lincoln himself sent me here with an important message for you."

"Yes?"

"The President sends you his regards, sir."

"Yes?"

"Yes indeed, General."

"I mean, did Lincoln say anything else?"

"Not really. It's so American of you to live in a tent," Evans remarked in admiration. "No European General would even consider it. They're just not democratic. But as they're inclined to be on the elderly side, perhaps I shouldn't speak harshly of them, because I expect sleeping on the cold ground loses its attraction in the long run, especially when you're eaten alive by these mosquitoes."

"I hardly notice them," Grant claimed, remembering an officer's duty to uphold morale. Conscious of being youthful, slender, dark-haired and handsome, if only in comparison with other Generals, Hiram Ulysses Simpson Grant tried to look indifferent to the mosquitoes. Puffing out lungfuls of cigar smoke, in passable imitation of a steam train at full speed, was the only defence he had found, but regrettably Grant was forced to put aside his cigars every so often to eat, when the mosquitoes, with commendable democracy, would ignore the lesser ranks all around, and promptly seize on the chance to make their own meal out of the unarmed General. It might have been warfare, but it was not warfare as taught at West Point. "You've just come from Washington, Dr Evans? What's the latest news there?"

"It was only neuralgia, as Mrs Lincoln said. I was able to reassure the President entirely. And one glance at your teeth, sir, tells me that I'm looking at a future President of the

United States: as soon as we are united again, of course."

"I'm no politician," said Grant in surprise. "I wouldn't have the least idea where to begin."

"You could start by dropping the Hiram," Evans suggested. "A pity Grant doesn't begin with an A. 'Vote USA for the USA.' What an election slogan it'd be! Who could have resisted it? Apart from the Southern voters, I mean."

"I'll never be President," said Grant without regret. "I don't have the slightest interest in politics."

"You'd bring a refreshing new insight to Washington," declared Evans. "Not for nothing were you given those teeth: Presidential teeth. The electorate would go wild with enthusiasm."

"I never voted but once," admitted Grant, "and then I voted for Buchanan. I've felt so guilty about it ever since, that I never dared vote again."

"Understandable, but every war we've ever fought has sent a General straight into the White House afterwards, and the future must not be denied. Where would France be now, if the Emperor Napoleon had worried about his lack of Imperial experience? You'd never guess, from all his achievements in the last ten years, the problems he's had with those Bonaparte teeth of his."

"Napoleon Bonaparte? Is he still going? I thought he died years ago at Waterloo, or someplace. But, as I said, I don't know anything about politics."

Grant was speaking to the right man if he required information on the subject of Emperors called Napoleon. In a mere matter of hours, that seemed but minutes to the engrossed Evans, Grant found himself overwhelmed with detailed intelligence concerning all branches of the Bonaparte family and their dental inadequacies. "The moment I've completed my mission here, I must get back to the Emperor as quickly as possible. I daren't neglect his teeth a second longer than necessary, and therefore as soon as you assure me that the North will definitely be the victor in this war, I can go on my way.

"Really? In that case, we'll certainly win," declared Grant. "Although I've heard that most people's money has been on the mosquitoes so far. Well goodbye. I'm sorry you have to dash away."

"Oh, don't worry, General, I can stay a little longer. I haven't said a word yet about the Empress Eugénie's family. Amazing teeth. You'd never guess the mother was British: well, half-British half-Belgian, to be entirely accurate, but the resulting teeth are spectacular. It's a complicated background, and takes some explaining but, luckily, my coach doesn't leave until the morning."

However, Grant found himself cheering up as the night progressed. Perhaps the bond of future glory made friendship inevitable between two men with such remarkable destinies to fulfill, each one instinctively recognizing the greatness in the other. Either that, or the wine Evans had brought with him from Paris was particularly potent.

****

Mission accomplished, Evans shot back across the Atlantic to his bereft Emperor, and hurried straight to the Tuileries Palace and duty, without even pausing to go home first.

Napoleon, feet up on his desk, was just in the middle of a relaxing half-hour with the most loyal of all the loyal newspaper editorials, when his dentist's abrupt appearance at the office door caused a cup of coffee to cascade over both news print and Imperial attire. "Evans!" exclaimed Napoleon in shock. "You can't be back yet. I thought you'd stay away months longer. Didn't you go to America?"

"Indeed I did, sire. A mere ten days separate us from New York now, your Majesty."

"And they call it progress," Napoleon commented sadly, as he abandoned the drenched newspaper and began to dab at his waistcoat with a handkerchief.

"I've spoken to Congressmen, to Senators, to Secretary of State Seward, to General Grant, to President Lincoln himself. Good man, Lincoln. Sound teeth."

"I'm glad to hear it," muttered Napoleon, weighing up his odds of getting out of the room unscathed. "However, most unfortunately, I haven't time enough today to discuss your trip. Perhaps tomorrow or next week, or even—"

"The Southern Confederacy is almost finished," announced Evans. "They haven't got a chance. Your Majesty was completely right to do nothing whatsoever about the war in that decisive fashion. Brilliant strategy, sire. General Grant himself told me that he'd never have thought of simply ignoring the entire situation; it didn't even occur to him to do so."

"Why not write me a letter all about your trip?" Napoleon suggested, making for the door. "I'm much too busy today. Affairs of state. Yes, definitely affairs of state. Urgent affairs of state, in fact. But next month, or rather next year, I might be able to spare time to —"

"You must put yourself first for once, sire," Evans replied firmly, blocking the Imperial escape. "Two months without me! I'll find work that needs to be done immediately; I'm sure of it"

But Evans was not half as sure as Napoleon.

****

Long articles in the French press praised the Emperor's

wisdom in so cleverly staying aloof and uncommitted throughout the entire American Civil War. The newspapers also spoke, as if with one scornful voice, of the machinations of a certain John Roebuck, a British Member of Parliament, who had been misguided enough to try and persuade his country that mere commercial prosperity, with mills full of lucrative Confederacy cotton, should be considered more important than the principle of freedom for all. The Emperor was particularly high-minded on the point, graciously permitting his stern words of reproof, directed squarely at the British in general and Roebuck in particular, to be quoted at length.

"Rather good, don't you think, Evans?" Napoleon said, after reading aloud some of the more expressive rhetoric. "Of course, the comparison to Racine and Corneille has been made before, though I always feel my speeches have a fluency about them that some of theirs are inclined to lack."

"Yes, indeed, your Majesty." But Evans sounded subdued. For once, he had walked rather than charged into the Palace, and even climbing the front stairs had failed to comfort his soul. "I've got the most appalling news to tell you, sire."

"I'm not having my teeth scraped yet again," declared Napoleon, "and I don't care what your tests say. Every tooth left in my head ached for a week afterwards last time, and I won't submit to such torture any more, however bad the news."

"Today's news is among the worst that I've heard in my life." Evans sighed deeply, unable to bring himself to say the words that he had come to deliver.

"Worse than scraping!" exclaimed Napoleon in horror. "Not that foot-pump drill thing again! No! Definitely not! Never! I refuse, I utterly refuse."

"Sire, I've just come from the American Legation —"

"Then couldn't you go back there?" pleaded Napoleon. "I mustn't keep you from your other patients, and I'm so very busy. I've decrees to sign, bills to draft, speeches to write —"

"Sire, Mr Lincoln's been shot."

"So, you see, I can't spare you a moment today, Evans. Perhaps tomorrow or next week or next—"

"Your Majesty, President Lincoln's been assassinated."

Napoleon's powerful intellect was immediately called into action as he digested the news. "Sounds as though someone didn't like him," he said at last.

"Your Majesty has summed up the dreadful situation with uncanny accuracy," declared Evans, sighing again.

"I've always been intuitive," agreed Napoleon.

"It seems that an actor shot President Lincoln."

"An actor!" repeated Napoleon, astonished. "I must cancel that visit to the *Comédie Française* at once!"

"If only President Lincoln had had such foresight," lamented Evans.

"An actor! I simply can't credit it. What business has an actor meddling in politics?" demanded Napoleon. "An actor's job is to stride up and down a stage in knee-breeches and shoulder-length curls, not to go around aiming guns at the nearest Head of State."

"Never was a truer word spoken," declared Evans with yet another sigh. "Oh, this is one of the worst days of my life."

"Then I insist you don't do any work at all for the rest of the month," Napoleon announced, the Bonaparte brain apparently working overtime that day. "Guard! Escort Dr Evans from the premises right now, at gunpoint if necessary."

The tone was imperially decisive, masterful and ringing, but the French were unworthy of such a quick-thinking leader, Evans was saddened to note, as he made his way home through the anger of placard-waving crowds.

70

5

"Demonstrations again!" the Emperor exclaimed indignantly, studying the police reports on his desk. "I can't think what on earth seems to have upset everybody so. Those miners had refused, absolutely refused, to end their strike. They just went on and on about more money, fewer hours, safer working conditions. I'd like all those things too, but you don't see me going on strike."

"No, not even once, sire," said Evans. "Your Majesty sacrifices himself for France."

"On a daily basis," agreed Napoleon, hurt that an ungrateful populace should have so little appreciation of his effective strike-breaking technique. "Naturally my soldiers had to open fire. What alternative did they have? It was the sole way to persuade those miners to go back underground. And then the troops only killed a mere handful of workers, no more than twenty-five or so. Twenty-six at the most. The way the story's been exaggerated, anyone would think a massacre had taken place, with blood everywhere and bodies littering the streets."

"Agitators, sire; Ignore them," advised Evans. "The newspapers have printed the truth. They support your Majesty entirely."

"And always will," declared Napoleon. "I'll see to that."

The Emperor certainly did see to it, and never more thoroughly than during a rather awkward incident involving his cousin Pierre.

The whole thing was entirely the fault of the two young journalists, of course, who had only themselves to blame for the unfortunate occurrence. As Pierre Bonaparte explained later, Ulrich de Fonvielle and Victor Noir had had the audacity to march up to his front door and knock on it, without the slightest invitation to do so.

Pierre was told that two gentlemen were waiting to see him, but the moment he looked over the banister down into the hall, Pierre knew that he had been misinformed. Two gentlemen? Two clerks perhaps, or two bank tellers, judging by their clothes. But two gentlemen? Never! Both had luxuriant dark hair, which irritated Pierre to start with, and de Fonvielle was tall and thin, which further annoyed Pierre. Noir was of a more tactful stockier build, but Pierre did not feel forgiving as the man was clearly no more than twenty years old at the most, and if Pierre had had any dearest friends, even they would have described him as short, fat, red-faced and ageing rapidly.

"Well? What do you want?" Pierre bellowed from the top of the stairs. Two clerks were not worth the effort of a strenuous descent to the hallway.

The young men looked up in surprise at the bellicose Bonaparte glowering at them. "Paschal Grousset sent us —" de Fonvielle began.

"Grousset! The journalist!" Pierre had heard enough. He was not the most easy-going of Bonapartes, particularly since his cousin, Emperor Napoleon III, had quite deliberately gone out of his way to marry and produce an heir, an infant of vigorous health who single-handedly wrecked Pierre's chance of one day inheriting absolute power, to say nothing of absolute money. It was typical of Louis-Napoleon's selfish nature and, more than a decade later, Pierre had still not mastered his disappointment. He seemed destined to remain a pensioned-off relative for the rest of his days, an also-ran Bonaparte, and the whole thing was simply not fair. "So Grousset hasn't the courage to face me, and apologize in person for his foul insult. The coward's had to send a couple of clerks to do the job for him. Well, you can tell Paschal

Grousset from me that it's not good enough."

"Well, actually, we're not clerks. I'm Ulrich de Fon —"

"I don't care if you're the King of Prussia," Pierre roared. "Is Grousset prepared to make a full and frank admission that he libeled me, maliciously libeled me, in that article of his?"

"Well, actually, no —"

"No!" shouted Pierre in disbelief. "No! He claimed in print, in print for the entire world to read, that I was wearing an orange coat at Longchamps. Orange! I wouldn't be seen dead in an orange coat. It was a delicate shade of salmon-pink, and very fashionable. Nobody's worn an orange coat for at least two seasons, as I said when I was interviewed for *L'Avenir*."

"We're here because of that interview in *L'Avenir*. You claimed he —"

"Inform Grousset that I demand an immediate apology from him. A public apology. A retraction on the front page. I'll accept nothing less than a full-page retraction of his foul libel."

"About *L'Avenir*. He sent us to tell you that he —"

"That he's gone into hiding!" Pierre cried triumphantly. "Wait until I get this into *L'Avenir*! He skulks underground, in a pathetic attempt to save his own miserable skin, and then sends two clerks —"

"He isn't in hiding, and we're not clerks." De Fonvielle wished that Noir would help him out a bit, but perhaps it was too much to expect from a nineteen-year-old, just started in a new job and encountering an enraged Bonaparte for the first time. "We're journalists, you see, and —"

"Journalists!" Already Pierre could visualize the misquotes and his topaz waistcoat described as yellow. "You're journalists!"

"Yes. And Grousset would appreciate an apology from

you."

"From me?" demanded Pierre in astonishment. "Me!"

"Well, you did say some fairly awful things about him in
L'Avenir," de Fonvielle pointed out, "and he's able to produce
his parents' marriage certificate on request at any time
convenient to you."

"You can tell Grousset that I'm going to get far worse
things about him printed in the very next edition of L'Avenir.
Orange indeed!"

"In that case, as you refuse to apologize, please name
your second."

"My second what?" barked Pierre.

"Your second in the duel."

"Duel?" Pierre had long known that all journalists were
totally insane, but this was the first time he had met one who
seemed to be raving as well. "What are you on about now?
What duel?"

"The duel between you and Grousset, of course," de
Fonvielle explained. "If you won't retract your insults, he
challenges you."

"He has the presumption to challenge me to a duel? Me!
But I'm a Bonaparte!" screeched Pierre. There was only one
possible response to such impertinence, and luckily Pierre
was foresighted enough to carry his revolver with him at all
times. He leaned over the banister, and began to fire
downstairs in sheer exasperation.

****

"I can't possibly have an appointment with you today,
Evans," declared Napoleon. "No free time at all. My cousin
Pierre has just killed a journalist."

"Oh dear. Press intrusion into a man's private life must be
an appalling experience."

74

"Pierre's always been on the quick-tempered side, and it makes Christmas a bit difficult at times, I can tell you. Lucky that he isn't a better shot, or we'd have had two dead journalists on our hands."

"There's generally some brightness in the darkest night, as the saying goes," remarked Evans. "Although that's a rather inaccurate observation, in my opinion, because I've never noticed any brightness whatsoever in the darkest night, but perhaps it's poetic licence or something."

"It won't be all that bright with Pierre in the dock on a murder charge — I mean, an accidental death charge," declared Napoleon.

"But surely he can't be charged with anything when it's a case of self-defence," said Evans in surprise.

"The man Pierre shot didn't have a gun. He had a witness instead," Napoleon reported gloomily. "Typical of a journalist, but I've told the police to take a second look at the body, and see if they find a gun after all, exactly as they should have hours ago. I've got to do everyone's job for them, and why these things always pick on me to happen to, I can't imagine. Other Emperors aren't lumbered with cousins who go around, armed to the teeth, taking pot shots at reporters."

"While we're on the subject of teeth —"

"We're not," snapped Napoleon.

The death of Victor Noir resulted in yet more street demonstrations and irrational cries of Imperial tyranny, which annoyed Napoleon intensely. As he told everybody, he had never once thought of aiming a gun in the direction of any member of the press, no matter what the provocation, and those journalists living in exile had been kicked out of France humanely, without so much as a single bullet to speed them on their way. Yet, despite the Emperor's protests, there was even a speech in the Chamber of Deputies that claimed

Napoleon was shielding his cousin from the full legal consequences of having committed cold-blooded murder, when the whole of Paris knew that Pierre's blood was usually close to boiling point. It was a very emotional speech, dwelling in detail on the grief of Victor Noir's widowed mother who, now that her son had been so savagely slaughtered, faced the world alone and unprotected in her silent house: a house that had once echoed with the merry chatter of a little child, a happy child, an only child, the sole comfort of his mother's tragic life — At this juncture, the speech was abruptly cut short, as the Deputy struggled unsuccessfully to control the tears that choked his voice. Jules Favre, the one-time incoherent defender of Orsini the hat-bomber, had since been elected to the Chamber of Deputies, and the other Members were no longer surprised by the sensitivity of Favre's compassionate nature. Indeed, the more heartless among them had been known to enliven the duller debates by placing bets on how soon into a rousingly patriotic beloved-motherland speech, Favre would be reaching for his pocket handkerchief, and he never disappointed his appreciative audience.

To show the disloyal agitators how ridiculous they were, with all the wild talk of a corrupt judiciary literally allowing Pierre Bonaparte to get away with murder, the Emperor decided that the trial should take place at once, before there could be even wilder talk of a lack of vigour in the police investigation. Despite being a Bonaparte, Pierre graciously agreed to attend his trial, and even condescended to address the court on the occasion although, as he pointed out, he had told the story so often at dinner-parties that he was bored, utterly and completely bored, with the whole thing.

Two violent thugs broke into his house, incited by their evil ringleader, who had earlier threatened to kill Pierre in a brutal three against one attack, and describe his waistcoat as yellow in the obituary. As Grousset had neglected to state exactly when the murderous assault would take place, Pierre naturally assumed it was happening there and then, and so with prompt Bonaparte instinct, he reached for his gun.

Impressed with the truth and logic of Pierre's evidence, the court acquitted him, but for some obscure reason, the public demonstrations against Napoleon continued. The fact that Victor Noir had undeniably been the cause of his own death was entirely ignored in the clamour for a re-trial. There were even calls for the Emperor to abdicate.

"An absurd suggestion!" said Evans. "Your Majesty mustn't take any notice."

"I don't intend to," replied Napoleon, not in need of that particular piece of advice.

It was 1869, the twentieth anniversary of Evans's first historic encounter with the teeth of Louis-Napoleon Bonaparte, and to celebrate, the Emperor decreed that Evans was to leave France, and accompany the Empress Eugénie to Egypt for the grand opening of the Suez Canal.

"I insist you go, Evans. As it happens, I'll be forced to stay here in Paris, so I want you in Egypt."

"No. Dr Evans must remain with you," the Empress declared. "He's not going anywhere with me."

"Yes, he is," stated Napoleon with equal determination. "I'm ordering him to go to Egypt."

"You're the one who needs a dentist on call. He must stay in Paris."

"He's going with you. I've decided."

"And I've decided that he isn't."

Evans was touched to see the Imperial couple, after sixteen years of marriage, still as devoted as newly-weds, in their concern for the welfare of each other's teeth. Neither would give way, and a toss of a coin finally settled the dispute. Eugénie was yet to discover that her husband kept a double-headed coin handy for such emergencies because, true to his Bonaparte genes, Napoleon had long since realized that fate appreciates a little assistance at times.

"Why not visit Greece while you're in the vicinity," the Emperor suggested. "And come to think of it, Constantinople isn't all that far away. A pity not to take in St Petersburg as well, and I've heard that Outer Mongolia can be rather attractive in the autumn. No need to hurry back."

"It'll be a bad enough journey as it is," Eugénie complained. "Nothing but sand and ruins all over the place. Why Cousin Ferdinand had to insist on constructing a canal in such an out-of-the-way spot, right in the middle of nowhere — well, it's a mystery to me. He's usually quite sociable."

****

On 17th November 1869, a fleet of fifty ships gathered around the French Imperial yacht at Port Said, a place greatly inferior to Atlantic City. For that first journey through the Suez Canal, the Austrian Emperor put in an appearance, as did the Crown Prince of Prussia, one of Queen Victoria's sons, several of the Czar's cousins, and some middle-European dukes whose identity remained unclear. Recognizing that he was the personal representative of ex-General now President Grant at the celebrations, Evans did not mention that the firework display was rather tame, when compared with the more magnificent American ones, or point out how disappointing the dimensions of the Canal were to somebody who had seen the Potomac in full flow, or even partial flow. Diplomacy was essential, Evans felt, and Europeans could not be held responsible for their more limited experience of the world, because not everyone can have the great good luck to be born American.

The very first dentist to go through the Suez Canal, travelling on the very first ship to use the route, Evans also claimed another record, when he became the first dentist to treat a patient while sailing through the Canal. The ship's captain insisted that nothing was wrong, and it could wait anyway, but Evans was firm, and as he said, he had nothing much else to do just then. The dreary miles of monotonous sand on either side of the yacht could not compete with the lavishness of scenery on daily display in his native Pennsylvania, and when the yacht finally reached the end of the Canal, the only thing to do was turn around and go straight back to Europe.

Perhaps because of the unaccustomed inactivity during that tedious journey up and down the Suez Canal, a brilliant idea suddenly hit Evans, with all the force of the electricity powering the very latest hand-held dental drills. So eager was he to share his inspiration that, on the very day he returned to Paris, he sent messages to all the richer American businessmen of his acquaintance in the city, instructing them to come to his office in the Rue de la Paix that afternoon at five o'clock precisely. They came in apprehension, each wondering uneasily what dental work was so urgent that it required an emergency appointment, and relief overwhelmed them on discovering that it was actually a mass rendezvous, with Evans merely wanting finance for a canal through Central America. Light-headed at their deliverance from his clutches, they were ready to chip in generously, and poor Ferdinand de Lesseps, shrivelled by the Egyptian sun and worn out before his time, found himself ordered to leave for Nicaragua, as though one canal were not enough to last a man his whole life. In vain did he protest that he was really just a diplomat, who had only constructed a canal to oblige.

"It was nothing more than a hobby," he tried to tell Evans, "a way of passing the time when I'd finished cataloguing my stamp collection. I never intended to make a career of it, and I only got the job through influence anyway. If my cousin Eugenia hadn't chanced to marry a French Emperor, nobody would have listened to me. I'm done with canals, and besides, I promised myself a holiday, a long holiday. I've been counting on it for absolute months, years in fact. I'm going somewhere nice and cool, with no heat or flies or mosquitoes or sand. And above all, no digging."

But de Lesseps's dentist was firm. Evans had decided on a canal; nothing less would please him. "And no, I don't want it through Sweden."

"What about Norway then?"

"Nicaragua," Evans said firmly.

"Nicaragua!" repeated de Lesseps in despair.

"Or possibly Panama, if Nicaragua proves to be unsuitable," Evans conceded. "But definitely Central America. Do you know how long it takes us in the States to go overland from the East Coast to the West?"

De Lesseps had no idea, and cared not a jot. Before the first shovel hit the ground, a canal through Nicaragua would mean endless surveying expeditions through malaria-infested swamps and sweltering jungles, with poisonous snakes and spiders as company along the way, possibly leopards and crocodiles too, and if he survived all that, there were years and years of being eaten alive by insects while he dehydrated like a particularly withered prune. "What about a nice canal on the Canadian border?" de Lesseps offered desperately. "It wouldn't be frozen over for more than a week or two each winter: a month at the most. Besides, I'm due to retire at any moment. You need a younger man."

"Age is merely a state of mind," decreed Evans. "I've booked your passage for Thursday, so you've plenty of time to do your packing, and New York's the place to shop for any equipment you might need; Europe can't compete. I only wish I could go myself, but you know the Emperor's teeth, although not as well as I do."

"I'm not going anywhere near Central America at my time of life, and I don't care if it takes six months or six years to get from New York to San Francisco overland. In any case, exercise is meant to be good for you."

"But the Empress is planning a big party to send you on your way," protested Evans. "You can't let her Majesty down. She's been working on the guest list all day. And the Emperor has graciously suggested that the new scheme be called the Napoleon Canal. Between you and me, I think he was a bit hurt that you didn't name the Suez job after him. His nature is as sensitive as his teeth."

"But I'm only an amateur —"

"An amateur whose name will be remembered forever in American history. Well, if anybody mentions the Napoleon Canal in Nicaragua, at any rate. This is your destiny, your chance to live on in glory through the centuries. Besides, the Emperor's decided that you can be a consul or an ambassador or something in Central America, as you'll be there anyway. He's always so practical."

De Lesseps promised himself that, should he ever return to Europe alive, he would patronize a French dentist and to hell with his teeth. He had more in common with Napoleon III than he realized.

****

Every July 4th, Dr and Mrs Evans held a party. The social event of their season took place, weather permitting, in the

81

garden, with American flags prominently on parade, and patriotic speeches instead of dancing. The 1870 celebrations were to be the most ambitious so far, with the entire American Legation invited to join the festivities: the entire American Legation above the rank of clerk, naturally.

The Emperor always took a great interest in these revels, often mentioning them as early as February or March. "Occasions like this need so much organization, Evans, that I insist you don't come to the Palace again before your party."

"I wouldn't be so selfish," declared Evans. "Not even Independence Day comes before your Majesty's teeth. I know my duty, and I can be here every morning before breakfast, if necessary."

"I never eat breakfast," claimed Napoleon. "And you must leave the city immediately after the party. Yes, a holiday, a long holiday's vital to help you recover from your exertions. It's of the utmost importance. Just go. Anywhere."

"Impossible, your Majesty," Evans replied, moved by the Emperor's generosity. "I wouldn't even consider abandoning the Imperial teeth for so long."

"Well, at least stay away until after your party," pleaded Napoleon.

It was the ninety-fourth year of American independence, and although Evans was already in the early stages of planning for the grand Centennial jubilee and inclined to regard less significant anniversaries as mere rehearsals, the day turned out to be a great success, with a gardenful of Americans, speeches by the dozen, fluttering flags, and not the slightest drop of rain. Knowing the Emperor's keen interest in the gala, Evans hurried to the Tuileries Palace at dawn the next day, so that Napoleon could have all the details at the earliest possible moment.

"Evans! I ordered you to stay away until after your party."

82

"But I did, sire. We celebrate July 4th on the 4th of July: yesterday," explained Evans, putting his instrument case down onto the Emperor's desk. "Everything went splendidly, thanks to your Majesty's great consideration. It looked like rain early on, and we feared the worst, but luckily —"

"I don't have time to see you today." Napoleon eyed the black case with considerable unease, and backed towards the door. "Perhaps next month, but probably not. I'm so very busy that I can't possibly —"

"I would never forgive myself if I neglected your Majesty's teeth another second," declared Evans. "A minute, no longer, will be all that I require."

But the last 'minute, no longer' had turned into a series of painful appointments that spanned several days and seemed more like weeks to the beleaguered Emperor. "I can't even spare you that minute, Evans, because — because — oh, yes, I remember. I knew I had an excuse: I mean, a reason. It's the Prussians; they're trying to grab the Spanish throne for themselves. They want to put Prince Leopold of Hohenzollern in Madrid: make him the new king, and they're even maintaining that he's the next in line to inherit the crown, yet Hohenzollern doesn't sound all that Spanish to me."

"This is disgraceful!" Evans's republicanism was affronted by such high-handed behaviour, and he spoke with all his customary passionate support for democracy. "The Prussians have no right to force a German Prince on Spain, no right at all. Your Majesty must be firm, and tell the Spanish people exactly who ought to be their monarch."

"Absolutely right," agreed Napoleon, encouraged by the success of his delaying tactic. "It's clearly France's duty to get our own man on that throne. After all, Spain's practically in France, and I can't have Prussians plotting to surround my country with German states. The next thing, they'll be claiming that Alsace is theirs and — Ow!" As underhand as any Prussian, the Imperial teeth chose that precise second to blast a bolt of lightning through Napoleon's head, but his rally was equally swift. "I bit my tongue, Evans. That's all. Nothing more."

"A few moments will be enough to determine the extent of the damage to the Imperial tongue, sire. We can take no risks with the enunciation of your Majesty's ultimatum to those devious Prussians."

"But there's no need. I haven't the time. There's nothing wrong."

"We must make the time. This is for France, your Majesty. Think of the Prussian King's teeth, assuming he still has some left. Can we in Paris lag behind, at such a critical phase in European politics? Besides, it'll only take me an instant to sort the problem out: why, less than an instant."

"No," said Napoleon.

"Yes," said Evans.

****

That 'instant' brought the Imperial Dentist to the Tuileries every day for the next fortnight, compelling the persecuted Emperor to take a stand.

"If the Prussians continue to be unreasonable, and they always are, Evans, I'll be forced to declare war on them."

"They won't dare risk it, your Majesty."

"Naturally, if it is to be war, I assume immediate command of the Army."

"And be an inspiration to the men, sire. They'll feel invincible with a Bonaparte at their head again, especially as they're unlikely to be fighting anywhere near Moscow or Waterloo."

"But I'll have to leave Paris far behind me, and once on the march to Berlin, I won't be making any trips back here until the Prussians are defeated, and that might take weeks, so I'll have to cancel —"

"I'm ready to leave with your Majesty at a minute's notice," announced Evans.

"No! You must stay here," Napoleon said urgently. "It's essential that you remain."

"But my patients never complain when I go away, sire. In fact, some of them actively encourage me to leave Paris more often. They know the importance of my missions for your Majesty, and are only too pleased when I postpone their appointments."

"As I'll be only too happy to postpone mine. You mustn't pursue me to the battlefield, Evans, absolutely not. I forbid it."

"But, your Majesty, regular check-ups are of such vital importance that I've got to accompany —"

"The Empress!" In so desperate a situation, even Napoleon's brain could be supple enough to do the gymnastics required for self-defence, and his words flowed with the glibness of inspiration. "Empress Eugénie will act as Regent while I'm away, and I rely on you to stay here, watching over her teeth."

"With my life, if need be," declared Evans, almost as though he sensed that his moment in history, his destiny, was nearly upon him. "But you only have to telegraph, sire, and I'll be there at your Majesty's side before you can look around."

"Yes, I'm sure of that," said Napoleon, and he was sure, very sure. "But you promise, you absolutely promise, to stay here? You'll give me your word as a dentist?"

"Your Majesty puts himself last, as always. Yes, sire, I'll stay in Paris."

"It looks like this war's going to solve quite a few problems for me," Napoleon remarked, with sudden cheerfulness.

6

On July 28th 1870, Napoleon III cancelled an appointment with Evans, assumed command of the Army, and named the Empress as Regent during his absence.

The rows of medals adorning the Imperial uniform glittered in the early sunlight, as the Emperor posed for a photograph on the terrace outside the Tuileries Palace, his fourteen-year-old son in a miniature copy of a Commander-in-Chef's uniform, without medals, at Napoleon's side. The Prince Imperial had successfully pleaded to be allowed to go with the army and see a genuine battle; his childhood box of tin soldiers simply could not compete with the thought of real cavalry charges that included real guns, and young Louis was ready to do his Napoleonic duty by brandishing a sword for the photographer. After Eugénie had joined her family and smiled for a second picture, all Bonaparte preparations for facing the Prussian enemy were concluded.

"Have a nice war," called the Empress, waving a handkerchief, as father and son turned towards the Imperial carriage that was to convey them to the railway station and glory. Napoleon paused to wonder whether a third photograph should be taken to commemorate so martial a departure, but then he abandoned his deliberations to stare suspiciously at a landau that was being waved through the Palace gates. The Emperor's misgivings were abruptly confirmed when Dr Evans jumped out of the still-moving carriage, and rushed up to him.

"I cancelled the appointment," Napoleon said in exasperation. "Evans, I cancelled that appointment with you. It was the very first thing I did this morning, even before I had a cigarette."

"Appointments aren't necessary, sire," Evans assured the

Emperor. "I'm ready to see your Majesty at any time and in any place."

"Well, you can't," Napoleon retorted. "I'm off to fight a war. In actual fact, I'm leaving now. This very second."

Evans knew that his words had touched the Emperor, for Napoleon sprinted to the Imperial carriage so athletically, Louis had to run to keep up with his father. Almost moved to tears, Evans turned to the Empress in order to pledge his support, as the carriage began to trundle down the driveway.

"I'm afraid I'll have to cancel my appointment with you as well, Dr Evans," said Eugénie. "As Regent, I can think only of France."

"Send for me at the first hint of the slightest discomfort. Your Majesty has priority."

"Thank you, Dr Evans, but I fear that it might not be possible to see you for some weeks, some months even. My duty to the French Empire must come first; dental appointments will simply have to wait."

Despite the years that he had known Eugénie, Evans was amazed at such selflessness. Before him stood an Empress prepared to sacrifice everything, even her teeth, for France, and no celebrated heroine of history or legend could have offered more. The courage behind the valiant declaration nearly overwhelmed Evans with emotion, and his voice faltered as he said, "Whenever your Majesty needs my assistance, I'll be ready."

"Thank you, Dr Evans." As she hurried away from her dentist into the sanctuary of the Tuileries Palace, Eugénie could not have imagined how soon that promised help would be required, or how grateful she would be to receive it.

****

Although temporarily relieved of his Imperial duties, Evans

enjoyed little free time. As a member of the International Red Cross, he had supplies to order and preparations to make for the field hospitals that were to support the army in North-Eastern France and, because of the gravity of the situation, he also summoned his Central American Canal Committee to an emergency meeting.

Everybody present in the Rue de la Paix office assumed that they had been convened to hear the latest survey report from the Nicaraguan Canal Expedition, and their minds were on snakes, spiders, ants, mosquitoes, alligators, swamps, quicksand and yellow fever, because Ferdinand de Lesseps was inclined to write rather dismal letters, assuring the Committee that a canal through Nicaragua was an impossibility, and that Panama would almost certainly be even worse. The Committee's collective mind was still jungle-bound, when Evans dashed into the room, and announced his intention of founding the American Sanitary Commission of Paris, the members of which were to be the Canal Committee, to save wasting time on a recruitment drive. Their vital work was to start immediately.

"But what is a Sanitary Commission?" the bewildered ex-Canal Committee wanted to know. "Something to do with drains?"

"It could be," replied Evans, and the members of the newly-founded organization looked even less enthusiastic. "Our spheres of activity will be wide-ranging. Sanitary Commissions are an American invention, like every other brilliant flash of genius in the modern world: desiccated egg and vegetables, for example, to say nothing of condensed milk. We either created them, or we used them first. Well, except for the railway, I suppose; although I did hear that Stephenson's father considered migrating to New York at one time, which would have made his son an American of course, and so the railway's practically a Yankee invention. Anyway, it was my friend President Grant himself who told me all about Sanitary Commissions, when he was nothing more than a General. He said that the Commissioners go around army camps and hospitals, looking at rats and maggots and putrid food."

Despite its Presidential origins, the information did not seem to enthuse Evans's audience, and he hastened to reassure them.

"We'll do a lot more than look at vermin, because our work will be extremely varied, and if there are any drains or sewers available, we can inspect them at the same time. I'm glad the subject's been raised. It's a most important task, and inclined to be neglected."

The Commissioners were not surprised to hear it, but meekly resigned themselves to their fate. If Evans had decided that they were to tackle cockroaches and sludge for the duration of the French war with Prussia, the Sanitary Commission's members knew they would be doing exactly that.

"So it's all settled. Excellent," said Evans, feeling the satisfaction of a job well done. "Oh, one more item: the President of the Commission. I'm perfectly willing to take on the job, if you insist. Of course, should anybody here have greater experience of rats and latrines, I'll naturally defer to him."

The meeting ended with a democratic vote to elect Thomas W Evans, the only candidate, as President of the Commission, and the members were then permitted to go home. For President Evans, however, there was no such relaxation. He began his duties immediately with a visit to the nearest printer's office to arrange for a new set of visiting cards, splendidly embossed and bearing the important tidings, in both English and French, that Dr Thomas Wiltberger Evans was President of the American Sanitary Commission of Paris. As soon as he was armed with proof of the honour bestowed on him, Evans felt able to concentrate on less crucial matters at Red Cross Headquarters.

****

In the August of 1870, as Prussian victory followed Prussian victory, the French began to turn against the Emperor and Empress. Bizarrely, people seemed to blame the Imperial family for the defeats, merely because their Army was ill-equipped, ill-trained and its commanders incompetent. These shortcomings would hardly have been noticed in a normal European conflict, but the Prussians had altered all the old, time-honoured, gentlemanly traditions of amateurism in warfare with an unsporting and relentless efficiency.

Throughout that summer's heat and brightness, the public notice boards around Paris began to fill with lists of places few had heard of before, but added to the information were columns of names that families and friends recognized with a blow that was physical.

Froeschwiller	August 6th	20,000 French casualties
Forbach	August 9th	4,000 French casualties
Colombey	August 14th	3,500 French casualties
Rezonville	August 15th	14,500 French casualties
Saint-Privat	August 18th	12,500 French casualties
Sedan	September 1st	17,000 French casualties

No loyalty, no patriotism, Evans thought sadly as street demonstrations increased in number. Of course, the demonstrators were undoubtedly the same troublemakers who took exception to shot strikers and dead journalists, and who displayed such little gratitude to the man who had voluntarily become their Emperor, without the slightest pressure having been put on him to do so. But Evans found it difficult to fit worrying about politics into his schedule, with a timetable that was already full, because the city hospitals were overwhelmed by the numbers of wounded arriving, in train after train, from the battlefields. The men had appalling injuries, their comrades were dead, their country in a desperate plight, and just when they thought life could get no worse, along came Dr Thomas W Evans to prove that they were mistaken. The French Army might be losing a war, but it was going to keep its teeth; Evans had made his mind up on that point. The soldiers could protest they had no dental problems, not the slightest twinge of pain, Evans refused to listen. They were going to enjoy the very best treatment, which naturally meant American treatment, no matter what they said; and the soldiers were inclined to say rather a lot, once they had recovered the power of speech but, by that time, Evans had moved on to other victims.

It was during the afternoon of Sunday September 4th that accurate news reached the city, and confirmed the rumours already circulating about the calamity at Sedan. Thousands more French soldiers were known to be dead, and yet the Emperor did not even have the common courtesy to be killed alongside them on the battlefield. Napoleon had surrendered to the Prussians at the first opportunity without a murmur, and managed to get himself comfortably installed in a castle somewhere, while the victorious German Army was marching *en route* for Paris. Desperate for the very latest information, the city's inhabitants, as so often before, started to gather in the streets.

****

That Sunday afternoon, the Empress was in the Tuileries Palace, busily defying Count de Palikao, the Minister of War,

92

who had just arrived in a panic from the Chamber of Deputies.

"It's a catastrophe, your Majesty, a disaster!"

"The beginning of the war might have proved unfavourable to France, Minister, but our gallant soldiers will soon reverse this temporary setback, and I too must be a soldier; therefore, I cannot desert my post," Eugénie announced imperially, feeling as if she were centre stage at the *Comédie Française*, with a rapturous audience about to applaud and cheer. "In the most dangerous place of all, there you will find me, ready to defend the flag, that proud Imperial standard of ours." Joan of Arc herself could not have put it better, Eugénie decided complacently.

"But the Chamber of Deputies has been invaded by a rabble."

"That's the worst of being so close to a road," Eugénie commented with regal indifference.

"Your Majesty doesn't quite grasp the gravity of the situation. The mobs are calling for a republic."

"But, Minister, we're an empire," said Eugénie in surprise.

As though the problems he already had were not enough with the Premiership and War Ministry foistered on him at a moment's notice, Count de Palikao thought bitterly, he now had an Empress on his hands who was determined to get herself guillotined. Everybody in the city seemed to be blaming him for the defeat at Sedan, merely because one of his job titles chanced to be Minister of War, and to hold him responsible for the French Army's lack of effort was decidedly unfair, in de Palikao's opinion, especially as he had been nowhere near the battlefield at the time; in fact, he had hardly left Paris since the war began. But would anybody listen? Oh no, they were far too busy saying the entire defeat was all his fault. "Your Majesty must leave the Palace right now, before it's too late," he said irritably. "This is another revolution."

"Duty insists that I stay here, and duty is a sacred trust," Eugénie declared. It was what Joan of Arc would have proclaimed. Though, come to think of it, Joan did have a rather unfortunate end.

"But the Palace might be stormed at any minute. There are crowds gathering in the Place de la Concorde." And it had not been part of either the Premier's or the Minister of War's job description, as far as de Palikao could recall, to die at the hands of an infuriated *canaille* in the Tuileries alongside a thick-headed Empress.

"My guards are loyal and trustworthy: men of the highest calibre, personally selected by the Emperor himself. Any mob that tries to attack the Palace will be forced to retreat." But where had Joan's guards vanished to, when the wood was being stacked for her own personal bonfire?

"Your guards have refused to fire on their fellow countrymen, and are standing down." De Palikao could speak with authority on this point because the sentries had told him exactly what they intended to do, not humbly asked his permission, and what was worse, they had actually dared to suggest that he might be Italian. All right, so he was dark, plump, sang tenor and had a surname ending with an O, but that was hardly reason enough to call a patriotic Frenchman an Italian. Modern soldiers had no respect, not even for the Minister who was practically their employer. "Nobody will be left to defend either your Majesty or the Palace by now."

What would Joan have said at the news that her guards were off like shots at the first hint of trouble? No, never mind Joan; what should the Empress of France say, just in case Count de Palikao happened to be taking secret notes for his future memoirs?

"I can face any peril for France, and if I'm to die, then it must be at my post, with honour." Even Eugénie was impressed with the line. All those years of theatre-going had obviously paid off, and de Palikao could write as many autobiographies as he liked. No Empress of France need fear any Italian, when she had the ability to produce such a memorable quotation on demand. "Leave me, Minister. I have work to do." Eugénie added grandly.

"Well, don't say I didn't warn you," de Palikao muttered. "I'm off."

****

Even though it was a Sunday, the Deputies had been fully occupied with an emergency debate about the war situation, when a mob, in no mood for reasoned discussion, surged into the Chamber. The Imperialist Deputies hastily recalled urgent appointments elsewhere, and left the floor to the less Napoleonic of their colleagues.

It was a day that the thirty-year-old Léon Gambetta had been certain would come, but even he was startled by the suddenness of its arrival. Short, overweight, shabbily-dressed Gambetta, with his untidy mane of dark hair, never managed to look like the lawyer he had been or the politician he had become, and looked even less like a leader of men. It was only his first year as a Deputy, and although he had often imagined himself, more revolutionary than the entire 1795 *Directoire* put together, delivering red-hot speeches all about the glorious dawn of freedom with the criminal Bonaparte usurper overthrown and the will of the people once again supreme, it had not occurred to Gambetta that he would require one of those historic orations quite so abruptly.

The remaining Deputies were rapidly being driven into a far corner of the Chamber by the sheer number of people pushing their way inside, and chairs and desks were overturned as the enthusiastic crowd waved red flags, attempted a spirited rendition of the *Marseillaise* with rather more passion than tune, and called for the Emperor's immediate removal from power. Somebody had to do something, Gambetta realized, before the next Government was squashed flat by the eagerness of its citizens, and he turned to the senior Deputy present.

"Announce the Republic!" he shouted urgently, over the pandemonium in the Chamber. "Quick! Announce the Republic! This is our chance to kick the Bonapartes out for good."

Historic moment or not, the word 'Republic' had that Deputy fumbling desperately in his pocket for a handkerchief. Life in the Chamber had done nothing to cure Jules Favre of the sensitivity that made his career in law such an emotional one, and many more clients than Orsini had been forced to suffer from a grief-stricken advocate, unable to continue their defence. Mention of the Republic was to Favre the equivalent of motherland, home, native soil, liberty, equality and fraternity all rolled into one, and he would be incoherent for hours, Gambetta knew, yet the other Deputies were looking with decided apprehension at the citizenry they preferred to encounter as a passive audience, rather than active participants in Government. It was an excellent opportunity, which Gambetta seized because, despite being the youngest and most inexperienced Deputy in the Chamber, he could recognize an opening for an inspirational speech when it came along. Making full use of a sudden nimbleness that he thought had gone forever along with his waistline, Gambetta jumped onto a chair, and feeling like President of the new Republic, he shouted "Attention!" and got it.

A youthful dream of becoming a great actor had been thwarted by his dumpy appearance and a practical aunt, who pointed out that lawyers never starved; but all at once it seemed that Gambetta's old ambition was realized, as an entire revolution obediently turned and looked up at him, in a scene too large for the stage of the grandest theatre. "Because of the present crisis that faces our beleaguered country," he announced in his most resonant tone, "I declare — I mean we, the elected representatives of the people, declare that Louis-Napoleon Bonaparte and all his dynasty are deposed." Gambetta kindly paused to allow the extras their moment of cheering, then he raised a hand to cue them to silence, and shouted, "Long live the Republic!"

"Long live the Republic!" shrieked the crowd, exactly as Gambetta knew they would, just as certainly as though they had all rehearsed from the same script. He stepped down from his chair in triumph, wondering if he ought to have led the company in a verse or two of the *Marseillaise*, but that might have been altogether too much for Favre, who seemed near to collapse as it was.

"I can't wait to go home and tell my Aunt Jenny about this," Gambetta remarked in awe, as the cheering continued. "France is a republic again, simply because I stood on a chair and said so."

Favre continued to sob.

****

The crowd in the Place de la Concorde shouted and cheered, in-between snatches of the *Marseillaise,* and the uproar could be clearly heard inside the Tuileries Palace, where the Empress Eugénie was being helped into a coat by her companion, Charlotte Lebreton. "Do you think I should go out onto a balcony and address the populace?"

"No," Madame Lebreton replied.

"Not even to try and bring them to their senses?"

"No."

"I'm rather inclined to agree with you, Charlotte," acknowledged Eugénie. "Is there a back way out of the Palace?"

"Yes, and the sooner you're through it, the better."

"You don't think I should disguise myself as a peasant, so that I can mingle unnoticed with the revolutionaries?"

"I think they'd notice a peasant in the middle of Paris nowadays."

"Oh well, it was just a passing thought. Will it take the servants very long to pack my dresses?"

"Forget the dresses," Madame Lebreton said in exasperation. "Come on!"

Charlotte Lebreton had been brought up at the court of King Charles X of France. She was a childhood friend of the Orléanist princesses, but also a childhood friend of Eugenia di Montijo, and even Eugenia's marriage to a man whose family background hardly counted as a background at all in Orléanist circles, had not ended that friendship. Charlotte was too loyal to desert any woman who had had to pay so appalling a price to become an Empress.

The back of the Louvre was behind the Palace, and with commendable foresight, a passageway had been constructed between the two buildings, so that by the time the mob trampled over the fallen railings and surged into the Tuileries Gardens, the Empress Eugénie and Madame Lebreton were already hurrying through the *Galerie d'Apollon* and past its great works of art, with more speed than an English tourist confronted with culture. However, there was no safety outside the Louvre. Madame Lebreton had hoped that the republicans would concentrate on storming the Tuileries Palace, yet in the Place St Germain, an excited crowd had gathered with no apparent purpose but to shout, and although the Empress wore a simple black outfit, her clothes were obviously expensive, and she had been photographed many times.

"What should we do?" asked Eugénie, glancing back at the Louvre in search of a possible sanctuary. "I doubt the mobs will have much interest in studying their national heritage today."

"But we'd be trapped inside, if they decided to loot the paintings. It's probably a better idea to keep moving." Madame Lebreton had little belief in her own advice, and as they tried to skirt the raucous crowd, her fears were confirmed when a small boy, much begrimed in shabby clothes, planted himself firmly in their way, held out a hand for charity, and then stared at Eugénie.

"You're the Empress!"

"No, of course she's not." Madame Lebreton attempted to laugh, but her heart thudded painfully, and Eugénie froze in terror. "What a silly thing to say."

"She looks just like the Empress."

"Nonsense."

"I saw her at the orphanage," the child declared stubbornly.

"If you're a runaway, I'm going to have to call a gendarme," said Madame Lebreton, trying to sound severe while she pressed her hands together to control their trembling. "It's clearly my duty to send you straight back to wherever you—"

The boy had disappeared into the crowd before Madame Lebreton could finish her threat, and Eugénie dared to breathe again, although shakily. "Little wretch! The poor are so ungrateful, and I opened some perfectly beautiful orphanages for them too."

"Not so loud," urged Madame Lebreton. "We've got to get

out of this crowd."

And then the impossible happened. In the Place St. Germain, on a Sunday, at that hour in the afternoon, right in the middle of a revolution, a free cab materialized before them.

"It's practically a miracle," Madame Lebreton assured the Empress.

As she hustled Eugenia into the cab, Madame Lebreton realized she had chosen the losing side, but at that moment, friendship cane before France. It was an instinctive choice, with no time for consideration. Eugenia needed her; the revolution did not.

The very French Charlotte Lebreton, a foreigner's idea of a typical Parisienne, with her dark hair, intelligent face and elegantly stylish appearance, found herself nervous of her own countrymen. Bellowing hordes of republican supporters swarmed through the central boulevards, obstructing the cab, and although Madame Lebreton attempted to talk loudly enough to mask the cries for the Spanish woman's death, she was unsuccessful.

"They always insist on calling me the Spanish woman," Eugénie complained. "Yet I'm just as British as I'm Spanish, and there's a Belgian grandmother thrown into the mix as well, but the French never mention the fact. And I've lived in Paris for so long now, I was more or less born here. They simply won't give me credit for that, and I can't think why not."

"I suppose they —" Madame Lebreton tried to think of a reason, and then decided it was easier to change the subject. "Will your friends be expecting you?"

"Oh yes, Napoleon had an escape plan ready from the beginning, just in case. Everything's arranged, and I'll be quite safe when we get to the Boulevard Haussmann. After all, Guy Besson's a State Councillor, so it's his job to be reliable. Once we reach the house, you can go home, Charlotte. I'll be fine."

It would not be of much comfort to go home, Madame Lebreton reflected. Her husband was a prisoner-of-war with the Emperor, and the Prussians were marching in the direction of Paris, but Eugénie only had time for her own problems. "Where will the Bessons take you?" asked Madame Lebreton. "Spain?"

"Why does everybody assume I'll head for Madrid the first chance I get?" asked Eugénie in exasperation. "No, I'm not planning to go anywhere near Spain. I'll travel with the Bessons to England. Paulina Metternich's waiting for me in Sussex right now. She smuggled my jewels there last week, and it's been so handy having a friend whose husband's an Austrian Ambassador. She never gets stopped these days, Paulina told me. Apparently she only has to begin explaining the more intricate details of the Schleswig-Holstein Question, and she finds herself more or less hurled out into the Dover streets."

Madame Lebreton had never before suspected Eugénie of having such strategic skills, and thought it was a shame that Napoleon, rather than his Empress, should have been the one to command the French Army throughout the disastrous war. "Will the Emperor know that you're in England?"

"Oh yes. I made him promise to send Louis straight to Hastings, if anything went wrong. And it certainly has gone wrong."

"Then the Prince is probably safe in England at this very minute," said Madame Lebreton, pleased to find something of comfort in the situation.

"I still think that fourteen's a bit too young to go to war, but darling Louis so wanted to see a battlefield. I suppose it's his Bonaparte blood, but even so I'm afraid that I spoil the child.

Anything he wants, toys, bonbons, cakes, wars; I can't refuse him."

The cab had finally reached their destination, but both women felt uneasy at the idea of leaving its security and venturing out among the rowdy demonstrators in the Boulevard Haussmann. Safety was only a few steps away across the pavement, but those steps seemed to stretch before them to the distance of a day's journey.

"It looks as though the entire population of the city's out there," Eugénie murmured.

"Impossible," said Madame Lebreton, with an assurance that she hoped sounded genuine. "At least a thousand were busy trying to storm the Tuileries when we left, and they couldn't possibly have finished the job and managed to get here before us. There are never enough cabs on a Sunday afternoon."

Eugénie took a deep breath, stepped down onto the pavement, and made her way through a crowd so preoccupied in calling for the Spanish woman's death, that nobody noticed her presence among them. Madame Lebreton struggled in the Empress's wake, telling herself that in another five seconds, they would be safe. Another four seconds. Another three seconds—

But the house was locked up, its shutters closed, even the servants gone.

"No, Charlotte, someone must be here," declared Eugénie. "The Bessons promised not to leave without me; they promised."

"It isn't safe to stay in the open like this. You could be recognized again." Madame Lebreton glanced around, fighting panic, and saw salvation in the shape of their cab, still at the roadside, temporarily unable to move as a part of the crowd surged in front of it. "Quick! Back into the cab."

"But I must stay here," Eugénie protested. "I might miss the Bessons when they return."

"Your friends have gone," Madame Lebreton said bluntly. "They've left you behind."

"No!" Eugénie had only been let down once before in her life, and it had happened earlier that same day, when the French nation abandoned their Empress, but the Bessons' desertion felt worse. "They'll be back at any second."

"No, they won't." Charlotte was right, and Eugénie knew it, although she still shook her head obstinately, forcing Madame Lebreton to grasp a plan at random. "Let's go to the American Legation and ask for protection. Revolutionaries should respect a republican flag."

"But the Americans wouldn't keep me there permanently, no matter how democratic a republic they have." Eugénie's greatest gift was her ability to write off the past, and finally accepting that the Bessons had deserted the Imperial side, she dismissed them from her mind. "A democratic republican! That's it! I'll go to Dr Evans's house."

"You've got toothache?" Madame Lebreton demanded. "But you can't have, not in the middle of a revolution; nobody could."

"Exactly!" Eugénie said in triumphant. "And nobody would imagine that I'd go voluntarily to see Dr Evans. I could hide in his house for weeks, months even, without anyone suspecting a thing. In fact, it's probably the safest place in Paris for me right now."

"The cab! Hurry!" Madame Lebreton led the way this time, one hand firmly anchored around the Empress's arm. If Charlotte Lebreton were to substitute for absent friends, she preferred to undertake her rôle away from public scrutiny, and as far as possible from the nearest guillotine.

"Even a cut-throat mob would avoid Dr Evans," Eugénie

remarked, as she climbed back into the cab.

7

After an early morning emergency call to the Prince de Beauffremont's house — and it was always an emergency with the old Prince, who gave his teeth no consideration whatsoever, yet expected them to behave like servants under his command — Evans had spent the whole of that Sunday at Red Cross Headquarters, preparing for the arrival of yet more wounded from the battlefields. The work was urgent, time limited and readiness essential; therefore, it seemed most unfortunate that he should be compelled to leave early. He postponed his departure until the very last minute, but so important a commitment could not be neglected, even in wartime. Great events constantly follow each other in rapid succession, and that very evening, Evans was hosting a gentlemen's dinner-party. The invitations had gone out the week before, could not possibly be rescinded, and Thomas W Evans was not a man to shirk his responsibilities.

A young American doctor, Edward Augustus Crane, travelled in the carriage with Evans. The International Red Cross had sent Crane to Paris, and his father had sent him to Evans. Benjamin Crane did not have a very high opinion of his son's competence, and the idea of Edward let loose in the middle of a European war made Benjamin wonder about the commonsense of whoever ran the International Red Cross. As Edward had once managed to get himself lost somewhere between the Liberty Bell and James Madison's house in Philadelphia during an instructive family outing, it seemed highly unlikely to Benjamin that his son would be able to locate any wounded soldiers in a strange country without considerable help and, luckily, Benjamin had an old college friend resident in Paris, who would be the ideal guide for a clueless young man in search of French battlefields.

Benjamin had not actually encountered his old college friend in more than twenty years, but he recalled that Tom Evans had been a zealous student, and according to Benjamin, anyone zealous must be practical: not at all the sort of person to mislay an ex-President's house. Thomas W Evans was therefore elected Edward's Parisian guardian without opposition. Not that Evans faced much competition in the matter, as Benjamin knew nobody else in Europe, apart from his disgraced sister who was the reason Benjamin had been forced to leave his native Massachusetts and start a new life in Philadelphia, after Caroline Crane shamed the family and herself by publishing her thoughts, feelings and opinions in poems for all the world to read, despite being a married woman. Any other husband would have stopped such nonsense in its tracks, but George Perkins Marsh had been a congressman with suspiciously liberal tendencies before his appointment as the first United States Minister to the newly-formed country of Italy, where he displayed an even more suspicious liking for European culture and art. Edward could not be allowed to venture near such dangerously polluted air, and so Tom Evans triumphed.

Edward A Crane was of average height and average build, not particularly dark, not particularly fair, not remarkably handsome, not remarkably plain, unusual only in his absolute American averageness. He had only been in France a few days, and had little understanding of the French and their customs, but was ready to learn more. "Odd how elated and busy everyone seems, considering the dreadful war news," Crane commented, as he looked out of the carriage window. "Why so many red flags?"

"They've apparently convinced themselves that crimson is the Emperor's favourite colour," Evans explained. "Actually, it's blue, but the people mean well."

"Those shouts —*mort*. Why are they shouting about death?"

"They'd follow the Emperor to death cheerfully. Or it could be *amour,* their love for the Emperor. Some of those working people speak very sloppily: no idea whatsoever of clear enunciation."

"Do they usually make such a noise?"

"It's Sunday," Evans said indulgently. "Their day off, and they've decided to spend it in a spontaneous show of support for the Imperial family. If you'd lived here as long as I have, Crane, you'd know how united this country is, behind their beloved leader."

"Just as well," said Crane, thinking of the Red Cross preparations. It was his first time away from home, as well as his first trip abroad, and he wanted Europe to be different. Should the French prefer to unite behind an Emperor who went in for *coups d'état* and disastrous war strategy, it simply made things more different. He knew that his father would not have regarded such flagrant un-Americanism so tolerantly, but his father disapproved of rather a lot — and Philadelphia was several thousand miles away on the other side of an ocean, Crane reminded himself yet again.

"You'll meet the American Legation staff at my party," Evans remarked.

"Really?" said Crane, impressed. "Every single one of them?"

"Well, the upper echelons, anyway. It's a *gentlemen's* dinner-party, after all. Some of my Sanitary Commission will be there as well, so the conversation should prove most stimulating. That's my house." Evans pointed, rather unnecessarily, because the building he indicated was the only one in the avenue with an American flag proudly flapping on a pole in the garden. "We're in good time for my party. It's taken a great deal of planning, and I've been exchanging telegrams with my wife about it for at least a week. She offered to come home early from her holiday in Deauville, but I wired back that I had everything under control and nothing can possibly go wrong. Well, not unless the Prussians arrive and begin shelling Paris right in the middle of the cheese course," he added merrily. But as soon as they climbed out of the carriage, Dr Evans was informed that there were two ladies waiting to see him in the library: two ladies who had told the servant that it was an emergency.

"And my party due to start in less than an hour!" lamented Evans, but he knew his duty to humanity, and also that he could probably get rid of any patient within half an hour, no matter what the problem, which would leave him twenty minutes, just time enough to change into his evening finery. "Of course, these days, appointments are made for my Rue de la Paix office: one of the best business addresses in Paris, but an expensive area's essential to make my aristocratic patients feel at home. It must be a dire emergency for my surgery staff to send the ladies here, so I'll have to desert you for a little while, Crane, but the very latest number of *Progressive Dentistry* is in the drawing-room, and you'll find it an absorbingly good read. Fascinating article on gumboils: a real conversation opener for my party."

With the first guest's entertainment off his mind, Evans crossed the hall and opened the library door. "Sorry to keep you waiting, ladies, but I was detained at Red Cross Headquarters, and only got home a few min—"

At the sight of his visitors, words failed Evans. But not for long. "Is your Majesty suffering great pain?" he demanded, slamming the door behind him in his haste to reach Eugénie's side. "If your Majesty had sent for me, I'd have gone straight to the Palace, despite my dinner-party. Your

Majesty shouldn't have taken the trouble of coming here, absolutely not. But such consideration! I'm overcome by the thought of your Majesty's consideration, and when I tell my dinner guests, they'll be astounded at your Majesty's generous determination not to deprive them of their host. But I'd willingly have made the journey to the Tuileries, even if it did mean being late for my own party, even if it meant missing the first course entirely. I would have sped to the Palace without a second's pause, without a moment's delay, without the slightest hesitation, without the least —"

Eugénie had only listened that far in sheer amazement, and she held up a hand to stem the rush of emotion. "Dr Evans, don't you know what's happened?"

"Happened?" Evans echoed.

"There's been a revolution," said Madame Lebreton.

"Indeed?" commented Evans, with polite interest. "Where?"

"Here."

"Here? You mean — here!"

"Yes, here in Paris. The Prussians captured the Emperor at Sedan. He's a prisoner-of-war."

"That's impossible, Madame Lebreton. The Emperor would have fallen on his sword rather than accept defeat."

"No, he preferred to hand over his sword quite unbloodied, and now people are in the streets, demanding a new republic, and the soldiers in Paris support them."

"I'm stunned!" gasped Evans.

"How could you have missed a revolution?" asked Eugénie.

"A mob stormed the Tuileries this afternoon," said Madame Lebreton, astonished that anybody in Paris could have failed to grasp the significance of an infuriated citizenry rampaging through the city's streets. "The Empress had to escape from the Palace."

"This is dreadful!" exclaimed Evans. "Dreadful!"

"Yes," agreed Eugénie. "I don't suppose I'll ever see my dresses again."

"Fashions change so quickly these days, you wouldn't have been able to wear them much longer," Madame Lebreton pointed out, before turning back to Evans. "The Empress is in great danger."

"Yes, I absolutely am," said Eugénie. "I must go to England as soon as possible."

"Then I'll take your Majesty there," declared Evans, undaunted. "No need to worry about a thing."

"But the Empress was forced to leave the Palace at a few minutes' notice," said Madame Lebreton. "There are no plans for such a long journey."

"Then we'll make some now."

"But, Dr Evans, how can the Empress get all the way from here to England?" asked Madame Lebreton, overwhelmed by the thought of the difficulties involved.

Luckily, heroes cannot be defeated by mere distance. "My wife's on holiday at Deauville. We'll go there, and hire a boat to take us across the Channel," Evans decided.

"You make it sound so easy," said Eugénie, but she looked doubtful.

"How on earth do we get to Deauville?" Madame Lebreton demanded. "It wouldn't be safe to go by train. Somebody might recognize the Empress."

But Evans had already thought of, and solved, the problem. "We'll begin the journey in my carriage, and hire another one when the horses are tired."

"That still leaves the problem of travel papers," said Madame Lebreton, who seemed determined to be the killjoy of the party. "We can't even get out of Paris without the right documents."

"As it happens, Charlotte," remarked Eugénie, "by a strange coincidence, I have some travel papers with me."

"Are they valid?" asked Evans.

"Oh yes. Oddly enough, for an unknown reason, they were sent to the Palace on the very day that war was declared. A bureaucratic mix-up, I suppose, but I chanced to have them in my hands at the very moment I was forced to escape from the Tuileries. It's such a coincidence."

"Yes, indeed," said Madame Lebreton, smiling for the first time that day. "The sort of thing the Paris Psychic Society would be keen to investigate."

"But what splendid luck for us! Good fortune is on our side, your Majesty," declared Evans, whose unshakeable belief that he and the universe worked in partnership gave him a self-assurance denied lesser mortals.

"I simply can't imagine how official documents from the British Embassy would end up at the Tuileries," the Empress claimed. It was lucky that Eugenia was not under oath, Madame Lebreton reflected, feeling suddenly cheerful.

"They're all stamped by the Prefecture of Police, here in Paris," said Evans, examining the papers. "Excellent. They're ideal for our purpose."

"How they came to be inside my writing-desk, I'll never know."

"A lucky chance for us, your Majesty," declared Evans, thoroughly approving of the way that fate had co-operated with his plans, only seconds after hearing them.

"The papers are for an English doctor, his lady patient, her brother and a nurse. Four people," said Madame Lebreton, taking her turn to study the documents. "Four. That's awkward."

"I'll have to find someone trustworthy —" But then Evans

realized that he had underestimated the efficient foresight of destiny, and he smiled with appreciation. "Crane! Of course! He's actually in the house at this very second, and Edward A Crane's the genuine article: a real doctor."

"Are you sure he's trustworthy?" asked Madame Lebreton, noting the assumption that she was to be a member of the escape party. It was also clear to her that Eugenia would insist on being a theatrical invalid, wilting the entire way to Deauville, while Charlotte Lebreton had to run around as the servile nurse.

"Trustworthy? Crane? Oh, absolutely!" declared Evans. "I'd trust him with my life."

"You've known Dr Crane for a long time then?"

"Two days."

"Two days!" repeated Madame Lebreton in disbelief. "But how can you be so certain that we can trust him?"

"He comes from Philadelphia," replied Evans.

****

As the drawing-room door opened, Crane looked up, bemused, from the correspondence page of *Progressive Dentistry*. Growing up in a sheltered background, he had not realized that passions ran quite so high on the subject of toothpicks, and the vehemence of the printed language startled him. It seemed that humanity might be risking its collective teeth with foolhardy abandon, and Crane was about to ask for a second opinion when Evans pressed a warning forefinger to his lips, closed the door carefully, and then announced, "You're not going to believe this, Crane, but the Empress of France is in my library."

"Toothache, on top of all the dreadful war news!" said Crane, with immediate sympathy. "That's just awful. When things go wrong, they really go wrong. I'm so very sorry to hear —"

"No, no. Listen." Evans glanced cautiously around the room, as though fearing the presence of a hitherto unobserved third person who might suddenly appear before him, and reassured he continued, "There's been a revolution."

"Really? Where?"

"Here." Evans looked surprised to be asked something so self-evident.

"Here!" repeated Crane in amazement. "You mean, in Paris? But when did it happen?"

"Earlier today. It's a nonsense started by a handful of agitators about a new republic, despite the Emperor's years of devoted service to France. Some people have no gratitude. The Empress actually had to escape from hordes of bloodthirsty mobs when they stormed her Palace."

"Nobody said a word to me about it at Red Cross Headquarters," declared Crane, astonished at the casual way that Europeans accepted revolution, without even a mention in passing of stormed palaces, escaped Empresses and bloodthirsty mobs: in fact, entire hordes of bloodthirsty mobs. How different, how very different, from life in Philadelphia where such unruly behaviour would almost certainly have raised several eyebrows.

"And, naturally, out of the whole of Paris, the Empress came straight to me for help," Evans reported complacently. "But I've always been so close to the Imperial Family, it's only to be expected that she'd turn to me for assistance. Crane, I feel as if I must have been born for this moment."

"Those bloodthirsty mobs you mentioned," Crane began, trying to sound untroubled. "The ones who stormed the Palace —"

"Yes? What about them?"

"Are they likely to follow Empress Eugénie here?" Crane was ready, indeed eager, to care for the wounded, but he had no particular wish to be included among their number, especially when imperialism was hardly his natural habitat. "Will any of those mobs come here?"

"Nobody has the slightest idea where the Empress is."

"Good!"

"Her Majesty wants to go to Britain immediately. Crane, the situation's both difficult and complex."

"I'll say!"

"Would you do me a very great favour?"

"Of course, if I can."

"The circumstances are particularly awkward, as you can imagine, today of all days."

"Yes, but I suppose everything's a bit tricky, when there's a revolution in progress."

"I don't like asking you to take on such a delicate task, Crane, but I daren't entrust this duty to anybody else. It's a great responsibility, requiring both resolve and discretion, not to mention level-headed astuteness."

Crane looked uneasy, aware that the job requirements probably ruled him out as the ideal candidate, but he asked, "What do you want me to do?"

"Be my substitute."

"Well, I don't actually know that much about dentistry, I'm afraid. Teeth were mentioned during my medical training, but not exactly in detail."

"No dental details are required, in this case."

"Then how can I be your substitute?"

"By taking on a great commitment for me," replied Evans. "As you know, I've a gentlemen's dinner-party due to start in less than half an hour, yet I can't leave the Empress to dine alone when she's in such distress. Crane, I know it's a lot to ask of anybody, but can I depend on you to host my party for me?"

"Well, I've never hosted anything before," said Crane. Being in charge of a formal dinner would be bad enough, but at least he was not expected to wield a pair of pliers over a panic-stricken patient, and he tried to look willing. "Of course, I won't know anyone at your party, but I'll do my best."

"I'm eternally grateful, Crane. You can tell my guests quite truthfully that I've been called away because of an emergency." His mind at ease, Evans felt able to relax for the first time since he had entered his library and seen Eugénie, but still he was compelled to add, "Naturally, you won't mention that the Empress is here."

"Perhaps your guests won't turn up." Crane, weighed down by his crushing new responsibilities, felt suddenly happier at the thought, and he smiled in relief. "They might just stay at home, with a revolution going on all around them."

"Of course they'll come," declared Evans. "They're Americans. We invented the modern revolution, remember."

"Yes, I suppose so," said Crane, his hopes dashed. "Still, at least the day's events will give them something to discuss over dinner. I've never been much good at casual conversation with strangers."

"Talk about sanitation and canals, if the conversation starts to flag. You'll find my guests are interested in both. Now, I must get back to the Empress." Evans turned towards the door, then stopped abruptly. "Oh, Crane, I almost forgot. Would you do one other thing for me?"

"Of course," Crane agreed absently. Sanitation and canals?

"Accompany me and the Empress when we escape from France tomorrow."

"Go with you!" gasped Crane.

"We need someone to pretend to be a doctor."

"But I am a doctor," Crane pointed out in bewilderment.

"Then you'll be really convincing in the rôle," Evans assured him. "This is for History, Crane. It's not often a man gets the chance to do something that people will talk about for centuries."

When leaving Philadelphia, he had expected to spend a peaceful war treating wounded soldiers, Crane reminded himself. He had not realized that part of his duties would apparently include charging about Europe in the company of a dentist and an empress, with hordes of bloodthirsty mobs in pursuit of him, while he tried to make casual conversation about canals and sanitation. "Tell me, is life in France always so complicated? I've only been here a few days, and already I'm involved in a war, a revolution, rescuing an empress, and hosting a dinner-party that's really my new dentist's dinner-party, and I don't know any of his guests." If Crane had ever dreamt of a similar situation, he would have considered it a nightmare.

"I knew I could count on you." However, it had not occurred to Evans that he would be unable to do so, because it was quite clear to him that Crane had been sent by Providence to be a faithful deputy. "The spirit of '76 lives on."

"Aren't we on the wrong side then?"

"The wrong side?" Evans looked puzzled.

"Shouldn't Americans be supporting a republic, rather than an empress?"

"Americans are on the side of freedom. In this case, it just happens to be an empress's freedom, that's all."

"I hope my father never hears about any of this," said Crane. "I'm pretty sure that he wouldn't agree with your analysis of the situation. You see, he's a staunch republican."

"So am I," declared Evans.

116

"But my father's the sort of republican who disapproves of emperors and kings."

"Oh, politics!" Evans dismissed the detail with a wave of a hand.

****

The front door closed behind the last departing guest, and Crane had never felt more relieved to get to the end of an evening in his life. Before the first course's remnants left the table, everything possible to say about a revolution had been said, but when Crane tried to introduce sanitation as the next topic, the conversation failed to take flight again. Evans had been wrong about his guests, very wrong, because none of them appeared to have any interest whatsoever in discussing sewage treatment while they ate, and the subject of the alimentary canal fared no better. If anything, it seemed to depress the diners, and they all refused the cheese.

"How did my party go?" Evans called from the second floor, and in his eagerness to get the very latest information, he leaned across the banister despite the grave risk of toppling over and shattering his teeth on the marble tiles in the hall below. "Did my guests have a good time?"

"I think so," lied Crane, as he wearily climbed the stairs.

"That's such a weight off my mind. Now I can really concentrate on the matter at hand. We'll spend the night here."

"Yes, you told me earlier, and we start the journey first thing tomorrow."

"I mean, we'll spend the night here, right here, in this corridor on guard outside the Empress's room."

"Here?" It was a pleasant corridor, one of the most striking that Crane had ever seen, carpeted in dark blue with chocolate-brown walls that were almost entirely hidden by two large pictures. There was a dramatic representation of Paul Revere, another celebrated American dentist, riding furiously to warn his fellow countrymen of an imminent raid by the dastardly British, and even in so dire an emergency, the black case containing his dental instruments could be observed tied to his saddle, a tribute to Revere's conscientiousness that had been added to the canvas by the artist at Evans's suggestion. Opposite the galloping dentist, the corridor was further graced by a particularly vivid depiction of the legendary Battle of Mullin's Pond, a colourful composition specially commissioned by Thomas W Evans himself. Yet, in spite of these manifold attractions, Crane still felt that he would prefer a bedroom for the night.

"Would you like a chair? Or perhaps you'd rather lie on the floor?" Guests in the Evans household were always treated with consideration, and the Dentist Imperial was anxious that Crane should enjoy every available luxury that night. "Feel free to make yourself at home."

"Do we really have to spend the night here?" But even as he spoke, Crane suspected that he was asking a silly question because, if Evans had decided on the corridor, Crane would probably have to resign himself to being corridor-doomed until the next day.

"It's vital that we guard the Empress's door. She's in constant danger."

"I thought that you said nobody knew she was here."

"But everyone knows that the Emperor and I are the closest of friends. Why, I've seen him practically every day for the last twenty years. You wouldn't believe how his poor Majesty suffers," said Evans, sighing in sympathy. "Luckily, I was one of the very first dentists to use the amazing Nasymth electric drill, although the Emperor appears to have a prejudice against it, merely because Nasymth invented the steam hammer as well, but I assured his Majesty that I wouldn't even consider employing a stem hammer, no matter how intractable the tooth."

"I'm glad to hear it, but you think people might guess that the Empress is in your house?" persisted Crane.

"I'm known the length and breadth of France as the Imperial Court Dentist, and my pioneering work with gold-foil fillings is celebrated throughout Europe. Princes and Grand Dukes come to consult me from as far away as Russia, because of my expertise." False modesty had never been a flaw in the Evans character. He knew that he was acclaimed whenever the topic of dentistry chanced to arise at social gatherings, and he saw no reason to pretend ignorance of the fact. "If the Imperial Court's mentioned, people instantly think of me. It's inevitable."

No matter how many times he thought of those bloodthirsty mobs, Crane found that the idea of them did not get any more attractive, and he suggested tentatively, "Perhaps we ought to start the journey at once, instead of waiting until tomorrow. Don't you think that, if the mobs do come here hunting the Empress, it might be better for us to be somewhere else?"

"But should the Empress have sought my help, the republicans would expect me to leave Paris immediately. It'd be the logical thing to do, and that's why I'm waiting until tomorrow."

"Illogically?"

"It's the best way to fool the revolutionaries. They'll think that the Empress can't possibly be here."

"Then why do we have to stay on guard in the corridor tonight?"

"In case they're not fooled, of course."

"I see." Crane stopped himself asking what was likely to

happen should any unfooled mobs arrive in the vicinity. He had the feeling that he would not care to hear the answer.

"Well, it's an early start tomorrow," Evans said cheerfully, settling down with as much ease as if he had spent every night of his life in a corridor. "Better get some sleep."

There was one thing to be said for having hosted another man's dinner-party, it made the rest of life seem considerably less difficult in comparison, Crane decided as he struggled unsuccessfully to relax in his chair. Even waiting for a horde of bloodthirsty mobs to storm the house was not as stressful as attempting to force light conversation out of strangers, who stubbornly refused to take the slightest interest in sludge dispersal, no matter how hard Crane had tried to enliven the topic with as many facts and figures as he could remember. The only consolation was that his father need never know about the disaster of the dinner-party, and putting three thousand miles between himself and family felt like the most sensible decision that Edward A Crane had made in his entire existence.

8

On Monday, September 5th, a cool and fresh morning, they began their journey just before dawn. The servants had been unpleasantly French and understandingly sympathetic about two lady patients staying the night while Mrs Evans was away, and the servants also appeared to think that his wife's absence gave Dr Evans an excellent opportunity to go on an impromptu holiday, accompanied by the same two ladies. Evans was disturbed to find such a lax moral standard in his household, but prudently decided to accept a temporary slur on his good name in the interests of security; however, it was particularly disillusioning to find that his strictly Calvinist coachman-gardener, who should certainly have had higher principles than the other less rigidly upright servants, was equally compliant and insultingly tactful about the whole situation. Célestin brought the landau and horses around to the front of the house, as calmly as if Dr Evans leaving home with two strange ladies for an unnamed final destination were an everyday occurrence, and it seemed that the servants had apparently expected such devious behaviour from the very moment Mrs Evans's train began to steam its way towards Deauville.

The landau turned a corner into the Avenue de la Grande Armée, where the tidy French already had street-sweepers out, busily brushing away the remnants of revolution; nor had the events of the preceding twenty-four hours been enough to disrupt the early morning milk-cart rounds, or to stop fruit and vegetable wagons trundling their way through the city gates with that day's produce from the outlying farms. By 1870, the French had come to regard the occasional urban uprising as so normal a part of life that yet another one was hardly worth making a fuss about, and certainly no reason to deny themselves the amenities of civilization.

"I'd always imagined that everything would be complete chaos in a revolution." Unable to believe that he was really travelling in a carriage with the Empress of France and fleeing republicans, Crane looked out of the landau's window at the serenity of the dark streets through which they were travelling. Americans had become rather half-hearted about rebellions, despite their nation's promising start, and Crane was relieved to note that all the bloodthirsty mobs had retired to rest from their labours of the previous day.

"We're coming to the Porte Maillot," said Evans. "Once past the guards at the gate, we're safely out of Paris."

"Once past the guards," repeated Eugénie.

"Yes, once past the guards, we'll be perfectly safe," Madame Lebreton added, in a tone that she hoped sounded confident. "Nobody will imagine that the Empress of France would dare to leave the city so openly. It's what my husband calls strategy."

"And your husband's a General who's just lost a war," Eugénie commented with wry acerbity. "But perhaps that's another part of his strategy."

"He didn't lose the war all by himself. My husband had to do whatever Marshal MacMahon ordered," Madame Lebreton said frostily, fighting the temptation to add that Marshal MacMahon had to do whatever the self-appointed Commander-in-Chief Emperor ordered.

"This time last year, I was getting ready to go to Egypt and open the Suez Canal," Eugénie recalled, ignoring Charlotte's coldness. "I had an escort of soldiers to protect me on the journey, and now those very same soldiers might throw me into prison at any second."

"Impossible, your Majesty," declared Evans. "They'll almost certainly be prisoners themselves in Sedan by now, assuming they're not besieged at Metz, of course. We won't have any trouble from them, and I've a plan to distract the guards here. Hand me my instrument case, Crane."

It was still dark as the carriage approached the city gate, and the nearby buildings were further obscured in the gloom of an early morning mist, but they could all see the sentry box under the gas lamp, as well as the soldier with fixed bayonet standing in front of it.

"Don't forget that you're an invalid," Madame Lebreton reminded the Empress. "Look ill."

Eugénie flung herself back against the carriage seat, and pressed a limp hand to her forehead.

"Not that ill."

"I feel 'that ill' at the moment," said Eugénie. "Besides, they always do ill like this at the *Comédie Française*, Charlotte."

"Yes, but you're an English invalid: open windows, cold air, sea-bathing, vigorous exercise."

"Yes, we must all think British from now on," agreed Evans, as the landau stopped. "Ignore strangers and never ask for coffee." He pushed down the door handle, and climbed out of the carriage to meet the guard approaching him through the shadows. There were two other soldiers as well, standing by the massively high closed gate, and all were armed. No matter, Evans assured himself; it was his destiny to rescue the Empress Eugénie, and rescue her he would.

"Purpose of journey?" Didier Lambert was too young and inexperienced for front-line service, but the excitement of feeling handsome in military uniform and keeping late hours without his mother's permission had worn off, even before August ended. He had been on duty all night, and was tired and cold, rather than alert. Outgoing carriages were of little interest to him; the Prussians were on their way to the city, not departing from it.

"I'm a British gentleman, and I come from Warwickshire," Evans announced in confident Philadelphian tones. "I'm returning to Britain with my British sister, who has her British doctor and British nurse with her, as she's a British invalid. We're hoping to get home to Britain as soon as possible, because that's where we all live, you see: Britain."

"Your papers, please," said Lambert, bored with the job of counting the number of papers, and then counting the number of passengers in the cab or cart. Foreigners had been leaving the city for hours, and it was all right for them, sheltered from the cold, in their comfortable carriages. If he were forced to do one more night on guard-duty, Lambert was quite certain that he would end up just as much of an invalid as any pampered Englishwoman with her own doctor and nurse.

"Our papers? Oh yes, of course: our travel documents. I always keep them in this case, with my dental instruments. Here they — My God!" Evans staggered back a pace in exaggerated horror, and gasped theatrically. "What an overbite you have! You need a lot of work done on those teeth of yours, and done at once. Perhaps I could give you some temporary relief before it's too late?" Evans swept up a handful of instruments from his case as he spoke, and demanded, "Now, where are those pliers?"

"Your papers are in order," Lambert said hastily. He was alert now, but too mesmerized by the contents of Evans's case to bother about checking either papers or passengers. The symbols of dental torment gleamed at him in the gas light with a menace more alarming than the advance of an entire Prussian army, and Lambert wished that he had followed his mother's advice and become a chef, even though the uniform was decidedly less romantic. "Your carriage is blocking the road. You must drive on. Immediately."

"Well, if you insist," said Evans. "But see a dentist as soon as possible, or you'll be in agony, absolute agony. And I don't mean one of your Army dentists. They're no better than torturers; in fact, they could teach torturers a thing or two. I saw a soldier only last week, a young man just like you with his whole life still before him, and you wouldn't believe what those butchers had done to the poor boy. I've always maintained that no man should be judged by his appearance, but let's hope he develops a captivating personality to compensate because he's certainly going to need it."

"Open the gate!" Lambert shouted to his comrades as he retreated rapidly to the sentry box. "Drive on, coachman. Drive on at once!"

Evans climbed triumphantly back inside the carriage, dental instruments within Lambert's sight to the last moment. Seconds later, they had passed through the gate and were on their way.

"It'll be easy from now on," Evans predicted confidently.

****

The morning mist evaporated after they had driven through the forest of Saint-Germain, and the day grew increasingly sunny and warm. Life in the countryside looked, to city eyes, tranquil enough to belong to another age, and the revolution seemed to have been left far behind with Paris. Crane had almost forgotten the reason he was travelling across north-western France with people he barely knew, when Evans suggested that the two of them should leave the carriage and walk up the next hill to lighten the load for the horses. As he climbed out of the landau, Crane could hear birds singing in the trees that lined the road, and the

125

September air still smelt of summer meadows.

"Beautiful day," remarked Crane.

"Splendid," agreed Evans. "We'd better plan what to do if somebody recognizes the Empress. We may have to fight."

"Fight!" Crane was brought back to reality with a thud.

"Stout denial certainly goes a long way," Evans continued, pensively watching Célestin amble beside the horses as he led them up the hill. "Yes, I believe my sister does resemble the Empress; we've been told so before. That might work, but if it doesn't, we fight."

Crane had an alarming vision of himself confronted by one of the bloodthirsty mobs that Evans dismissed so casually, and he demanded, "But how can we possibly fight hundreds of revolutionaries?"

"We could hit them over the head with something," Evans suggested, after a few seconds of reflection.

"What sort of something?" Crane wondered uneasily how many of 'them' there would be, and if 'they' were prepared to stand still, in obliging fashion, while he and Evans went around knocking out each one in turn.

"We could try using a rock, perhaps?" Evans said meditatively, surveying the landscape for a suitable weapon. "Yes, let's collect some rocks, and put them in the carriage. But don't tell the ladies why we're doing it. They might be afraid."

As well they might; Crane could certainly sympathize with those timorous ladies. "Won't they think it's a little odd, if we suddenly start filling the carriage with rocks for no apparent reason?"

But Evans was not the dentist to be thrown by a mere detail. "We'll say you collect fossils."

"Surely I wouldn't be collecting them at a time like this."

"You're a fanatic when it comes to fossils."

126

"Wouldn't you be more convincing as the fanatic? I don't know anything much about fossils."

"Neither do I, and the Empress might wonder if I suddenly become a fossil fanatic, after never once mentioning the subject to her in twenty years. You have to be the fanatic, Crane. It's the only solution and we might just need those rocks."

Crane tried to imagine himself saving the day, armed with only a rock. It had worked for King David of course, but he had been lucky: only one Goliath, not a whole bloodthirsty mob of them. Then an even more terrifying thought abruptly cleared Crane's mind of all Goliaths, and he demanded, "What on earth do I say if the Empress asks me a question about fossils?"

Evans took a momentary pause from his roadside rock review to consider the point. "You could talk about Charles Darwin," he said at last. "Hasn't he got something or other to do with fossils?"

"Darwin!" Crane had not realized how much worse things could get, but he sighed in submission to fate. "I hope my father never hears about all this. If he thinks I've been studying evolution, and doubting the Biblical account of creation, I won't be allowed to go home again."

"He'll never hear a word about your fossil collection from me," Evans promised. "And he's unlikely to correspond with the Empress or Madame Lebreton. Now, look for rocks that are heavy, but small enough to be held firmly in the hand."

"Are they the ones with fossils in them?"

"I've no idea. I was thinking more about their usefulness as a weapon."

"What if we hit somebody over the head, and he doesn't fall down?" asked Crane, spotting a potential flaw in the Evans plan for the disposal of bloodthirsty mobs.

"We hit him again, of course," Evans replied briskly.

"I'm not sure that a doctor ought to go around knocking people out with fossils," said Crane. "And I'm certain the International Red Cross wouldn't approve."

"This is an emergency."

"But even in an emergency, I wouldn't dream of hitting anybody over the head with anything."

"Oh, patients often have to endure a little pain: at least, mine do. It's for their own good in the long run." Evans straightened his back, and glanced with approval at the assortment of rocks that he had gathered. "These should be enough for the most diligent of fossil collectors. You can keep them as souvenirs: if we don't need to use them, that is."

"Being alive, at the end of all this, will be souvenir enough for me."

"Of course we'll succeed in our mission," declared Evans, surprised that there could be any doubt in the matter. "We were sent to France to rescue the Empress. It's our destiny, plain and simple."

"As long as our plain and simple destiny doesn't include us being guillotined later today."

"Oh, no, we couldn't possibly be guillotined today, Crane: not on the very day they captured us. It'd take far longer than that. You don't know the French. They're all paperwork and bureaucracy. They can't do anything without fifty different forms being signed by fifty different officials. Why, it would probably take them months to get around to guillotining us, perhaps even as much as a year."

Yet, despite such emphatic reassurance, Crane did not seem to find Evans's words of much comfort.

****

The horses needed water, and Evans needed food. It was

a long time since his pre-dawn breakfast, and the inner dentist demanded immediate attention, although his companions appeared more preoccupied with other concerns. As Célestin led the horses to a trough in front of a roadside wine shop, a lone nod to civilized living in the midst of wheatfields and stubble, Evans decided that he had to be firm.

"We're only twelve miles from Mantes now, and I'd better find out how far the news from Paris has travelled, and whether or not they're searching for your Majesty around here. I'll pretend to be looking for food, and make a few casual inquiries about the political situation."

"I suppose it would be sensible," conceded Madame Lebreton, although the idea of anybody leaving the seclusion of the landau alarmed her.

"The whole of Paris will be missing me by now," Eugénie declared, and it served the ungrateful city right to wake up and find itself empressless.

"Crane, stand outside the carriage and make sure nobody approaches it," ordered Evans, but the command seemed unnecessary because the road was deserted and the sunshine full of birdsong.

"I can't believe yesterday happened," remarked Crane, climbing out of the landau. "It's like a dream now."

"A nightmare," said Evans. "You've left your fossils in the carriage. Better find some more quick, just in case."

Crane hastily collected a few rocks from the side of a ditch, and offered one to Evans. "Do you think we'll actually have to use them?"

"There won't be any choice if we're attacked by an angry mob."

"But won't hitting republicans make them even angrier?"

"Their problem, not ours." Armed with his fossil, Evans

opened the wine shop's door, the brightness of the day making it difficult for his eyes to adjust to the dark interior and do a survey for possible danger. Although calling itself a shop, the large room looked more like a kitchen, something Evans noted with hope because a kitchen should mean that food was on offer, as well as wine. There were no other customers, an indication that any available food might not be locally acclaimed, but Evans was too hungry to need gastronomic excellence. Bread and cheese would be fine, he assured Madame Fontaine who, broom in mid-sweep, had paused to smile, revealing unexpectedly attractive teeth.

Stoutly middle-aged and bustlingly active, Géneviève Fontaine seemed too cheerful to be a crazed revolutionary, in Evans's opinion, but a dentist could not be overcautious when dealing with a possible misguided French republican. "Any news?" he asked so casually that the question hardly appeared worth mentioning.

"News?" repeated Madame Fontaine, apparently more interested in slicing cheese than in current events.

"I think I heard that something had happened in Paris," said Evans, counting out money to show how little the answer mattered.

"Yes, I heard something too. Another traveller was in here earlier today."

"What did he say?"

"There's some fuss or other about the war, a republic and the Emperor. I forget the exact details. How much cheese do you need? How many people are in your party?"

"Just two of us and the coachman," Evans lied smoothly. "I'm travelling with my nephew: the young man you can't see at the moment because he's hidden by our carriage. He collects fossils. In fact, we're on a fossil collecting expedition. The whole British scientific community's mad about the

Theory of Evolution, as you probably know, and this area's famed for the excellence of its fossils."

"Is it? Most visitors seem more attracted by the local wine."

"And who can blame them? I've never tasted better, but you need a clear head when you're collecting fossils." Evans picked up a yard-long loaf from the table that doubled as a shop counter, paid the bill without a quibble although prices had been inflated for a foreigner, and he retreated into what felt like a different season after the cool dimness of Madame Fontaine's kitchen.

"What's the news?" Crane whispered urgently, hurrying to meet Evans.

"I've only been able to get bread and cheese, but they both smell very good."

"I mean the news about you-know-what."

"Not so good. There are rumours about the Emperor and a republican *coup d'état*."

"Oh no! What are we going to do?"

"Be very careful in Mantes."

****

On a highway bordered by orchards and vineyards, they were fast approaching the town of Mantes. It was nearly eleven o'clock, and the sun was shining with oppressive heat on the tidily cultivated fields that stretched to the horizon on either side of the road. The carriage was thickly coated with white dust, and Evans, who had a low opinion of provincial standards, hoped that it made his expensive landau look almost shabby enough to pass for a countryman's cart. The horses were tiring, and Evans decided that the party in the landau would remain on the outskirts of the town, while he ventured alone into Mantes to reconnoitre and hire a second carriage, driver and team. Célestin could then go into the town with the empty landau, and stay there until the horses were rested enough for a return journey to Paris.

"Nobody should pay any attention to travellers with tired horses, but Dr Crane will stand guard in the road until I get back. You can add to your fossil collection at the same time, Crane."

"Yes, I suppose I can," agreed Crane, uncertain which was the worse prospect: facing curious republican farmers or an Imperial cross-examination on the subject of fossils.

"I'll try and find a Paris newspaper while I'm in Mantes."

"What a pity the Emperor didn't have you, Dr Evans, instead of Marshal MacMahon to advise him on strategy," Eugénie commented.

"Destiny had already decided what my rôle was to be in this war," declared Evans. "That same destiny will guide me to wherever the livery stable is in Mantes, and produce our next carriage."

A walk of less than ten minutes brought Evans into the town, where destiny had the thoughtfulness to locate the livery stable on the very road that the Imperial Dentist trod and, impressed but not surprised at such celestial organization, he went inside. As his eyes grew accustomed to the gloom of his new surroundings after the glare of sunlight, Evans became aware of a thin, gnarled man in a corner scowling at him.

Octave Druon had run his business in Mantes for over three decades. Once upon a time he had been polite, enthusiastic, helpful and kind, but years of dealing with the public had warped a fine and generous nature, and made him look as though he were rapidly approaching his bicentenary. However, on the plus side, his teeth appeared to be in fairly good condition.

132

"I want to hire a carriage, horses and driver," Evans announced briskly. "We're a party of four."

"Oh," said Druon.

"We plan to visit friends in Pacy-sur-Eure. British friends. We're British too, you see."

"Oh," said Druon.

"I've got my own carriage, naturally, but it broke outside town —"

"City."

"Yes, of course, city. Well, as I was saying, we're stranded on the road, and I had to leave my sister there, waiting in the landau. She's an invalid, so I really must get back to her as soon as possible."

"Oh."

"Therefore speed is essential."

"Oh."

"Have you got a suitable carriage?" asked Evans, attempting to hide his impatience with such a lethargic attitude towards business. "Or should I try another livery stable? Perhaps you could recommend one."

"I've got a carriage you can hire," conceded Druon, resenting the call to action, but prepared to co-operate when the alternative would mean losing money, although the order to harness some horses to a brougham was given at his own pace.

"Tell me," Evans said casually, heartened by making progress at last, "is there any news?"

Druon looked blank on principle. "News about what?"

"I heard there was some trouble in Paris," said Evans, trying to sound even more casual.

"There's always trouble in Paris," Druon said scornfully. "I've got my own problems."

"Do you get newspapers here? I mean, the Paris

newspapers: ones like *Le Figaro*, for example. Are they available in Mantes?"

"Of course we've got them," Druon replied, indignantly cross. "What do you think the city of Mantes is? A backwater?"

"Not with such a first-rate livery stable," declared Evans.

No smooth-talking foreigner was going to get around Octave Druon that easily. "There's nothing in Paris that you won't find right here in Mantes. And better."

"I don't doubt it. And will the newspapers have arrived from Paris yet?"

"Of course. Hours ago. They come by the railway. It's all rush, rush, rush these days. My business is being ruined. Now that people can speed all over the country in a train, who wants to hire a carriage?"

"I do," Evans pointed out. "How soon will the brougham be ready?"

"They don't even think of going by road," Druon continued relentlessly, not to be tricked out of his pessimism. "Though why anybody needs to leave Mantes in the first place —"

"And where do they sell the Paris newspapers?"

"Well, you could try asking at the newsagent's along the way. He might be able to make a guess." But so benighted was the foreigner that he did not even notice the fine example of sparkling Mantes wit. Evans merely left the stable without another word, and hurried down the street in search of his newspapers. And that was the last time Druon would ever condescend to share a joke with an outsider. God, how he hated tourists.

****

Evans was in a fever of haste to get back to the Empress, although he knew she was safely hidden inside his landau on

134

a highway that had seemed as deserted as the surrounding fields; but to see the carriage standing exactly where he had left it, under the shade of a tall tree with fossil-laden Crane on guard in the road, was an immense relief. Frozen-faced and sullen Dominique Druon, their newly-hired driver, was a true son of both his father and Mantes, determined to show no interest whatsoever in his temporary employers, even to the extent of deliberately staring at the far horizon, while the passenger transfer took place. The Druon brougham was not as large or modern as the late landau, but an empress cannot demand luxury when escaping bloodthirsty mobs, and luckily, as Eugénie observed to Madame Lebreton, the revolutionaries had waited until crinolines were quite out of fashion, before commencing their activities. Five years earlier, forcing their skirts into such a small carriage would have been considerably more of a problem.

Crane seized one of the newspapers as he sat down inside the brougham, almost expecting to see a *Wanted Dead Or Alive* poster, with his name prominently displayed in the middle of it, emblazoned across the front page. "What does it say about us in the papers?" he asked, uncertain whether or not he really wanted to be told.

"I've no idea yet," replied Evans, calmer now that the carriage had started moving. "I've only had time to glance at the main stories in each paper."

"You mean, I'm not the main story?" said Eugénie in surprise. "But what else do they have to write about?"

"The war. The new Republic," reported Madame Lebreton, rapidly scanning the contents of *Le Figaro*. "Provisional Government of National Defence. New Ministers."

"I can't find a word about me in the *Journal Officiel*," Eugénie said indignantly, as she turned page after page. "Not a single solitary word! It's extraordinary."

"There's nothing at all about you in the whole of *Le Figaro*," Madame Lebreton concluded, after further hurried searching.

"Or in *La Presse* either," said Evans, perplexed.

"Hasn't anybody even noticed that I've gone?" Eugénie demanded. "I've been missing for an entire day now."

"It says here that the Prussians are on their way to Paris, and they might bombard the city into submission." Evans thought of his house, before remembering that it was decidedly unheroic to worry about the furniture at such a time.

"And after everything I've done for the French people, not even a mention of my name, not a single thought for my safety," the Empress complained. "All they can think about is some army marching to shell them. It's utter selfishness when I wore myself out going to banquets and the theatre and parties on their behalf. Why, I was ready to die at my post in the service of France, defending the Tuileries from the Prussians; but no, I was forced out of my own Palace by the very nation I'm Empress of, and yet not a word of apology anywhere."

"Your Majesty's an example of duty and steadfastness to us all," declared Evans.

"Absolutely. I'd have shown the French how to die unafraid. But what did they do? Forced me to go to the dentist's instead, and now they're forcing me to go to England. It's all so inconsiderate." Eugénie pictured herself on the ramparts, assuming that there were some in Paris, an inspiration to the devoted soldiers around her, just like Joan of Arc defying the English when they besieged Orléans. Or had the English been inside Orléans, while Joan herself did the beseiging? And was it Orléans at all? Eugénie always had a problem sorting out the Hundred Years War from the

136

Thirty Years one, but whichever the war and wherever the city, she knew that she would have been a second Joan, although hopefully without the voices. Poor Joan must have found dinner-parties an absolute nightmare, sorting out who said what to her, while trying to keep the general conversation running smoothly.

"Do you think it's odd: the newspapers not mentioning the Empress?" Crane murmured to Evans.

"Yes. Obviously the republicans don't want us to know what they're doing. They've probably telegraphed her Majesty's description, and mine, along possible escape routes. We'll just have to be as inconspicuous as we can." But Evans was not unduly worried, because he felt that, with destiny and American determination on his side, the French were already outwitted. It was no contest.

However, he had yet to discover that destiny seemed to have lost concentration somewhere on the road to Pacy-sur-Eure.

The drive there had been so uneventful, that even Crane was beginning to relax. Nobody showed the least interest in the brougham or its occupants, whenever they stopped to water the horses, and the smooth highway between towns was free of both cut-throat mobs and gendarmes with arrest warrants. A few more changes of carriage, and they would be on the coast, Evans told himself, and once at Deauville, a mere trickle of water was between them and safety in Britain. By that time, the Emperor should have negotiated peace terms with the Prussian King, and be planning his triumphant return to a chastened Paris. After all, his Uncle Napoleon had experienced a defeat or two along the way, and the French did not seem to hold those hiccups against him, unlike the British with their tactlessly named railway stations and squares. France would settle back into prosperity and

Bonapartism, as Napoleon III was succeeded, on a day in the far distant future, by Napoleon IV with his wonderfully American-tended teeth, and history would remember Dr Thomas W Evans with gratitude. There would almost certainly be a boulevard named after him, perhaps even a park, and generations of French children would be told the story of the daring dentist whose scientific zeal had brought hope to European mouths, when he was not otherwise occupied with rescuing empresses. Evans began to imagine the speeches made in his honour, the banquets, the firework displays —

Then, around two o'clock in the afternoon, they arrived at the hamlet of Pacy-sur-Eure, and destiny began to shilly-shally in a most un-American way.

"But you must have a carriage for hire," Evans said firmly. "And horses too. We need them."

"Everybody goes by train these days," Madame Everard said, with equal firmness.

"Well, we don't."

"Perhaps not, but I haven't bothered with carriages these past ten years. There's no call for them now."

The inn was run-down, most of its former trade lost since the coming of the railway, but Sophie Everard kept going because she was old, yet still active, and knew no other way of life. She was dressed in many layers of faded and shapeless clothes, but her teeth were surprisingly good for such a dilapidated place, quite as good as those that Evans had seen in the vicinity of Mantes. He found this surprising, for in the wilderness of provincial France, the attentions of a properly qualified dentist were unlikely to be at hand, yet the teeth on display were a credit to their owners. Perhaps something to do with the local water supply?

"The station's up that road. Turn left at the second elm

138

tree, and when you come to a signpost, ignore it. Keep going until you see a stubble field, then cross—"

"We don't want to travel by train. My sister dislikes them," Evans explained glibly. "They make her ill — iller than she already is, I mean, and she's an invalid to start with. We must have a carriage at once: immediately, in fact."

"Why don't you wait until your horses are rested? You could stay here," suggested Madame Everard. "Overnight, if you like. I've plenty of rooms vacant at the moment, as it happens, and —"

"No. We need fresh horses now. And a carriage. And a driver as well." Evans gave the list to destiny, and waited impatiently for some co-operation. "We must leave Pacy-sur-Eure without delay."

"Impossible!" But Madame Everard found herself wavering before the American certainty that what you want in life is what you get, and Evans wanted a carriage and horses, and he wanted them right there and then.

"Well — I do have a — well — it's probably not —"

"Yes?" demanded Evans, his suspicions confirmed. He had known all along that Madame Everard must be concealing a carriage somewhere on the premises, and no doubt horses too. Impossible had always been a word that annoyed him.

"Well, there's a carriage, an old carriage, a very old carriage, at the back of the stable," Madame Everard admitted. "But it hasn't been out on the road in years, and I'm not sure if it's exactly —"

"We'll take it," said Evans. "Horses. Where can we get some?"

"I don't keep horses now," Madame Everard claimed, trying to recover lost ground, unaware that she was dealing with fate as well as the Imperial Dentist.

"Then who does keep horses around here?" Evans asked briskly. "Somebody must. You can't plough fields by train."

Madame Everard capitulated. "My son has two horses on his farm. He lives further down the road, a few minutes walk."

"And he can be our driver. Excellent! Dr Crane and I will get the carriage out, while you send for your son and his horses. What sort of carriage is it, by the way?"

"Oh, just a carriage sort of carriage. I really don't remember. It's been so long since anybody wanted to travel anywhere by road."

Evans could not have put a name to the contraption either. It had been repaired and altered so many times over its long life that the carriage had become unique, a mixture of every vehicle made in France over the previous hundred years, but that was not the most startling feature of its appearance.

"Inconspicuous, you said," Crane recalled sadly. "That's our best chance, you said, to be inconspicuous."

In a one-time Everard flurry of artistic exuberance, the carriage had been painted green with yellow wheels. Age could not wither the vividness of the colour scheme, and although dust and cobwebs had made a valiant attempt, they too were defeated. The green was so very green, and the yellow so very yellow, that even Dr Thomas W Evans felt taken aback, but only for a few seconds. A man of destiny cannot be conquered by a lack of colour co-ordination, no matter how unfortunate.

"Nobody's going to look for the Empress of France in that," Evans declared. "It's ideal for our purpose."

"But won't everyone stare rather a lot, when we drive by in such a — such a — such an unusual vehicle?" said Crane.

"Some people might stare," conceded Evans, "but only at the carriage, not us. It'll be good camouflage."

"You're sure about that?" Crane wondered why he

bothered to ask. He had already realized that his new dentist was sure about everything.

"It might be a good idea to leave the cobwebs on the windows, then nobody would be able to see who was inside," Evans said reflectively. "I wonder if her Majesty has any objection to spiders?"

A woman did not become Empress of France by objecting to the presence of arachnids. After all, Eugénie had been prepared to marry Louis-Napoleon Bonaparte to achieve her aims. Madame Lebreton, however, was only a companion, and therefore had higher standards.

"People might wonder why we're in such a desperate hurry, we wouldn't even stop five minutes to get the carriage cleaned. We don't want to raise unnecessary suspicions, and I'd certainly be suspicious if I saw anybody travelling in such a filthy vehicle." She might be on her way to the guillotine, but Charlotte Lebreton preferred to arrive there dust-free, and without spiders scurrying through her hair. The world had turned upside-down in twenty-four hours, and she was trapped in a hazardous twilight existence of homelessness and husbandlessness, so any detail still under her control took on greater important than it normally would have.

Madame Everard was ordered to dispatch a servant to clean the carriage, her son arrived with the horses, and Evans felt as triumphant as a successful conjurer with an extremely large hat. He was even prepared to forgive destiny for the momentary lapse, as long as it did not happen again.

"Don't forget your fossils, Crane."

Bloodthirsty mobs, nights spent in corridors, on the run from republicans with an empress and her dentist, false papers, fossils, and finally green and yellow carriages. Crane's once well-ordered and predictable days in Philadelphia seemed to belong to a past so distant that the memories might have been of a book read years previously. Changing continents had changed his entire life at the same time: a transformation that he feared might actually be for the worse.

****

The green and yellow carriage creaked and rattled as though about to fall apart at any second, and its occupants had to lean forward and speak loudly to be heard. The vehicle was the sort that dogs barked at, and small boys tried to hit with rocks, Evans thought with satisfaction; no Empress in her right mind would dare to attempt an escape in so noticeable a conveyance.

"Another town safely passed," he said, mentally congratulating himself.

"Another town where they don't seem to care who rules them," complained Eugénie, wounded by the ingratitude of her subjects. "They just get on with their lives, not even pausing for a moment to worry about my fate."

"Most won't have heard the news from Paris yet," said Madame Lebreton.

"When they do, then your Majesty will see loyalty," declared Evans.

"They weren't very loyal to their queen eighty years ago," retorted Eugénie. "Marie-Antoinette tried to escape from the Tuileries in a carriage as well, and just look what happened to her."

"The situation's entirely different. She went east; we're going west." And Marie-Antoinette did not enjoy the great good fortune to be escorted by an American dentist, Evans could have added, especially an American dentist who was a graduate of Jefferson College.

"Let's not talk about such long-gone horrors," said

Madame Lebreton, recalling that Marie-Antoinette had been captured after an eighty-mile bid for freedom: a fact making Charlotte uncomfortably aware that, just then, the green and yellow carriage chanced to be approximately eighty miles from Paris. "Look at the scenery: those hills over there. I think they're chalk, aren't they?"

"Yes," agreed Evans, "every last one of them solid chalk. Just consider how much toothpowder you could get out of those hills. Why, there must be enough to fill tins by the thousand, the million: plenty for generations to come. We can only marvel in awe at the wonders of nature."

The marvels of the natural world, and its unbounded generosity in the supply of toothpowder to humanity, silenced the Imperial Dentist's fellow passengers, and Evans was able to expand his theme to include the vital importance of cleaning teeth after each meal, as well as the horrendous consequences of neglecting so fundamental a duty, until the Empress's mind appeared to have left Marie-Antoinette far behind. The hour spent on so absorbing a topic felt like mere minutes to Evans, but by the time they reached Evreux and stopped at the horse trough outside the *Café Cantilope*, it was after five o'clock, yet the town looked deserted, streets and shops empty in the late afternoon sunlight.

"I'll go and buy some food while nobody's around," Evans announced, opening the carriage door.

"What's that noise?" asked Crane.

"What noise?" Then Evans heard it too: shouts in the distance, applause and cheering. "Oh, that noise."

"Yes, that noise. What is it? It sounds like a crowd." Crowd seemed a more reassuring word than mob to Crane.

"If they don't bother us, we won't bother them," declared Evans, determined to seem untroubled. "I'll buy enough food in the café to last until tomorrow, then we can travel through the night, and should be able to reach Deauville by tomorrow morning some time. It's a straightforward run from here to Lisieux, and we can hire another carriage at the next —"

"The crowd's getting closer," Crane said uneasily. "In fact, I think it's coming this way."

Then suddenly a mob, raucously excited, boisterously rowdy, surged into the street in front of them, and the shouting was no longer muffled, but all too clear.

"Long live the Republic!" Loud cheering.

"Long live France!" Loud cheering.

"Death to the Emperor!" Even louder cheering.

"They've found me!" Eugénie gasped. "They know I'm here! They know!"

"Your Majesty's a British invalid," Evans reminded her. "We've got the papers to prove it, and I've often been told that my sister resembles the Empress, though she's said to be a lot taller."

Now that he was actually confronted by a bloodthirsty mob, Crane found the scene had the unreality of a dream. Despite the fact that events were unfolding before him, he was more bewildered than afraid, and his one instinct was to run away, but Crane felt certain that, if he tried to do so, his legs would refuse to move, in nightmare-like fashion. "Speak French badly." It was all he could suggest.

"No, speak it well," urged Madame Lebreton. "Everybody thinks the Empress has a Spanish accent."

"They can't know who we are," Evans declared. "It's impossible. I refuse to believe it."

"Then why are they charging straight at me?" Eugénie demanded.

There must have been several hundred people in the street by that time, and they were all shouting and laughing, blocking the road, yelling the *Marseillaise*, heading directly for

144

the carriage.

"Tell the driver to turn the horses around," cried Eugénie. "Let's get out of here."

"There's no time," said Evans. "And a British invalid has nothing to fear from a French crowd, no matter how republican."

Eugénie tried to summon up Joan of Arc, pictured a bonfire instead, and wished that she had never heard of the wretched woman. "We can't just sit here, and do nothing."

"Dr Evans is right," said Madame Lebreton, the remnants of childhood superstition compelling her to touch the wooden side of the carriage for luck. She hoped that whatever was about to happen would happen quickly, but time seemed to be slowing to a standstill. And all because of Eugenia di Montijo, Madame Lebreton thought in despair; one should choose friends so carefully.

"Too many of them for fossils," muttered Crane, as the crowd cheered its way towards the carriage. But there was comfort to be had, even in the bleakest situation; at least he would not be around to face his sternly egalitarian father's reaction to the news that son Edward had been guillotined for his part in an Imperialist plot to rescue the Empress of France from her just deserts.

"Crane," Evans murmured, "do you know how to handle a gun?"

"No," Crane whispered back in alarm. "Have you got a gun with you?"

"Of course not," replied Evans. "Why would I carry a gun? I don't know how to load or fire one."

"Neither do I. I'm from Philadelphia as well, remember."

"Then there isn't much point in overpowering a gendarme."

"None whatsoever," Crane agreed thankfully.

145

"We'll simply have to trust in our American wits and remember we're British. We'll be fine, as long as we keep our heads."

"Better not let the Empress hear you use that expression."

The crowd, roaring their enthusiastic version of the *Marseillaise*, had reached the carriage, and began to surge around it. Eugénie awaited her fate with closed eyes, while Evans held the travel documents in front of her like a shield, clutching one of Crane's fossils in his other hand.

"They're going right past us!" Madame Lebreton exclaimed suddenly. "I think it's only some sort of demonstration."

"Really?" Eugénie opened her eyes cautiously, and saw that Charlotte might be correct. The noise was even louder as jubilant faces went past the windows, but the crowd had no interest in a carriage or its occupants. The day was one of rejoicing, not suspicion or vengeance.

"They've probably just heard that a republic's been announced in Paris, and are celebrating." It was too late to recall his last word, but Crane made a hasty attempt, although the Empress seemed too busy recovering her breath to listen to him. "I mean, demonstrating — I mean, protesting —"

"Some half-witted firebrand's persuaded them that the revolution's good news," said Evans. "They'll regret this day with bitter self-reproach when they finally come to their senses."

However, nobody else in the carriage showed interest in the future remorse of the Evreux citizenry. Being alive, with a renewed chance of staying alive for some years to come, was more important.

"If the Emperor's ever restored to power, I'll make sure he raises the taxes in this town immediately," said Eugénie, with a shaky attempt at cheerfulness. "Long live the Republic, indeed! So tactless on an Imperial visit, even though it does happen to be an incognito one. And should they want an orphanage opened, I'll refuse to do it, simply refuse."

"Serve them right too," declared Evans. "Still, at least we're safe."

"Safe for the moment, but let's get out of here as soon as possible," said Madame Lebreton.

9

The sun was low in the sky, and the shadows of roadside elm trees grew longer and longer. Evans decided to stop at the very next livery stable or inn that they came to, where he would hire a new coachman, and change carriage and horses. The journey could then continue overnight, hopefully on roads free of republican demonstrators, gendarmes and cut-throat mobs. The whole strategy was neatly worked out in Evans's mind, but destiny had the nerve to disagree with him, and a mile or so outside the village of La Rivière de Thibouville, a whiffletree snapped.

"A what's snapped?" Crane asked blankly, as he stood in the road with Evans, and watched their driver crawl back under the carriage for a further inspection.

"A whiffletree," Evans replied in exasperation. "It would be a whiffletree. It's always a whiffletree. Everard won't be able to fix it. No man born of woman can fix a whiffletree. They refuse to be fixed. Whiffletrees! They can't stay in one piece for more than five minutes at a time."

"So it's very bad news?" ventured Crane.

"Whiffletrees are continual bad news. We need another carriage, and there's no way around it. Whiffletrees! It was a whiffletree that made me arrive late for the Philadelphia Dentists' Conference, and I missed an entire discussion on the most effective method of persuading a patient to hand over his gun. 1847 that was, 1847! And yet, here we are, more than twenty years further on, in the most scientifically advanced century mankind has ever known, still at the mercy of the whiffletree. Not the slightest progress made, no advance whatsoever, when it comes to whiffletrees."

"I think this carriage probably dates back further than 1847," said Crane. The green and yellow glowered at him, brazen in malicious glee, despite the darkness of the night: a mutinous vehicle gloating in its power to thwart. "1747 wouldn't surprise me."

"It's all the same to whiffletrees," Evans declared moodily. He would not have criticized destiny for worlds, but if it did have to go around snapping whiffletrees, how much more convenient to snap them in a large town, with a livery stable right at hand; yet Evans refused to be baffled by a mere whiffletree, and was already working out his solution.

"I'll walk down into the village," he decided. "There's bound to be some sort of inn or livery stable where I can hire another carriage, and it's time we changed horses anyway. Crane, I entrust the ladies to your care. Be alert, be vigilant, and above all, watch the driver. This so-called accident might actually be a ruse, if he suspects anything."

"Why would he want to stage his accident in the middle of nowhere?" asked Crane, attempting commonsense although it offered him little comfort. "Wouldn't a town be better, with gendarmes close by?"

"Perhaps, and perhaps not. I'll get back as soon as I can." Still muttering to himself about the malevolence of whiffletrees, Evans lifted one of the carriage lanterns from its hook, and set off down the road. Crane watched the light bob along through the dusk, until it was finally lost in darkness and he realized uneasily that he had been abandoned with his fossils and a monosyllabic driver, who was possibly a republican supporter, to guard two ladies from any bloodthirsty mob that chanced to come along. The horses jingled their harness while they nibbled the roadside grass under the trees, and an owl hooted in the distance. But was it an owl, or some sort of signal? Everard, however, showed no sign of insurrection as he placidly pulled up handfuls of grass to feed his horses, and so, to avoid the chill of the night,

Crane climbed back into the carriage, where suddenly the whole situation seemed ridiculously impossible. He was sitting in a green and yellow monstrosity that was apparently possessed by an evil-natured whiffletree, stranded on an unlit road outside a village that he could not have placed on a map, and opposite him sat the Empress of France.

"Fossils must be a very interesting area of study," said Madame Lebreton, kindly making conversation as the young man looked ill-at-ease. "How long have you been collecting them, Dr Crane? You must tell us all about the subject. We've plenty of time."

Yet, oddly enough, the young man looked even more ill-at-ease.

****

The inn was called *Le Soleil d'Or*, which seemed rather inappropriate when a frosty night breeze stirred the roadside pines. It was an old, square building, with stables at one side that Evans trusted would provide immediate transport capable of foiling the malice of whiffletrees. He opened the inn door, and despite his short stature, had to duck to avoid hitting his head on the lintel, before he stepped directly into the warmth and brightness of a large dining-room. The innkeeper, Madame Desrats, paused as she served supper to the dozen or so customers who were sitting at a long table that stretched out from the kitchen doorway, and the diners followed her gaze to inspect the newcomer with automatic hostility.

"Stranger," thought Madame Desrats. She meant troublemaker.

"I'm a British gentleman," announced Evans, and the farm labourers turned back to their food, unimpressed. "I want to hire a carriage and horses to take a British party of four to

Lisieux. I want a driver too."

And Clémence Desrats, thin and worn and middle-aged, bored with a life of constant cooking and housework, wanted to order everybody out of her inn, bolt the door behind them, and go straight to bed. She was not to get her wishes granted that evening, any more than Evans would get his.

"I don't keep carriages here now."

"Then where's the nearest livery stable?"

"In Bernay."

"Bernay!" Evans could hardly believe how badly destiny was letting him down: first the obstreperous whiffletree, and now another stubborn innkeeper. "You must have a carriage," he said firmly.

"No."

"An old carriage, left at the back of a stable."

"No."

"There must be," said Evans. "A very old carriage. Somewhere. Something. Anything with wheels."

"There are no carriages. None at all."

"But there must be. How do you travel without a carriage?"

"I don't travel," Madame Desrats replied austerely. "But if I did, I'd go by train. It's no more than an hour's walk to the station."

"But my sister's an invalid. She couldn't possibly walk all that way."

"Oh." Subject closed, Madame Desrats turned back to her customers. She did not deserve to have such sound-looking teeth.

"You're quite certain there are no carriages anywhere around?" Evans asked incredulously. "Not a single one?"

"None whatsoever."

Destiny was simply not pulling its weight. "We'll have to stay here tonight, in that case, and send to Bernay for a carriage in the morning. I need four rooms."

"I only let two rooms."

"Then two rooms it'll have to be," Evans said impatiently.

"They're already taken."

What was destiny thinking of? "Is there another inn?"

"Yes."

"Where?"

"In Bernay."

"But how can we get to Bernay without a carriage?"

"I couldn't say."

The diners almost applauded Madame Desrats. No foreigner should be allowed to charge in during their peaceful supper, insisting on carriages and rooms as though by right. The next demand would doubtless be for a journey by hot-air balloon if such arrogance were allowed to continue unchecked, and Madame Desrats was just the woman to be reliably unaccommodating.

Evans was accustomed to getting his own way, whether in the matter of front doors, treating reluctant patients, or refusing to permit the French Government to recognize the Southern Confederacy, and no provincial innkeeper could stop him acquiring a room for the night when he had decided that he was to have one. "Where are the people who've taken your rooms? I'd like to meet them."

Would the troublemaker never give up? Reminding herself that the general public provided *Le Soleil d'Or*'s only source of income, Madame Desrats pointed to a man sitting by the fireplace on the opposite side of the room, and called, "Mr Branwell! A countryman of yours wants to speak to you."

Evans almost faltered, but a dentist learns to roll with the punches early in his career, and he resolutely crossed the room. "Ah, you're British too, sir. I didn't realize. Which part of our beloved homeland do you hail from?"

Jonathan Branwell had been feeling lonely. His wife and daughter were already upstairs, and everybody in *Le Soleil d'Or* stopped understanding French whenever he spoke it to them, but at last he had a companion. His round and cheerful face looked even more round and cheerful as he replied, "I'm from London, sir."

"London? Then my accent will sound a little strange to you," said Evans, hoping to quell suspicion before it was aroused. Branwell might appear pleasant enough, but Evans knew the British. Mullin's Pond and the Emperor's hat were not to be forgotten merely because a man seemed inoffensive. "My home town's hundreds of miles away from London."

"North or west, sir?"

"West. Very far west."

"The West Country!" exclaimed Branwell. "What a happy coincidence! I live in London now, but I came from Truro originally."

"Though I haven't lived out west for some years," Evans said hastily.

"We'll have a lot to talk about, even so."

"Yes. Yes, I'm sure we will. Yes, indeed. Perhaps, as you're a fellow westerner, I could ask a favour?"

"Certainly. Which part of the west do you come —?"

"My sister, also of the west, is an invalid. Our carriage has broken down, and we can't replace it until tomorrow, so we're stranded here without rooms for the night, and I —"

"Another coincidence!" It was uncanny, Branwell thought: the kind of amazing twist of fate that he had often read about in the newspapers under a *Truth Is Stranger Than Fiction* heading. "We're stranded here overnight as well, waiting for a carriage. Which part of the West Country are you from?"

"The part most distant from Truro. As we have so much in

common, could I perhaps ask you to give up one of your rooms for my sister the invalid?" Evans hurriedly produced a handful of coins, in case fellow western feeling required a little assistance, and added, "She must rest before the journey tomorrow."

"Of course she must," agreed Branwell. "I'd refuse your money, of course, but I might find myself in need of cash soon. Apparently there's been yet another French revolution, and we could find ourselves trapped on this side of the Channel."

"Away from our British homes? Let's hope not! Thank God we don't have revolutions and lawlessness out west."

"You're forgetting Trelawney," said Branwell. "The Tower."

"Oh. Yes. So I am. Yes, Trelawney. Yes, of course, Trelawney. Who could forget Trelawney the Tower? Excuse me, please. So much to do. I must speak to the innkeeper. And get back to my sister. The invalid. She's waiting for me." Evans beat a hasty retreat across the room, before further gaps in his western knowledge could be revealed: gaps that might turn an obliging stranger into a possible enemy.

"We'll have a long talk later on," Branwell called after him. "Share our fondest memories of the glorious West Country."

"I'm already looking forward to it," declared Evans, his heart sinking at the prospect.

******

"But you haven't brought us a new carriage," the Empress said in surprise, as Evans climbed back into the Machiavellian whiffletree's stationary vehicle. It had not occurred to Eugénie that her dentist would fail to achieve what he had set out to do.

"We can get one from Bernay in the morning." Evans hoped that it sounded like part of an ingeniously devised master-plan instead of defeat, and as further proof of his resourcefulness, he added, "That should fool anybody attempting to follow us."

"I'd sooner start walking to Bernay right now, than sit here until tomorrow," said Eugénie. "It's getting really cold in the carriage."

What an Empress, thought Evans in admiration: prepared to walk all the way to Deauville, if she had to, and yet the misguided French were trying to replace her with republicans, who would probably insist on taking a cab if they needed to cross a road. How the nation could have so little political sense baffled him, but Europeans were usually beyond comphrension anyway.

"Walk?" Crane would have been in the cab with the republicans. He had already missed one night's sleep, and knew that he was destined to miss another, should Evans have decided on a route march through the darkness. "How many miles is it to this Bernay?"

"Ten, more or less, but we're not tackling them. We'll be staying at the inn tonight."

"An inn!" said Crane in relief. "Wonderful!"

"I was able to get a room for the ladies, but that was all I could get. Crane, you and I will be sleeping on a floor. I hope you don't mind?" It was not a question.

"Do I have a choice?" said Crane. That was not a question either.

"Well, you could walk to Bernay now, and get us a carriage for the morning."

"I'll take the floor," said Crane, resigned to his fate.

"Al least we're better off than our driver. Everard will be in the stable with his horses, unless he prefers a dining-room chair, I suppose."

"Are you sure it's safe for the Empress to stay at an inn?"

asked Madame Lebreton, but wanting reassurance rather than an overnight hike to Bernay. "I think that people who live in a village would notice strangers."

"Perhaps, but they won't be expecting the Empress Eugénie of France to appear in their midst," declared Evans. "Besides, we're British travellers, and should anybody ask, all from the west. Though nowhere near some place called Truro. Oh, and the revolution makes us think of Trelawney, which is either a tower or a man, or it could be a town, or possibly a battlefield."

"Are we going to be cross-examined in British history?" Crane asked uneasily.

"Only if we're very unlucky." But Evans believed in self-reliance and courage, not luck, unless whiffletrees were involved and that owed more to bitter experience than superstition.

"I know everything about the English Civil War," declared Eugénie. "Or do I mean the War of the Roses? Though I always think that sounds far too pretty to be a real war. Anyway, I read a novel, all about whichever English war it was, but the story had a very sad ending. The heroine got married."

"I saw a production of *King Lear* once, in London," said Madame Lebreton. "But I couldn't follow the plot."

"I can't remember any British history at all," lamented Crane. "Well, apart from 1066."

"No, that's French history," Eugénie pointed out.

"If anybody tries to talk British history, simply change the subject," Evans said firmly. He had not brought an empress half-way across France, only to be betrayed by a scheming Britisher, determined to discuss a history so rightly shunned by other nations. "Tell him you're only interested in ancient history, Crane, and don't forget your fossils."

After the warmth of the day, the night felt as cold as winter, and despite the lantern that Crane held awkwardly in one hand, as he tried to push fossils into his pockets with the other, the road was very dark, criss-crossed with constantly moving shadows of the pine trees that lined the way down the slope to the village. An owl hooted again. Or perhaps it was another signal, Crane thought apprehensively: a signal announcing that they had left the carriage.

"*Le Soleil d'Or* is the very first building we come to, on the outskirts of the village," Evans was saying, when Crane suddenly stopped walking.

"Horses!" he exclaimed.

"Off the road! Quick!" Evans ordered. "Get behind the trees. Put the lantern out, Crane."

They stumbled over unseen roots and slithered on pine needles in their haste to take cover, hoof beats steadily approaching all the time, ringing out through the night air like hammer blows.

"Perhaps it's just our driver," said Madame Lebreton, trying to remain calm. "Everard will want to get his horses to the stable as soon as possible."

"Yes, but he wouldn't make tired horses trot," declared Eugénie. "Besides, it sounds more like a squad of soldiers to me."

"It can't be," Evans said reassuringly. "By great good fortune, all of your Majesty's soldiers are either dead or prisoners-of-war by now."

"It might be gendarmes then."

"How could they know that we're here?" asked Madame Lebreton. "How could they, or anybody, even guess which road we'd be on by now?"

"There are only two of them, whoever they are," Crane whispered with relief, as the horsemen came into sight. After his vivid mental picture of a bloodthirsty mob charging after him on bloodthirsty horses, to discover that he was actually pursued by a mere two men seemed an almost tolerable situation.

The riders went past, but the shadows that hid the road made it too dark to see if they were in uniform, too dark to see if they were armed. The horses slowed to a walk, and then stopped outside *Le Soleil d'Or*.

"Crane, give me some of your fossils." Evans whispered. "You tackle the one on the left. I'll get the other. This will be easy."

"But I've never done any fighting," Crane protested. "My father disapproves of it."

"So do I," said Evans. "Teeth can get broken. But desperate times, desperate measures."

The inn door opened, spilling light over the riders as hey dismounted, and Madame Desrats stood, dramatically illuminated, on the threshold. "Pascal? Come in."

"Can you give us some supper, Aunt Clémence?" called one of the men. "We're out chasing that poacher again, but he's too clever for us."

"Put your horses in the stable."

"Gamekeepers!" said Evans and, reprieved from a roadside brawl, he handed his fossils back to Crane. "Just gamekeepers."

"Lucky I didn't wear a hat with feathers in it," commented Eugénie, attempting nonchalance.

"Let's get inside while they're busy with their horses."

Crane returned stones to coat pockets, happy that his début as a street-fighter was postponed indefinitely, although a skirmish might have been worth it to get rid of a few of the fossils, he reflected; they were ruining the shape of his coat and weighed a ton. How other fossil collectors managed,

Crane was unable to imagine. They were obviously not the most fashion-conscious of individuals, but perhaps devotion to science raised their minds above more worldly considerations. Crane's own spirit, however, failed to soar to such abstracted heights, and he felt closer to a scarecrow than a palaeontologist.

They crossed the road to the inn, and entered its brightness in a huddle, with Evans in front of the Empress, while Crane and Madame Lebreton guarded either side. From his fireplace seat, Branwell called out a cheery greeting that Evans acknowledged with a wave of a hand as, in close formation, the Imperial party clattered up the narrow wooden stairs to the ex-Branwell room. It was isolated, right at the top of the house, with a passageway leading to a single door, and for anybody with the necessity to hide an empress inside a country inn, that particular room might have been specifically designed for the purpose.

"Crane, you and I will sleep in the passageway," Evans informed his assistant. "Then no one can get to the ladies without disturbing us."

"I'm not so sure," said Crane. "I'm tired enough to sleep through an earthquake."

"They don't have them in this part of France." Evans opened the door of the room as he spoke, and looked apologetically at the Empress.

"I'll take supper immediately," decided Eugénie: "a light supper, I think. Soufflé perhaps, or an omelette with herbs and —"

"I did try to arrange a cooked meal," said Evans, "but unfortunately, there's no room service."

"No room service?" repeated Eugénie in astonishment.

"We're very far from civilization now."

"So I gather." Eugénie glanced around at the bare walls

159

and wooden floor of the room that was to be hers until the next day, and she laughed. "Well, at least nobody can say I don't share the suffering and privation of my people."

"There's bread, cheese and coffee available, however. I'll fetch some from the kitchen, and we can share that."

"How very egalitarian," the Empress remarked. "The republicans would thoroughly approve."

****

Supper with an empress in her own bedroom. At last there were things in Crane's formerly blameless life that he would never be able to tell his father. The room was sparsely furnished and severely unornamented, as far from a palace chamber as it could possibly be, and Eugénie, child of aristocratic parents, cousin of dukes and counts, wife of an emperor, would never have expected to occupy such lowly accommodation in her life, but she had already recognized that to escape from a revolution with two democratic Americans might mean encountering some equality along the way, sooner or later.

"I'll never forget this evening," said Crane, as he and Evans adjourned to the passageway. And he also knew that he would never forget the night either, sleeping in a draughty wooden corridor on a draughty wooden floor, with a dentist on one side, and a collection of fossils on the other.

"We were chosen by destiny to be on this floor, Crane." Now that he had been fed and rested, Evans was prepared to overlook the whiffletree lapse, as long as destiny reported promptly for duty again, first thing the next day.

"I wish destiny could have managed a bed for the night," commented Crane. "My back will feel like a plank of wood in the morning, and that's assuming I get any sleep at all, which seems unlikely."

Then, suddenly, Evans was shaking him. "Wake up. Crane, wake up."

"What? What is it?" Crane demanded in panic, scrabbling desperately for a fossil. "What's going on? Oh, my back! What's happened?"

"Nothing," replied Evans. "It's nearly five in the morning. The ladies are already up."

"Five? It can't possibly be five. I've only just closed my eyes." Crane tried to move, but his back objected so strenuously that the floor reclaimed him as its own. "You're sure it's tomorrow?"

"Quite sure. I've been stepping over you this past half-hour, but I thought you'd appreciate a bit of a sleep-in. I want to leave before my British friend wakes up, because we've got to avoid that western reunion at all costs."

"You've found a carriage already?" said Crane in bewilderment. "But however did you manage that?"

"There's no carriage. We're going to walk to —"

"Walk! The ladies can't walk all the way to Bernay, and neither can I: not with my back."

"We're not going to Bernay. I've decided to chance the train as far as Lisieux. We can hire a carriage there, be in Deauville this afternoon, and across the Channel tonight." If destiny had chosen to falter on the job, then Evans was perfectly capable of being its substitute without a moment's hesitation.

"The train? Do you think we should? Will it be safe?" Crane almost forgot his aching back, as he pictured himself attempting to defend the Empress from a mob of bloodthirsty railway workers. "Won't the republicans be watching the stations?"

"They can't watch all of them, and the railway might be safer than staying here any longer, with a British traveller who could denounce me as a fraud at any second. The English have never got over losing our War of Independence, and they'd enjoy some revenge at last."

"They did burn down the White House in 1812."

"Which simply goes to show the sort of nation we're dealing with," declared Evans. "The British are an embittered people, without the slightest compunction at having made President and Mrs Madison homeless, and the sooner we're out of *Le Soleil d'Or*, the better."

"But how are we going to get to the station?"

"We walk, of course. It only takes an hour or so, apparently, and my invalid sister made a miraculous recovery overnight."

"I am a good doctor," remarked Crane.

"And you recommend an hour's walk as the best possible thing for her."

"I don't recommend it for myself. I can hardly move."

"You'll feel better after you've had some breakfast," said Evans, knowing that a mere backache would not be allowed to interfere with destiny. "I'll go downstairs now, and see what can be done about this no-room-service nonsense."

However, Madame Desrats had had enough of invalid sisters, demanding a continual supply of suppers and breakfasts to be carted up steep stairs and down narrow passageways. It was time to liberate herself from troublemaker guests who refused to eat conveniently in the dining-room with the more cowed of her customers, and she began speaking the moment Evans reached the foot of the staircase. "The gentleman over there by the fire —"

Evans looked around in alarm, expecting West Country Branwell with his unfortunate British teeth to appear in front of him, happily chatting of Trelawneys and Towers, but the sleekly dark-haired, middle-aged man, harmlessly drinking coffee, was a stranger. "What about him?" Evans asked warily.

"He's having breakfast while he rests his horses. I was telling him about your sister, and he's offered to drive you all to the —"

"You mean he's got a carriage!" Destiny had woken as early as Evans, and was obviously prepared to atone for the whiffletree.

"He'll take you to the station, if you like."

"Wonderful! I'd be so grateful to have transport to the —" Evans paused, and then added cautiously, "He isn't British, by any chance, is he?"

"No, it's Monsieur Mauger." Madame Desrats had heard that the English as a race were stand-offish but, nevertheless, surely they would accept a lift, when stranded in the middle of a foreign country, even if the carriage owner chanced not to be a fellow Briton. With that stilted outlook hampering logistics, it was surprising that The Hundred Years War had ended as soon as it did.

"Monsieur Mauger! Excellent! I must thank him." Evans hurried across the room, and grasped the hand already extended towards him. "I'm very grateful for your offer to drive us to the station, sir: most kind of you."

"Don't mention it. I'll be glad of the company." Laurent Mauger was plump, genial, and happy to do anybody a favour, with teeth as appealing as his nature. "I understand that you're English."

"Yes, indeed, all four of us," Evans agreed cheerfully, "British to the very core."

"My daughter married an Englishman," Mauger said, as though he had just announced a piece of news that Evans would find particularly delightful. "I often visit her, and was in Hampshire for a month last Christmas and New Year."

"Then you probably know the country better than I do," declared Evans. "I've lived abroad for many years now. And so has my sister. And her doctor and nurse."

"We'll still find plenty to talk about, I'm sure. Which part of England do you come —?"

"I'm afraid my sister's too weak to talk much at present. She's an invalid."

"Yes, Madame Desrats told me." Mauger's tone was at once sympathetic, and he lowered his voice to a suitably sombre pitch as he added, "I hope your poor sister isn't suffering too much this morning."

"She's never really well these days, but her doctor doesn't think it's contagious any more, so that's one less thing to worry about."

"Oh. Yes. I see." Mauger exchanged compassion for caution, and his expression became somewhat less amiable. "She has — I mean, she had an infectious illness then?"

"She was bedridden for months, in absolute agony the whole time; yes, agony, there's no other word for it. But, happily, her doctor says that he's almost certain she's over the worst. He's a very young and inexperienced doctor, but I guess he knows what he's talking about. It's an odd coincidence, but he's full of aches and pains himself this morning, exactly as my sister was until only a week ago. I do hope he hasn't caught it. Such a virulent illness, but he'd probably pull through in a couple of months, simply because he's so young."

"On second thoughts," said Mauger, his cautious expression now combined with prudence, "my carriage might be a little too crowded for the poor lady, if I rode inside with you. I wouldn't want to disturb your sister. Or her doctor."

"He's a strange young man," Evans confided. "Insisted on filling the carriage with rocks yesterday."

"Rocks?" repeated Mauger, looking startled.

"Yes, rocks. We didn't like to thwart him."

"I suppose not." Mauger had been conditioned by centuries of French civilization, and felt unable to retract the freedom of his carriage, but he could, and did, keep his distance from the pestilent sister and her symptom-ridden doctor, who was indeed worryingly weighed down with rocks. Somehow, Mauger managed to keep a welcoming smile on his face, but consoled himself with the thought that he would have his carriage fumigated at the earliest opportunity.

****

Long before eight o'clock, Mauger's carriage left them at La Rivière de Thibouville station, where the wind was cold and the sky dark with rain clouds. The few other passengers huddled around a small booking-office, the only available shelter, but Evans led his party out beside the track, as everybody knew that the British had an eccentric fondness for fresh air.

Without waiting-room or benches, the station was on a branch line, but trains passing through La Rivière de Thibouville went to Serquigny, barely three miles away, where travellers could change onto the Paris-Cherbourg line, and Serquigny itself was only one stop from Lisieux, a whole fifteen miles jumped in a single leap, and once there, Deauville and the Normandy coast were a mere eighteen miles further west.

"According to Mauger's timetable, we leave here at five past eight, catch the Cherbourg express at eight-fifteen, and arrive in Lisieux at twenty past nine. We'll save hours with the train, and it'll be easy to hire a carriage and horses in a big place like Lisieux. We should get to Deauville long before evening." Now that he and destiny were as one again, Evans allowed himself a moment of congratulation. Then the Empress spoke.

"The station-master keeps staring at me. Perhaps the republicans have telegraphed an alert across the whole railway system."

"Ignore him, your Majesty," said Evans. "If we seem in any way self-conscious, it might add to his suspicions: if he has any, that is."

"He's still looking at me," the Empress reported, and then added indignantly, "No, not looking, leering."

"Stand behind us, ladies," commanded Evans. "Crane and I will watch him."

"Do you think the station-master suspects something?" Crane asked anxiously, as Eugénie and Madame Lebreton, attempting unconcern, took cover.

"I'd hit him with one of your fossils, but it might delay the train if somebody missed him," said Evans with a sigh of regret. "I wouldn't mind knocking his teeth out though."

"You don't think that might be a bit ruthless?" Crane suggested, taken aback.

"Believe me, I'd be doing the man a favour. Did you get a look at those teeth of his? I've never seen any in such a disgraceful condition, not anywhere in the whole of Europe, not even inside a British mouth. I could save that man years of suffering, by hitting him in the mouth with a rock." There was real yearning in Evans's voice, as he lamented having to deny himself the satisfaction of battering the offensive teeth out of their jaw.

The shameless station-master continued to leer in the Empress's direction, and it seemed hours before the engine steamed ponderously towards them. Evans located an empty compartment, and as soon as the train could be said to have stopped, he hurried the others on board, although uncertain

166

whether he was leading them to safety or into a trap, because the instant they were securely locked inside a carriage, the station-master could telegraph either Serquigny or Lisieux at his leisure, and inform the authorities that the Empress Eugénie was rapidly approaching them.

"The station-master's looking through the window at me," complained Eugénie.

"No, no. He's just checking to see that we've shut the carriage door properly. It's part of his job." Madame Lebreton hoped that she was right, but it would be so like Eugenia di Montijo to get herself noticed by every available man, even when she was supposed to be incognito. Eugenia simply did not know how to be ordinary. She never had.

"He's leering again." Eugénie was now offended, as well as apprehensive. The French might have declared a republic, she was fully prepared to concede, but the working-classes were getting decidedly above themselves, when they went around leering at empresses.

"It'd be a humane act to knock those teeth out," Evans said wistfully.

The train gave a shudder and then began to move slowly along the track, mercifully saving the station-master and his leering teeth from any imperial dentistry, although Evans still sighed for lost opportunity, saddened that his three score years and ten were so brief a period for all the tasks that needed to be done in the world to ensure each person's fundamental right to life, liberty and the preservation of teeth.

"We're safe now," Madame Lebreton said optimistically, as the train left La Rivière de Thibouville behind. "I'm sure the station-master didn't suspect a thing."

"He could be telegraphing both Serquigny and Lisieux at this very second," declared Eugénie, able to believe any treachery of so loutish an individual.

167

"Even the most radical of republican railway workers wouldn't be expecting the Empress of France to patronize his whistle-stop branch line station," Evans pointed out. "And he's most likely too busy collecting tickets right now to think of anything else."

"I should hope that he is concentrating on the work he's paid to do," said Eugénie. "The nerve of the man: leering at me like that."

"Do you think we're safe?" Crane whispered to Evans. "Or do you think the station-master will send a telegram?"

"We'll soon find out," Evans replied grimly.

The sky lowered ominously in purple and yellow as a cloudburst threatened the bleak stubble-field landscape, and Crane passed the short journey wondering what on earth the *Jefferson College Quarterly*'s obituary page would make of his death by public execution in France, but Evans was already deep in strategy. Only a few minutes separated La Rivière de Thibouville from Serquigny, yet Evans barely needed such a generous allowance of time because, even before the train had started to slow down, the finalized plan was ready to be revealed to his audience.

"If the station-master has telegraphed, they'll be expecting to see a party of four people, so I'll get out first and watch any officialdom hanging around. They might simply overlook a party of only three."

"What should we do if they don't?" asked Crane.

"We deal with it," replied Evans. "In fact, we tackle it head-on. The suspicions of a provincial station-master won't count for much against the authorized documents of British travellers, especially if we act condescendingly amused at the man's wild imagination. Self-assurance is everything."

"Everything," echoed Madame Lebreton, aware that she, alone of the party, had an appearance that all too obviously proclaimed French nationality.

"Follow me onto the platform after a few seconds, but if I'm talking to any gendarmes, ignore me and get on the Cherbourg train," ordered Evans. "Don't forget your fossils, Crane."

Serquigny station was busier than La Rivière de Thibouville had been, but still offered little chance of hiding out in a crowd, even though the express from Paris was steaming its way into the junction. Evans crossed the platform, noting that there seemed to be only one official within sight and he was a guard, idly waiting until all the passengers had left the branch line train. On the grounds that a fugitive would shun anybody in uniform, Evans dashed up to the man and did his best to imitate a bewildered traveller.

"I'm British," he announced, "going home to Britain, you understand, and I need to find the Cherbourg express."

"You've found it," the guard said, barely glancing up, and clearly more interested in shifting his weight from left to right foot.

"Thank goodness for that. I feel quite lost in France, being British. I've hardly ever left Britain in my whole life." The guard continued to look unmoved by the information, and Evans felt safe enough to hurry away and scan the express in search of the empty compartment that he knew destiny would have reserved for him. It was no surprise to find what he sought, and moments after Evans had taken possession, he was reunited with the rest of his party.

"No one seemed to take any notice of me," said Eugénie. "Am I safe now?"

"It looks like it, your Majesty," replied Evans, shutting the door and standing with his back to it, in the hope of discouraging any passenger who might try to storm their sanctuary.

"There's still Lisieux to face," said Eugénie.

"We'll bluff our way through that station as well," declared Evans.

"What did the guard say to you?" asked Crane, who had been close to a nervous breakdown at the sight of Evans chatting to a railway worker.

"Nothing worth mentioning. I informed him that I was British, in case he's questioned about the people who changed trains."

"Shouldn't we be leaving Serquigny by now?"

As Madame Lebreton spoke, the engine jerked forward, and nearly sent Evans sprawling across a seat. With a second jolt, the express crept out of the station, and then made a belated attempt to live up to its name as it gathered speed. Serquigny was left behind, and rain misted the view of orchards and fields that Crane had seen only days earlier after his arrival in France, a time that now felt as distant as his childhood. Presumably, he had passed through Lisieux on that journey to Paris, but Crane had no memory of the station, and could recall no premonition that its name would come to sound so menacing to him. And even more menacing it became during the long hour of that non-stop journey from Serquigny.

The outskirts of Lisieux looked dingy and defeated through the train's grimy windows. Rows of sooty houses imprisoned people in drab lives that nobody would ever celebrate, yet any one of those lives had to be better than arriving at a station where a horde of gendarmes might be waiting to drag their victims out to a bloodthirsty mob. Crane glanced at Evans for guidance, and was not disappointed as the express slunk to a halt.

"If there's any sort of alert, they'll still be seeking a party of four people, so we'll split up again, in twos this time," he

170

announced. "Crane, you get out first with Madame Lebreton."

Feeling as though he had just been ordered to climb the steps to a guillotine, Crane opened the carriage door.

"You've forgotten your fossils, Dr Crane," said Madame Lebreton, gathering up his collection.

"Oh. Yes, of course. The fossils. Thank you." Crane reflected gloomily that his coat would never recover its shape, and then reminded himself that a baggy overcoat was hardly the most immediate concern for somebody faced with the possibility of a public execution.

"I'll carry a few of those fossils for you, Crane," said Evans. "Off you go. And don't forget that you're British travellers. Above suspicion."

Both Crane and Madame Lebreton had never felt so suspicious-looking in their lives, but neither thought of disputing Evans's leadership, and they left the express with the resigned air of martyrs about to be fed to some particularly anti-Christian lions.

"Unusual young man," commented Eugénie, as she watched them move with the crowd towards the ticket barrier. "Odd for someone his age to be so obsessed with a fossil collection, of all things."

"He comes from a very scientific background. Anyway, we'll get out now, your Majesty. Walk slowly, and remember that there's nothing in the least remarkable or noteworthy about us." Clutching an armful of rocks and with his dental equipment case in the other hand, Evans stepped down from the train.

To be in the middle of a slow-moving crowd was good camouflage, he decided. Evans could not see any gendarmes ready to pounce, and no plain-clothed detectives appeared to be watching the passengers. Rain clattering on its glass roof, Lisieux station resembled any other provincial station on a wet weekday morning, as impatient business men, obviously on their way to the office, hurried to the ticket barrier, while travellers struggled with luggage and called for porters. There seemed to be nothing out of the ordinary at all. Then the Empress caught her breath.

"The station-master's stopping Dr Crane!"

Evans had been too busy looking around for republicans to concentrate on the welfare of his front line, and he gave a startled glance ahead, before saying, "It's only the ticket collector."

"Tickets!" Eugénie exclaimed, smiling in relief. "Yes, of course, tickets. I'd forgotten all about them. It's been so long since I had to have one for anything."

"Even if somebody was suspicious of Crane, there's nothing to connect us with him or Madame Lebreton. We'd still be safe."

The words sounded callous, however, and even though an empress clearly outranked both Crane and Madame Lebreton, no conscientious American lightly abandoned a fellow countryman and a lady who could not be held responsible for her French nationality. On the other hand, Evans knew that he had been sent by the forces of destiny to rescue Eugénie, and that he was duty bound to complete his mission because history demanded it of him. After that, he would be quite free to return to France at his leisure, and democratically rescue both Crane and Madame Lebreton from whichever prison they had been thrown into. They would just have to wait a bit, that was all.

"You don't think people might notice that both you and Dr Crane are carrying a black case in one hand, and fossils in the other?" suggested Eugénie. "It's a sort of connection."

"People aren't aware of details. They only see what you want them to see."

The Empress hoped that Dr Evans had not underestimated French observational skills. She herself was of the opinion that carrying fossils around by the armful looked decidedly odd, but to doubt her rescuer seemed ungrateful. And indeed, the ticket collector had allowed Dr Crane through the barrier without a second glance, so perhaps fossil collecting was more wide-spread among the lower bourgeoisie than in Imperial circles.

"Another few minutes, and we'll be safely out of here," Evans murmured, as they approached the ticket collector. Heart pounding, Eugénie shielded her face with both hands and pretended to adjust her hat, expecting the raucous shout that would denounce an empress, but no cry came. However, instead of a sense of deliverance, Eugénie felt almost hurt that the man should be unaware he was collecting the ticket of the most eminent traveller ever to pass through his dull provincial station. The Empress of France had posed for so many portraits and photographs that she was astonished to find herself able to walk anywhere in Europe without being instantly recognized because, after years of close attention from all the newspapers, she had assumed that her every action was of deep interest to the entire reading population; yet there she was, anonymous in a crowd of ex-subjects, none of whom apparently had the slightest concern about the events that had led to her unexpected personal appearance in their midst. Such apathy was convenient, but still it rankled, and although Lisieux might be indifferent to Imperial displeasure, it now had an irrevocably blemished character in Eugénie's eyes.

They were through the ticket barrier unchallenged, with the station yard in sight and Evans triumphant. "That's the most risky bit of the journey over," he declared. "We're as good as in Deauville right now."

"We haven't got a carriage yet," Eugénie pointed out.

"We'll have one soon."

Rain was falling heavily, and the wind grew ever stronger and colder, but they hurried past the few remaining cabs, whose horses were restlessly shaking raindrops out of their manes, while drivers huddled inside waterproof coats and hats. Overnight, the season had jumped from summer to autumn, and further up the road, Crane and Madame Lebreton, in the absence of any instructions from Evans to stop, were battling on against the weather.

"Couldn't we hire one of those cabs?" asked Eugénie, but instinctively knowing that comfort would not be obtained so easily in a thoroughly democratic escape.

"It'd make us too easy to track," replied Evans. "I don't want there to be any sort of link between us and this station."

"But we are safe? Yes, of course we are. This rain's enough to dampen down the most red-hot of revolutionaries."

"And we can walk quickly without attracting attention on such a wet day. The rain couldn't have come at a better time. Destiny's on our side, your Majesty."

"Then I wish destiny had thought to remind me to carry an umbrella. I'll never attempt to flee from a revolution without one again," said Eugénie, the rain hitting her squarely in the face and trickling down her neck in icy rivulets.

"As soon as we're out of sight of the station, your Majesty can take shelter in a shop doorway, with Crane and Madame Lebreton, while I get a carriage. There's bound to be a livery stable somewhere nearby."

A room in a country inn overnight, and then a morning in a shop doorway; life in a republic could not compete with Imperialism when it came to comfort. Eugénie wondered uneasily if Evans would expect her to cross the Channel in a fisherman's boat, accompanied by mounds of pilchard and mackerel. She was devoted to her people, of course she was, no Empress more so, but they did have a depressing tendency to lead rather dreary lives in even drearier surroundings.

****

Eugénie had imagined herself taking refuge in the doorway of Lisieux's finest emporium, with a window full of hats or jewellery to enliven the time spent waiting for her carriage, but Evans failed to share the vision, and he led his party to a building that Eugénie would not have recognized as a shop, so small was its window: a window that had the additional disguise of iron bars, chillingly reminiscent of a prison cell.

"Nobody leaves the house to look at carpets in weather like his," declared Evans. "There won't be any customers going in or out, and the staff will be too busy making the next carpet to notice anyone sheltering from the rain in their doorway."

"Wouldn't it be better if we went to find a livery stable with you?" suggested Crane, appalled by the responsibility of being an empress's defender in so public a place.

"I don't want the people around the livery stable to see a group of four. The station-master might have sent a telegram that somehow got delayed, and a livery stable's bound to be one of the first places the republicans would visit, if they're tracking us. Splitting up again is the safest option, but I'll be as quick as I can."

Evans splashed his way down the street, and Crane regretted not having had the sense to offer himself as the seeker of livery stables. Guarding the Empress Eugénie in deserted country roads had been bad enough, but to be left on Imperial protection duty in the middle of Lisieux took an

175

already alarming state of affairs to horrific proportions, even though it was not a day for passers-by to linger in front of shops and notice sheltering strangers.

"We shouldn't be here for long," Madame Lebreton remarked, to encourage herself as well as the others. "We'll be on our way again very soon."

"Let's hope so," said Eugénie, leaning against a bale of wool that almost blocked the shop entrance. "I'm sure Lisieux's an enchanting place, but I've no wish to explore its possibilities any further."

Small talk with empresses was not a field in which Crane thought he would excel, and he glanced out into the street again, alert for any sign of danger. His imagination still pictured a cut-throat mob, rather than an individual, as the main threat, and a male voice from the interior of the shop took Crane completely by surprise.

"Excuse me, Mesdames, Monsieur —"

Fossils clutched tightly, Crane swung around, and saw a dark-haired young man, in shirt sleeves and workman's long apron, gazing at the Empress.

10

Englishmen, barging into a peaceful livery stable without the slightest of formalities, demanding carriages for invalid sisters, who had to rush to Deauville at a second's notice. Jacques Guérin, plump as an oversized apple, was not used to being hustled, and he resented it. Usually, the English were prepared to stand about meekly half the day, and wait until he finally got around to harnessing a horse or two, but that particular Englishman was as forceful as an American, stating precisely what he wanted and expecting immediate results. He also wanted newspapers, Paris newspapers, not the local one, as though nothing ever happened in Lisieux worth reporting.

"I need good horses and a good driver," Evans had announced without preamble. "And a good carriage too. A very good carriage," he added, remembering the treachery of whiffletrees.

Guérin had spent forty years telling people what they needed. He was unaccustomed to being ordered about like a servant, and did not plan to get used to it either. "All my horses and carriages are good," he replied, affronted. "This is the best livery stable in Lisieux." It was also the only livery stable left in Lisieux, but Guérin saw no reason to reveal the lack of competition at the top.

But even the privilege of standing within Lisieux's finest livery stable could not shame the Englishman into deference. "My sister's been desperately ill, and she needs sea air at once; her doctor said so. It's essential that we start for Deauville this instant."

"Well, you can't. Not until I've harnessed the horses," Guérin said obstinately. He still had, despite his years, the tenacity of youth, as well as his own teeth, but Evans had already noted that, with the exception of the leering station-master, the standard of dental health in north-western France appeared to be much higher than in Paris. Something to do with the soil, perhaps, or a simpler diet? It was indeed a matter worthy of study, but even the manifold blessings of sound teeth failed to mollify Guérin's stubbornness. "Your sister will just have to wait at her hotel, until the horses are ready, and that's all there is to it."

"But she's not in a hotel," said Evans, sighing impatiently. "I left her in a shop doorway."

On such a wet and cold day? After a desperate illness? Those English invalid sisters were a hardy breed, Guérin reflected.

It seemed to Evans as though several hours had passed before the carriage finally reached the road. His confidence in destiny was absolute, but still he had the uneasy feeling that somebody must have recognized Eugénie the moment the Imperial Court Dentist left her side. There was Crane as assistant Imperial guard, of course, armed with his fossils, but Evans could not fool himself about his deputy's ability; Crane might be a useful subordinate, but he was no resourceful man of action. Despite the risk, despite the rain, Evans knew he should have insisted that the Empress accompany him to the livery stable because, although she hid it well, Eugénie was half-British, and had a heritage of trudging through downpours to sustain her. Every manner of calamity rushed through Evans's mind, and as the carriage turned into the road where he had left — no, abandoned — his responsibility, he expected, at the very least, to see the leaders of one of those cut-throat mobs, so prevalent in Paris, dragging the Empress and Madame Lebreton guillotine-wards, while the rank and file rabble battered Crane senseless with his own fossils.

Instead, Evans saw a peaceful scene that he would never forget: the Empress of France, quite safe and sound, half-sitting half-leaning on a bale of wool in a shop doorway, with Madame Lebreton and Dr Crane attempting to shield Eugénie from passers-by, even though the few pedestrians enduring the cloudburst were huddled beneath dripping umbrellas, as they scurried around puddles without noticing the presence of an ex-empress. She had been their sovereign only days before, the centre of Imperial Court life, the lauded guest of foreign nations, and now Eugénie was just a woman who had taken refuge with her companions in a carpet shop's entrance on a rainy Tuesday morning in the small provincial town of Lisieux.

"Next stop, Deauville," Evans called, as he opened the carriage door.

"I'm so glad to see you safe," said Eugénie, hurrying across the pavement, and the relief on her face showed how much more slowly time had passed for the deserted three than for Evans. "I thought you might have been arrested."

"For hiring a carriage? Not even in revolutionary France. We'll be in Deauville before evening." Evans was back in command and nothing dare go wrong from then on because he would not allow it.

"Such a nice young man in that shop. He offered to bring us chairs," said Eugénie, shaking raindrops off her dress as the carriage began to move, allowing all four of its passengers to breathe freely again. "Vincent is the owner's son, and he was left in charge this morning because his father's taken some samples of brown carpeting to Monsieur Ambrose's house. I've no idea who Monsieur Ambrose might be, but I looked suitably impressed."

"It would have seemed suspicious to move to another doorway in such a downpour merely because somebody spoke to us," said Crane, aware of Evans's reproachful glance at what was apparently deemed outright neglect of duty.

"No customers came in or out," added Madame Lebreton, "so it was safer to stay exactly where we were."

"Besides, I told Vincent that the very next time I chance to need a carpet, I'll patronize no other business, and he wouldn't want to deprive his father of a possible new customer," declared Eugénie. "The minute the war's over and the Republican Government's overthrown, Vincent's father will be appointed Imperial Carpeter, and that should put the puffed-up Monsieur Ambrose in his place, and serve him right too, after forcing Vincent's father out on such a miserable day."

"Your Majesty's thoughtfulness for the wellbeing of the lower classes is beyond compare," said Evans, and it was like a holiday to be back in his old world of Imperial adulation for a few seconds. "But, of course, your Majesty's empathy for hard-working carpeters has long been celebrated worldwide."

"Yet I don't suppose you'll find a word about it in the newspapers today," commented the Empress, a distinctly barbed tone entering her voice.

Imperial intuition proved itself to be impeccable. There was still no mention of the vanished Empress in any of the newspapers that Evans had bought, and Eugénie was astonished at the continued neglect, after so many years of headlines, detailed reports of all her activities, and comprehensive descriptions of every gown and jewel that she wore. Once upon a time, whole paragraphs had been devoted to her beauty and modesty, to say nothing of the occasional effusive poem in her honour, because a husband who controlled the newspapers certainly ensured a first-rate press; but, without Napoleonic guidance, the journalists wrote of nothing but war, casualty numbers, ruined harvests, Prussians on the march toward Paris, the superior German armaments and the probable French defeat: information so utterly depressing for everybody that the Emperor's policy of only allowing good news to be printed was going to be sorely missed.

"It's bad enough when awful things happen, without having to read about them beforehand," complained Eugénie. "The editors are simply not making the slightest effort to see the brighter side of life."

"Perhaps it's as well to get a little warning, when your country's about to be destroyed," Madame Lebreton suggested tartly. "Much less of a shock than if you wake up one morning and find that a Prussian shell has just landed on your roof."

"I'm sure the editors could manage to warn people without being quite so dismal in the process."

"France won't be destroyed," declared Evans. "The Emperor wouldn't permit such a thing, and he's certain to be negotiating the peace treaty at this very second, and we all know how politically astute his Majesty is."

There was a moment's silence.

"I wonder if it's raining in Deauville," said Madame Lebreton.

****

The road to Deauville was smooth and tree-lined, passing through river valleys and farmland misted by the rain. Evans was triumphant at being so near the coast, but to Crane things seemed to be progressing too easily, and when he worried, he felt that he was doing something positive to avert whatever disaster lurked in wait for them at Deauville. "Do you think the republicans will be watching the ports?" he asked apprehensively.

"Oh yes, and Deauville in particular," declared Evans. "They're bound to have detectives following my wife around the place, even as we speak. It's inevitable. My connection with the Imperial family is so well-known."

"Wouldn't it be wiser not to go anywhere near Deauville in that case?" suggested Madame Lebreton, alarmed.

"But they'll assume that we will go somewhere else," replied Evans, proud of his reasoning. "They'll imagine Deauville is the last place on earth we'd head for, so it's obvious that we should go straight there."

"But if they think we'll be somewhere else, why would detectives bother to watch Mrs Evans?" asked Crane.

"In case we do turn up in Deauville, of course."

"So the hotel will be watched by detectives, but they won't be expecting us to go there," said Crane, trying to sort out the good news from the bad.

"Precisely," declared Evans, "so it'll be easy to fool them. Just before we get to the *Hotel du Casino*, the Empress and I will leave the carriage, go into the hotel through the garden door, and up to my wife's room. Crane, you and Madame Lebreton will continue on to the hotel in the carriage, and take rooms there like ordinary travellers: rooms on the first floor, if possible, near my wife's." Evans sat back, and reflected that it was no wonder destiny had chosen him, out of all humanity, to save the Empress Eugénie from a revolution. No plodding Deauville detective could hope to outwit such ingenious strategy, in Evans's opinion; but any man who had survived twenty-five years as a nineteenth century dentist without being lynched was certain to have resources beyond the ordinary.

In Pont L'Évêque, they stopped to feed and water the

horses at the *Lion d'Or*, where the invalid sister stayed hidden in the carriage with her doctor and nurse, while Evans went in search of bread, cheese and coffee. After the drama of Evreux republican demonstrations, whiffletrees and leering station-masters, the *Lion d'Or* felt like a haven of safety. Nobody saw the Empress, and nobody had the least interest in the self-proclaimed British Evans. A picnic lunch inside the carriage, and then the journey's final stage began, through the hamlets of Coudray and Bonneville, past Touques, and across the bridge separating Trouville from Deauville. It was just after three in the afternoon, and to be on the Normandy coast, with only the Channel between them and freedom, gave an odd sense of having come home.

As they approached Deauville, the town looked bleak and deserted on that cold, wet afternoon, the very conditions Evans himself would have selected for their arrival, he noted with satisfaction, because when destiny and modern dentistry worked in joint partnership with the weather, anything could be accomplished. The carriage was stopped in a quiet road of grey, storm-battered houses, close to the shore, and the Evans plan for smuggling empresses into hotels commenced.

"My sister and I are staying in this road with friends," Evans explained to the coachman who, hunched under a waterproof jacket with rain cascading from his hat, looked more depressed than enlightened. "We never go to hotels. We wouldn't even consider going inside one. My sister dislikes hotels intensely. That's why we're leaving the carriage now. Because we're not staying at the *Hotel du Casino*. We won't even go near the place. Not once. My sister would refuse to. Absolutely refuse." Confident that he had allayed any suspicion the coachman might have otherwise harboured, Evans and the remarkably strong-minded invalid sister stood in the rain-soaked road and waved the carriage on its way.

****

The *Hotel du Casino*, expansive and imposing, would normally have awed Crane, but he was far more concerned about republicans that day than crimson velvet, gold paint and a sycophantic clerk at the reception desk.

"Two single rooms on the first floor for the night," repeated Gaston Buffet. He had recognized the situation immediately, and flattered himself that the older woman, if given half a chance, would reject the dull young man at her side for the Gallic charm and sultry good looks of one Gaston André Buffet. "Adjoining rooms, naturally."

"Naturally," echoed Madame Lebreton, glad that her husband was not there to witness the ease with which his wife took on the rôle of woman with young lover. "My nephew and I will find adjoining rooms most convenient."

Startled that anybody could possibly mistake him for a sophisticated man of the world, Crane tried to look blasé at the prospect of adjoining hotel rooms with a married woman, but felt more like an embarrassed schoolboy, especially as the clerk seemed to scorn both Crane and fossils with one bland glance.

"Dinner's at eight," announced Buffet, tactfully not mentioning the lack of luggage, and therefore evening dress. "But you'll prefer a quiet supper in your room — I mean, rooms —rather than go to the dining hall, of course."

"Of course," said Madame Lebreton.

"You'll find our room service menu upstairs, should you require anything further." Buffet smiled a tacit understanding of the lady's needs, telling himself that one night in the hotel meant a fool of a husband had swallowed the old chestnut about his wife staying with her mother, and Buffet's only

184

regret was that there were no similarly resourceful and obliging married women among his acquaintanceship.

"I don't think the clerk was suspicious of us," Madame Lebreton whispered to Crane, as they left the reception desk, relieved at the effortless way a cover story had been provided for them.

"If we're arrested, it won't be for empress smuggling." To check into a hotel with another man's wife would be considered a far worse crime back in Philadelphia, and Crane felt rather proud of himself to have so defied his puritanical upbringing. It was just unfortunate that the scandalous behaviour existed only in the mind of a clerk.

****

The Empress no longer lamented her lack of protection from the downpour, because even the mightiest umbrella would have been defeated by the storm that roared in from the sea. After a lifetime of luxury, Eugénie found herself wet, cold, hungry, tired and beginning to lose interest in whether she survived the revolution or not. Dr Evans marched her into the hotel garden, where leaves were being torn from the trees and roses stripped of their last petals, while the sea wind boomed like great guns, and her dentist talked cheerfully about crossing the Channel as soon as he found a boat. Eugénie had had enough of the whole preposterous situation. Any further privation, and the Empress of France would be tempted to hand herself over to the nearest revolutionary committee, and have done with it all.

"There don't seem to be any detectives around. Perhaps they've all gone out with my wife," Evans was saying. "We'll get into the hotel through the reading-room, because nobody's ever in there. It's always empty. Who bothers with newspapers and magazines when they're on holiday? That's the door we'll use, your Majesty." The entrance he indicated could only have been described as a side one, and yet, out of loyalty to the Imperial cause, Evans did not hesitate to overlook his usual claim on the front door, as even his stern egalitarianism could make a temporary compromise in an emergency. He opened the second-rate door for Eugénie, and then followed her into the warmth of the hotel.

A large, middle-aged American man, with large American teeth, looked up from the writing-desk, and said in surprise, "Hello, Evans. I didn't know that you were in Deauville."

"Oh — hello, Fenby." Evans was utterly flummoxed for once, frantically searching for a glib reason that would explain why he had been caught furtively entering the hotel with an unknown and beautiful woman. Clarence Fenby was from Philadelphia, had met all of Evans's sisters and cousins, and would not be fooled by the abrupt addition of an extra one. Fenby was also a long-established and dedicated gossip, guaranteed to start sharing any secret with everybody in his address book seconds after confidential information had been revealed to him.

"And Mrs Evans too — Oh, I do beg your pardon." Fenby stood up to offer a hearty American welcome to the stranger, waited for an introduction, and then realized that he was not going to get one. "Er — excuse me, please — I have to hurry to — to get there in time." With a pretence of tactfulness, Fenby backed out of the room, colliding with a magazine rack *en route*, before stumbling over the waste-paper basket in his haste to reach an audience, and commence the self-appointed duties of town-crier.

"I fear that your reputation's now in shreds, Dr Evans," said Eugénie with amusement, and suddenly she felt better, much better.

"Fenby's got more to worry about than my morals,"

186

declared Evans. "A long history of mouth ulcers, to say nothing of receding gums."

A gentleman prepared to stay in the same hotel as his dentist? That was taking democracy to the limits, Eugénie thought in astonishment; but she had not realized that a dentist's wife would frequent such good quality accommodation, complete with reading-rooms and carpeted hallways. She had been expecting a repeat of the previous night's inn, although with a somewhat rowdier atmosphere, judging by an apparent connection to a casino. Perhaps the hotel might not be quite the one that Eugénie herself would have patronized, even during her pre-palace days, but it was definitely acceptable after the excess of social equality that she had encountered in the preceding forty-eight hours.

"I hope my wife isn't out with her detectives," said Evans, "though it doesn't really matter because Madame Lebreton should be here by now, and your Majesty can hide with her, if need be." Cautiously, he walked along the corridor towards his wife's room, and gently pressed the door handle.

Agnes Evans had been idly looking through rain-lashed windows at a restlessly choppy sea, and as the door slowly opened, she glanced around in search of more interesting entertainment and found it. "Thomas! What on earth are you doing here? And why didn't you reply to my telegram? I've been so worried about your dinner-party. Was it an absolute disaster? Of all the inconvenient times for the French to have one of their revolutions, they would choose the very day of your party. Did nobody turn up? I'm so sorry. Such a disappointment for you, after all that planning."

"No, no, Agnes, the party was fine, I —"

"So why didn't you telegraph? I've been imagining every type of calamity from rancid butter to fetid cheese. I even began to have my doubts about the wine, although it's supposed to be such a good vintage, and Monsieur Laval himself told me that Crown Prince Rudolf of Austria refuses to drink anything else. Apparently he —" Disastrous dinner-parties and Crown Princes were abruptly driven from Mrs Evans's mind by the astounding sight of the Empress of France standing in the doorway.

"Have the police questioned you about me?" Evans demanded.

"The police? No. Why? Thomas, what have you done?"

"He's rescued me from the revolution," said Eugénie, surveying her surroundings. Not a bad room, and a view of the sea as well. Dentists' wives certainly lived better than an empress would ever have suspected.

"I did read a line or two somewhere about the palace being stormed by a mob," recalled Mrs Evans.

"A line or two!" repeated Eugénie, with considerable bitterness.

"Yes, your Majesty, but it didn't say a word about Thomas being there, rescuing anybody."

"I'll tell you the details later," said Evans, regretting that his story was not going to be quite so dramatic as Agnes clearly expected. It would have been glorious to defy a mob at the stormed palace, and taken charge of the rescue right from the start. He felt almost cheated, and the fact that the Empress had managed to escape from the Tuileries perfectly well without his assistance was not the point, because destiny should have arranged for him to be at the Imperial side from that very first moment.

"And I suppose there wasn't a single word about me, in any of the Deauville newspapers either," said Eugénie, tight-lipped.

"I'm afraid I didn't study them very closely, your Majesty," confessed Mrs Evans. She had been far too busy, thinking how shattered poor Thomas would be by the failure of his dinner-party, to have much time to spare for the lesser problems of France and the Imperial family. Yet despite her husband's assurance that the party had been as successful as his empress rescue, something still puzzled Agnes Evans. "Thomas, why are you carrying those rocks?"

"Rocks? What rocks?" Evans asked, before remembering the weapons that he had prudently armed himself with. "Oh, these rocks. They're part of Dr Crane's fossil collection."

"Dr Crane?" queried Mrs Evans. "Who's Dr Crane?"

"A fossil collector. He's a fanatic about them."

"But who is he?"

"Benjamin Crane's son."

"And who's Benjamin Crane?"

"Someone I was at college with. He hosted my dinner-party for me: the son, that is, not the father, who couldn't possibly have done it, because he's in Philadelphia."

"But why didn't you host your own party?" And why on earth bother with somebody's fossils in the middle of a revolution? A whole house crammed to the rafters with their possessions, and Thomas chose to salvage an armful of old rocks and transport them half-way across France. There were times when Agnes Doyle Evans felt that she still did not fully understand the man she had married, even after twenty-five years.

"I'll explain everything later. Crane should be here soon with Madame Lebreton, and then —"

"Who's Madame Lebreton?"

"Agnes, there's no time for long discussions. Crane and I have got to go and find a boat."

"Why?" demanded Mrs Evans. "What boat?"

"Oh, I don't know yet," replied Evans, impatient with Agnes's slowness. "Any boat I can get."

Any boat? Eugénie knew, she just knew, that before long the Empress of France would find herself sailing out into the middle of a Channel gale, democratically knee-high in fish.

****

The wind was even stronger on the quay, but at least the rain had temporarily eased, although dark clouds were again gathering over the Channel, and boats creaked and rolled at their moorings, as waves swirled against the sea-wall, sending arcs of salt-water crashing down onto the wharf. Evans and Crane began their slow tour of inspection, but it was not the most encouraging time to think about setting sail, when even the gulls were headed inland.

"I don't like the look of those fishing boats," said Crane. "They seem too small and fragile to last more than a few minutes in such a rough sea."

"And the fisherman might have a misguided loyalty to the new Republic, and report strangers trying to get to Britain," Evans added.

Bent into the wind, they struggled further down the quay, their coats billowing like sails. "What about that boat?" asked Crane, pointing towards a more substantial vessel in the distance. "Isn't it flying the British flag? Yes, that's definitely the Union Jack."

"British? We can't trust the British," declared Evans. "Nobody can trust the British. They're a treacherous nation. The Emperor had a new hat once, a completely original design, utterly unique, and yet the very first time he wore it, the British conspired with an Italian anarchist to blow his hat to bits. In shreds, it was; you wouldn't believe the destruction. The Emperor could never wear it again. The whole thing was a typically British act of vandalism."

They walked along in respectful silence for the late-lamented hat, but as they drew nearer the yacht, Crane spoke again. "It's called the *Gazelle,* and I don't think you'll find a better boat in the whole harbour. It's either that, or trust one of the fishermen. "

"But a British flag." Then Evans recalled the vital importance of his mission. Perhaps destiny was offering the English a chance to atone for the detonation of Napoleon's hat by helping to rescue his Empress, because Crane was probably right when he said that the yacht was the most suitable craft docked in Deauville that afternoon, and Eugénie's safety came first, but still Evans felt frustrated by the limited choice on offer to him. Hiring a boat to cross the Channel had seemed the least complicated part of his escape plan; there were always boats at the seaside, and Evans had imagined being able to select the ideal vessel from a vast array of candidates, yet the *Gazelle* appeared to be the only contender. As they approached the yacht, he could see a crewman in dark-blue guernsey and denim trousers leaning against a broom handle on deck, apparently fully occupied with gazing into the middle distance, and despite being a possible British national, the man looked harmless enough. "I'll ask who the yacht belongs to," decided Evans, telling himself that a mere inquiry committed him to nothing.

"Make up a story," said Crane, finally getting into a conspiratorial frame of mind. "You could say we're travellers stranded here because of the revolution, and pretend that, being British, when we saw the Union Jack, we —"

"We can't be British on board a British boat, so we're Americans until further notice."

"Are we? Good!" Crane felt better than he had done for days, because if Evans allowed him to be an American again, Crane realized that the most disconcerting time in his life was about to come to an end, and hopefully without him taking the leading rôle in a public execution. Better yet, his father need never know a thing.

Fighting the wind, Evans and Crane walked alongside the yacht, and each step convinced them that they were looking at their best option. The *Gazelle* was perhaps eighty feet long, as white as milk teeth, and seemed impeccably clean and modern after the rejected fishing boats. Evans glanced around, but was unable to see any detectives lurking behind the mounds of ropes and nets that lay scattered among the puddles on the quay, and he waved a hand to attract the idle crewman's attention.

"Excuse me! Or should I say ahoy? Whichever, we're Americans, and we think we know this yacht. Doesn't it belong to a man called Fenby?"

Hubert Poldray had been completely fed-up with life. He was on duty with nothing, in his opinion, to do, while the other five crew members were let loose among the fleshpots of Deauville; and although Deauville was not exactly seeing the world, it still beat gazing at a wet dockside all night, if you happened to be a fair-haired man in your early twenties and considered rather fetching in a favourable light. However, talking to a couple of Americans was a better pastime than brooding on his wrongs, and Poldray made an effort. "This is Sir John Burgoyne's yacht."

"Burgoyne. Yes, of course. That's the name I meant to say. I can't think why it slipped my mind," declared Evans. "Is Sir John on board by any chance?"

"He's on board all right," Poldray replied gloomily. If Sir John Burgoyne had not been on board, Hubert Poldray could have been somewhere else as well.

Evans climbed gingerly onto the gangplank, hanging onto the roped sides as the wind buffeted him. "Give Sir John my card, and ask him to see me for a few minutes. Tell him that it's very urgent, extremely urgent. A matter of the utmost importance: absolutely vital, in fact."

"Vital!" Poldray repeated, intrigued. Life was unexpectedly livening up. "I'll tell him," he promised, with a sudden smile that appalled Evans, because Poldray had distressingly typical British teeth, as degenerate as their country of origin.

"Sir John Burgoyne," Crane said doubtfully, as Poldray left. "Wasn't there an English general called John Burgoyne in the War of Independence?"

"Yes, but no match for our American troops. He surrendered at Saratoga Springs, too cowardly to fight to the death."

"I hope this Burgoyne's no relation. He might hold a bit of a grudge against Americans."

"Of course he will. Every Britisher there is has spent the last ninety-odd years sulking about that defeat, but we have to work with what we can get," declared Evans, trying and failing to sound tolerant.

****

Sir John Montagu Burgoyne, 10th Baronet, was tall, thin, plain and fifty. He was also bewildered. Why should a Dr Thomas W Evans, President of the American Sanitary Commission of Paris, want to see him on a vital matter of extreme urgency? He turned the card over, but there was no message written on the back.

"Well, yes, I suppose he can come on board," said Burgoyne.

"He's already on deck," reported Poldray. "And there's another man with him."

"Where's his card?"

"I don't know. He didn't give me any card."

And what was a Sanitary Commission anyway, Burgoyne wondered; something to do with drains? Or were they the people who wrote to the newspapers about the disgracefully unhygienic state of restaurant kitchens? Or, more worryingly, was some sort of public health inspector on board, ready and eager to start his inspecting?

"There isn't any — well — any vermin on the *Gazelle*, is there?" Burgoyne asked uneasily.

"Certainly not," declared Poldray. "They can inspect anywhere they like, and they won't find a single rat, mouse or cockroach on this yacht. Not if I can have five minutes to make sure, that is," he added prudently.

"I'll keep them talking for as long as I can." Burgoyne gave an anxious glance around the stateroom as Poldray went out, and as no vermin seemed to be returning his gaze, he examined Dr Evans's card again, but a message had not appeared on its back since the last time Burgoyne checked, and Sanitary Commission still read Sanitary Commission. The explanation was approaching, however, because he could hear footsteps outside his stateroom door, and at once felt guilty, without being exactly sure what he was supposed to have done wrong.

"Dr Evans?"

"I'm Dr Thomas W Evans, and this is Dr Edward A Crane."

Two doctors! The danger to public health must really be serious, Burgoyne thought even more uneasily. "You both work for this Sanitary Commission in Paris?"

"Work *for* it! No, indeed. I'm the President," said Evans so reprovingly that Burgoyne found himself mumbling an apology. "And Dr Crane's been sent to France by the International Red Cross."

"The International Red Cross!" repeated Burgoyne, more startled than impressed by such exalted credentials.

"As it happens, I'm a member of the International Red Cross myself," Evans said, determined to put the Britisher in his place, "as well as being the President of the American Sanitary Commission."

The vermin situation in Deauville must be absolutely appalling, thought Burgoyne in horror, if the International Red Cross had been called in to deal with the emergency. There ought to be warnings to stop a blameless yacht owner docking in so contaminated a port, yellow flags along the quay at least, and Burgoyne wished that he had avoided Deauville like the plague. Plague?

"Do you want to inspect the yacht?" he asked miserably, wondering what the first symptoms of plague were. "Try the food perhaps?"

Evans relaxed a little towards the British. He had always heard that they were coldly reserved to the last man, yet here was a Britisher urging the freedom of his boat onto strangers, with a pressing invitation to dine thrown in. "That's very kind of you, but I'm afraid we'll be forced to refuse."

Did the International Red Cross and the American Sanitary Commission believe that the poor *Gazelle* was so badly infected that they dare not carry out any sort of inspection at all? Burgoyne pictured horrifying scenes of himself, his wife and crew, all imprisoned in a medieval quarantine hospital, and doomed to expire in fearful agonies, one by one.

"However," continued Evans, "we do have a favour, a very great favour, to ask you."

"Yes?" replied Burgoyne. Were they planning to send the *Gazelle* up in flames without further ado?

"You've heard about the revolution in Paris? The storming of the Tuileries Palace?"

"Yes," Burgoyne agreed absently. Lucky he had not gone

to all the bother of having the London house re-roofed for the winter. Someone else's problem now.

After days of lies and being British, Evans found himself reluctant to trust anybody with the truth; yet how could any sister, no matter how much of an invalid, demand the Burgoyne yacht for a personal cruise across the Channel? It was a wild leap of faith for Evans to share his secret with a Britisher, but the only alternative seemed to be a rickety French boat that might have perfidious republican tendencies, as well as a cargo of wet fish. "Sir John, can we rely on your absolute discretion? What I say is told only in the strictest confidence, and you must be prepared to guard the information with your life."

It was plague! Plague in Deauville! People were gasping their last breath all over the place, and the International Red Cross had the nerve to expect him, Sir John Montagu Burgoyne, 10th Baronet, to be part of a cover-up! Never! He had his integrity, and would refuse point-blank, without hesitation, without compromise, without equivocation, to lower his principles. "Well, I don't think that I could — well, I'm not sure I — well, you see — it's a bit much to try and rope me into a —"

"I'm asking you to help save a life," said Evans. "I rescued — somebody — from Paris, you see, and —"

"A plague victim!" exclaimed Burgoyne.

"Oh, no. I'd have taken a plague patient to the nearest hospital and reported the case to the public health authorities, not transported her half-way across the country. Although the air does seem very bracing in Deauville, I must admit: in fact, almost as good as Atlantic City. No, it was the Empress Eugénie I rescued, when a bloodthirsty mob stormed her Palace." Evans paused, to allow time for a few words of congratulation on the success and daring of the mission, but Burgoyne merely looked vacant, and Evans continued his story, somewhat offended that rescuing an empress should be taken so casually. "With Dr Crane's assistance, I brought the Empress here to —"

Evans got a reaction at last. "Here!" gasped Burgoyne, glancing around in alarm. "On board the *Gazelle*!"

"No, she's in the town, but we must cross the Channel as soon as possible, and the ferry to Southampton's far too dangerous, so we need a private boat. Will you help us?" Evans waited with supreme confidence for the answer.

"I'm afraid not."

Evans smiled in gratitude, and opened his mouth to thank Burgoyne, before registering what he had actually heard. "You won't help us? You refuse?"

"But surely you've got to help," said Crane. "The lady's in great danger, exactly like Marie-Antoinette, and Dr Evans isn't asking much: just a boat ride. You could be saving a life."

"But I can't do something that might have political repercussions," declared Burgoyne. He was on his own territory now and, happily, it was far removed from plague victims and quarantine hospitals. "I'm a lieutenant-colonel in the British Army, seconded to the Diplomatic Service at present."

"I left my patients, my career, my house and everything in it, because a lady needed my help," said Evans, scorning what he perceived to be downright cowardice.

"But the lady is the Empress of France," Burgoyne pointed out. "Or rather, *was* the Empress of France."

"That's why she needs your help," said Crane. "That's why she's in such danger." And so was Burgoyne, because Crane feared that, at any moment, Evans would be tempted to seize a fossil, knock the Baronet out cold, and commandeer the yacht.

"Crane, there's nothing further to discuss with a man who's more interested in saving his own skin than taking a risk for a fellow human being," announced Evans. "But let me tell you, Burgoyne, no American would be so cravenly spineless."

"It's nothing to do with my spine," claimed Burgoyne, wondering how to bring the Grenadier Guards into the conversation without seeming to brag. Not that there was a great deal to brag about in his military career, he would be the first to concede, and the sight of those final mess bills had probably killed his father, but even that was one of England's glorious traditions.

"It wouldn't be much of a risk," urged Crane, trusting that nobody would ever figure out that his own wish to get the Empress Eugénie on board the *Gazelle* had a lot to do with him hoping to avoid a French prison. "You'd be across the Channel before anyone realized what had happened."

"But if I were involved in any sort of rescue scheme, it could cause all sorts of difficulties," protested Burgoyne. "The new French Government might conclude that Britain favours the Imperial régime, and that we oppose the change of power. The Republicans could even suspect Westminster of plotting to restore Bonaparte, and as for Prussia —"

"Oh, don't be so stuffy, John." Lady Burgoyne, a shameless eavesdropper, opened the door and walked into the stateroom. "You're not so important that people assume the British Government meekly follows in your wake."

"Well, no," Burgoyne admitted. "But, Amy, the Service doesn't sanction any meddling in the politics of a foreign country."

"You're bored rigid with the Service," Lady Burgoyne informed her husband briskly. Like him, she was tall, thin, plain and fifty, but there the resemblance ended. "You'll have an excellent excuse to resign, and the newspapers would give you a splendid write-up, for once."

"But the Foreign Office wouldn't approve of a lieutenant-colonel who deliberately intervened to —"

"It'd be headline news; I can see the columns of newsprint now. Baronet to the rescue. Empress saved from guillotine. Without thought of career or personal safety, Sir John Burgoyne dashingly leapt into action to rescue the beautiful Empress Eugénie from barbarous execution at the hands of a ferocious mob."

Burgoyne was taken aback, never having pictured himself as any sort of reckless hero. His conditioning, however, made one last stand. "But what about future relations with the new French Republic?"

"Oh, let somebody else worry about them." Daughter and wife of army officers, Amy Burgoyne had endured more than three months' diplomacy, and the strain of polite conversation, forcing a smile at Consular wit, and looking fascinated by Ambassadorial anecdotes had taken their toll. Another month, and she would be ready to join the Anarchists. "Just think, John, if you did resign, we'd never have to attend another Embassy dinner-party again."

All men have their price. "Bring the Empress on board as soon as you like, Dr Evans," Burgoyne said cordially. "We're planning to sail on the six o'clock tide tomorrow morning: although not if the wind gets any stronger, of course."

"It won't," Evans decided.

Triumphantly, he went ashore with Crane, and the sound of Poldray's furious scouring of the galley accompanied them half-way across the quay.

****

199

"Where's the Empress?" demanded Evans, the moment he opened the door of his wife's room.

"She's with Madame Lebreton. Did you get a boat?" Not that Mrs Evans needed to ask. She knew that if Thomas went out determined to acquire a boat, he would not return until that boat was securely his.

"We found a yacht, but I didn't think much of the owner. British. Though I'll say one thing for him and his wife," Evans conceded grudgingly, "they both appear to have looked after their teeth."

"I'll start packing."

"It might be better if you stayed in Deauville." Even with the successful end of his mission so close, Evans was not prepared to take any chances with the Empress's safety. His wife, of course, was an entirely different matter.

"Stay here? Why?"

"There might be detectives following you."

"Following *me*? Why would detectives bother to follow me?"

"Because you're the wife of the Imperial Court Dentist," Evans pointed out. "I expect the society columns in the local newspapers were full of your arrival here."

"No. I don't think that my name was in any of the papers."

"They pretended not to know who you are!" marvelled Evans, staggered by the cunning of such a ruse. The enemy was smarter than he had suspected, but he could still see through their wily subterfuge. "They're trying to lull us into a false sense of security."

"They managed it as far as I'm concerned," admitted Mrs Evans. "I haven't noticed a single detective following me anywhere: not that it ever actually occurred to me to look for one. Are you sure the police wouldn't have something better to do with their time, than trail around Deauville after me?"

"As the Emperor's closest friend and confidant, I'll have been the first person they thought of, when they tried to work out who the Empress would turn to for help, and when they discovered that I'd left Paris —! Well, it doesn't take much imagination to know what happened then."

"Anybody watching me walk along the shore has had a pretty dull time."

"Good," said Evans. "Unfortunately, we can't sail until tomorrow morning, and if you check out of the hotel now, your detectives might start to search the boats."

Having shared a home with a dentist for twenty-five years had made Mrs Evans resilient, and being abandoned in the middle of a revolution, to be trailed by unseen detectives, while her husband sailed away into the unknown with an empress, could not faze her. "How long should I stay here in Deauville?"

"Until the yacht's safely out of the harbour. You can follow us then, if you like, on the ferry to Southampton."

"Is that where you'll be? Southampton?"

"No, Hastings," replied Evans, and his normally decisive tone became uncharacteristically hesitant when he added, "The Marine Hotel, Hastings."

"The Marine Hotel?" repeated Mrs Evans in surprise.

"The Imperial family agreed to meet there, should they ever be separated."

"Not in a castle or a palace?"

"No. The Marine Hotel, Hastings."

"It sounds like the sort of place a shopkeeper would take his family to, for a week's holiday," commented Mrs Evans. "Are you sure that it's the Marine Hotel?"

"That's what the Empress told me, but perhaps the hotel's more promising than its name suggests," said Evans, trying to seem optimistic: a struggle in which he did not altogether succeed. "After all, the Emperor himself chose the rendezvous."

"And where will we go after the Marine Hotel, Hastings?"

"I don't know." It was the first time that Evans had properly considered his future, since the startling appearance of the Empress of France in his library, and for once he had no plan. "The Prussians are marching on Paris, and just about everything we own is there. The French are going to be annihilated, unless the Germans begin listening to the Emperor. He's the only man who can keep the peace in Europe."

"Oh well, we started married life with very little," said Mrs Evans, and she tactfully refrained from pointing out that the Emperor had hardly fostered European peace by declaring war on Prussia. The good sense that accompanied Agnes Doyle Evans through life did not let her down, even at the prospect of German shells aimed directly at the flag-pole in her garden, and she dismissed the past without repining. "What we've done once, we can do again somewhere else."

"Yes," agreed Evans. "Luckily, people are always going to have toothache."

11

A little after eleven o'clock that night, the roar of an agitated sea greeted the Imperial party when they left the *Hotel du Casino* by its garden door, and walked into a cold wind that drove smoky black clouds across the moon, abruptly snuffing out the sky. Evans led the way along a road that skirted the sea shore, and the other three followed in his wake, stumbling over rocks as they tried to avoid puddles that were almost invisible before the fugitives had blundered into them. Deauville's lighthouse, a beacon of safety, glowed through the darkness, but Evans guided his group onto a footpath that crossed some open fields, and added mud to the hazards of their journey.

Crane decided to worry again because things seemed to be going too well. Mrs Evans was stationed in the reception area of the hotel, to distract those watching detectives, but Crane felt certain that there were gendarmes behind every wall, every tree, and at the side of every building. He was sure that he could feel their gaze on the Empress, although how the police could see Eugénie so clearly from a distance, when Crane had considerable difficulty making out the ground beneath his own feet, was a mystery left unsolved as he slithered through mounds of wet earth, almost dropping the fossils held in readiness for a possible attack. The footpath ended, and after clambering over a boulder that acted as a stile, Evans permitted his mud-spattered followers to rejoin a road, but only because he had no choice, even though the Rue du Casino forced them to cross the Place de Morny where the lights from a café illuminated part of the street with the clarity of daytime.

Then, suddenly, Evans stood still.

"What is it?" Crane asked apprehensively, before he too

heard the sound that had alarmed Evans: the *Marseillaise*, sung so loudly and enthusiastically that even the bluster of wind and sea was unable to mask the exuberance of the words. After staging his *coup d'état*, the Emperor Napoleon III had wisely banned such a rabble-rousing song, and it was yet another sign of changed times that the French should again feel free to sing the *Marseillaise*'s inflammatory verses without fear of arrest.

"Stay here. I'll go check what's happening." Evans headed toward the brightness of the café, and Crane clutched his fossils, hoping that he would find it easier to hit somebody when the night was too dim for a face to be seen clearly.

"It can't be a Republican demonstration at midnight," said Madame Lebreton.

"They sing quite well, for a mob," remarked Eugénie, who prided herself on refusing to let prejudice cloud artistic judgment. "The enunciation's very precise: almost as good as a trained choir."

"Perhaps they're just rehearsing for a demonstration," suggested Crane.

"At midnight?" Madame Lebreton sounded doubtful.

"They're probably forced to hold late rehearsals," said Eugénie. "They must be kept very busy rioting by day, and yet it's a necessity for them to learn the words of the *Marseillaise* sometime, if they want a proper revolution. As Empress, I've come to understand the difficulties that face the lower classes in society."

Then Evans was back, looming out of the dark night like an image in a developing photograph. "It's all right. Just some people in the café, a café that's served far too much wine, if you ask me. How else could they lose their senses so completely, and sing that particular song?"

"Yes, anybody would think the French preferred a republic

to an empire," agreed Eugénie. Her subjects seemed unable to appreciate how much more fun life had been for them, with a splendid Imperial Court to brighten their dull lives as they read newspaper reports of receptions, balls, concerts, foreign visits, presents, and admiration for France's beautiful Empress. If Republicanism meant following a dentist from one uncomfortable situation to another, through muddy pools of rainwater in a windy street at midnight, the French people had plainly been hoodwinked by deceitful agitators.

Evans steered his party to the far side of the road to avoid the light spilling out over the pavement from the café, but the vigorous singing followed them defiantly. And she had been prepared to die in her Palace for those very same people, thought Eugénie. It was the ingratitude that hurt, the lack of response to the generosity of her self-sacrificing nature, and she felt glad that to go on living had seemed a more sensible option; although had she known that escape would lead her to a pitch-black quay that smelt of an overabundance of fish and oily rope, with the daunting prospect of a stormy Channel voyage ahead, she might have had second thoughts about abandoning the Tuileries.

The Rue du Casino led almost directly to the *Gazelle*'s moorings, and it was even colder by the gangplank where, lantern in hand, Poldray glumly awaited the sanitary inspectors' arrival. He also had instructions to watch out for gendarmes, detectives, soldiers, or any sort of official, although what Burgoyne expected Poldray to do about such an influx of authority was left unsaid. Of course everybody knew that vermin were nocturnal, but even so, a midnight inspection seemed rather excessive to Poldray.

The sanitary group approached slowly, picking their way carefully between stacks of timber and tangles of fishing net. Lady sanitary inspectors? France was a surprising country, and things were definitely on the up, Poldray reflected happily.

****

Thank God, thought Eugénie, a fairly decent-looking yacht even though Sir John Burgoyne was merely a baronet. The *Gazelle* could never be considered on a par with the Imperial yacht, but it was a cut above travelling in the company of mackerel, and Eugénie stepped onto the gangplank, more concerned about her chances of plunging into the darkness of the rough water below, than with the fact that an empress of France had just taken what might be her final steps on French soil.

The last time Eugénie went on board a yacht, there had been flowers, spectators, reporters, a band, several tons of luggage, attentive naval officers, and the local mayor determined to make a long speech in her honour. Now the Empress was about to leave the country as furtively as a criminal on the run, wearing borrowed clothes and with only a dentist and doctor on Imperial Protection Duty. Not being a fortune-teller, Mrs Evans could hardly be blamed for having bought a coat in a shade that veered suspiciously close to Prussian blue, and the sturdiness of the material certainly disguised Eugénie's famed hourglass figure; however, on the plus side, a fairly acceptable dress, almost fashionable, though it would not have been her first choice of escaping costume, but Eugénie was far too generous to let Mrs Evans suspect the wide gulf that separated Imperial from lower bourgeois attire. After all, any old thing was good enough to travel in when there were no admiring audiences, and to judge by Lady Burgoyne's sensibly English appearance, her wardrobe would offer no better alternative.

"Thank you for the invitation to share your voyage to

England," said Eugénie, in case the Burgoynes should feel overwhelmed by the presence of an empress on board their lesser-ranking yacht. "Such a pretty boat: so compact."

"Do come and inspect the cabins," urged Lady Burgoyne, for Poldray's benefit, as the crewman seemed greatly struck by the beauty of one member of the Sanitary Committee.

"It's a great risk that you're asking me to take," Burgoyne muttered to Evans.

"The greater the risk, the greater the glory," retorted Evans.

"And the greater the penalty if one gets caught."

It was the type of defeatist talk that Evans had always despised, but he forced himself to be content with a disapproving silence, because Poldray stood close by, and he would doubtless share any enthralling gossip about confrontational sanitary inspectors with the five other crewmen, all of whom were British and therefore untrustworthy by birth. Even though the Empress was securely on board and hidden in a Burgoyne cabin, Evans felt unable to relax. He was certain that only his determination and alertness kept Eugénie safe, and that if he stopped concentrating before the *Gazelle* left port, something might happen merely because he had neglected his duty by being off guard. The solution was to stay resolutely on guard, and so, ready to repel invaders, Evans stationed himself on deck close to the gangplank, facing land that the night made too dark to see.

"The wind seems to be getting stronger," Crane commented, as he brought some coffee for the self-appointed sentinel. "I hope the yacht can sail in the morning."

"Of course we'll sail," Evans said firmly. He was in no mood to stand any nonsense from the weather.

"You won't need me any more then," Crane continued. "I'll

wait until the boat's safely out of the harbour, pitch my fossil collection into the sea, and go back."

"Go back?" repeated Evans in bewilderment. "Go back where? Philadelphia?"

"No, Paris."

"Paris! But, Crane, you can't!"

"I have to."

"No, you can't. The Prussians will be there soon."

"I know."

"But they'll shell the city," Evans protested. He had imagined that Crane would be a meekly unquestioning assistant, until he received a dismissal in due course, and it felt to Evans almost as though he had a mutiny on his hands.

"The Red Cross sent me here to work in a field hospital, and the French need all the doctors they can get. I have to go back."

It came as a surprise to Evans to remember that Crane did have a life of his own, and also the right to make decisions about that life. After all, he had managed to get himself across the Atlantic Ocean without any instructions or guidance from Evans, and could presumably find his way back to Paris by train, yet the instinct to take control of Crane was hard to relinquish. "Are you sure you'll be safe? The republicans will be looking for me, and they're bound to have been informed that you hosted my dinner-party."

"But nobody realizes that I met the Empress, and I think a few Prussian shells flying overhead should give republicans more to worry about than whether or not I hosted a dinner-party." After his unexpected survival of bloodthirsty mobs and a possible trip to the guillotine, Crane felt that the job he had been sent to France to do would be practically like returning to the regular world where, despite the stupidity of the war, he could be known by his real name and deal with crises that he was trained to cope with. "I'm an American doctor with the International Red Cross. That should keep me safe from any French officialdom."

"You're right, of course," Evans admitted grudgingly. "Crane, I must thank you for standing by me in such a dangerous venture."

"I only hope that my father doesn't hear a word about it, because he wouldn't approve at all of me helping to rescue an empress. If he ever discovers what I've done, I'll find myself disowned and disgraced."

Though should he be forbidden to return home, Crane reflected, he would never again have to face paternal criticism of his inadequacies, and the rest of life would be one long holiday, free of restraint and disapproval. In a sudden startling flash of awareness, Crane realized that, just as he had decided to leave the rescue group without consulting Evans, so he was free to decide not to go back to Philadelphia. Nobody could force him to return home, and nobody could stop him living wherever he wanted, because he was as much a part of the world as anyone else, not placed in it on sufferance to apologize for his ineptness, and choosing to live far away from blood relatives would turn out to be his own personal revolution against oppression. Some people have to die for the cause of freedom; Edward A Crane simply stayed on in Europe.

****

Just before the dawn of Wednesday, September 7th, Crane stood on the quayside, drenched by rain and sea spray, while he threw his fossils one by one into the Channel, and watched the *Gazelle* leave Deauville harbour. He had passed another of Evans's sleepless nights, sharing sentry duty on deck and wondering how he would be able to repel invaders if talk of British invalid sisters failed to hoodwink whichever officious governmental authority stormed its way on board. However, the only disturbers of that cold vigil were the returning crew members, and even Crane had not managed to convince himself that the raucous version of *Araminta Fair* was a French Republican subterfuge, although the noise brought a nervous Burgoyne out of his stateroom like a jack-in-the-box.

The south-west wind was strengthening and the waves might be high, thought Evans, but they were at sea with no other boats in sight, and therefore safe. The Imperial Dentist, who had crossed the Atlantic several times, scoffed at Burgoyne's misgivings about the weather because, on any map of Europe, the Channel appeared to be little more than a river, and Evans was confident of their arrival at Southampton in a matter of hours, without any more interruptions to his plan. The great adventure was almost over, and the place of Dr Thomas W Evans in history secured.

The Empress seemed pensive, taking no part in the conversation, as Evans chatted happily to Madame Lebreton and Lady Burgoyne. He approved of the yacht, with its comfortable stateroom and trim cabins, and was almost prepared to pardon Burgoyne for being British. After all, it would be unreasonable to blame anybody for the faults of a previous generation, because no man could be held responsible for parents who had been too stick-in-the-mud to migrate to the States, and even the most superior of families, such as Evans's own, could not boast complete freedom from the taint of British ancestry.

"There's nothing like a sea voyage," Evans said cheerfully, as the stateroom swayed and dipped. "You'd be surprised how many of my patients have left on long voyages, after consulting me. They've often gone to the other side of the world."

"England's quite far enough for me, in weather like this," replied Lady Burgoyne. She had as little enterprising spirit as the rest of her retrograde nation, Evans thought with pity.

"The storm's getting worse." Madame Lebreton felt she ought to be more conscious of the fact that she had just left her native land perhaps for ever, forsaking, at the same time, her husband to whichever prisoner-of-war camp had claimed him, but all sensitivities stayed firmly in the background. She had never liked the sea. It was unruly, did not know its place, and she could hear waves washing over the deck with a noise like thunder, battering the sides of the *Gazelle* as though determined to smash the yacht into fragments, and making the stateroom buck like a restless horse. Madame Lebreton did not like horses either.

"We must be near the British coast by now," declared Evans. It was lunchtime, and he wondered why none of the crew seemed to be doing anything about a meal; but perhaps the *Gazelle* was so close to Southampton that Burgoyne planned to put them ashore unfed. The British just did not understand hospitality, Evans concluded scornfully; why, at least three meals would have been served on an American boat by that time, with several snacks in between.

Then Burgoyne the inhospitable appeared, and cold air swirled around the stateroom, as he struggled to close the door behind him. "The wind's veered north-west," he said. Not a mention of a meal: not even an apology for its absence.

"North-west?" repeated Evans, unenlightened.

"We've lost the spinnaker boom, so the mainsail's been reefed, and the jib run down."

"It all sounds most efficient. When will we reach Southampton?"

211

"We won't, in this weather," declared Burgoyne. "It's impossible to hold our course."

"Then land anywhere you like on the British coast," Evans said tolerantly.

"You don't understand. We're nowhere near England."

"But we've been at sea for six hours," Evans pointed out, appalled by such un-American incompetence.

"We haven't been able to make any headway against this wind," claimed Burgoyne, no doubt first cousin to Benedict Arnold. "I think we'll have to turn back to the French coast for shelter."

"Absolutely not!" stated Evans.

"It might be our only chance of survival," maintained Burgoyne the feeble.

"We can't turn back," announced Evans. "We won't turn back. And we will survive."

Then the Empress spoke. "Wasn't it during a September that the *S.S. Arctic* went down, Dr Evans? I remember how upset you were about your sister and her family. I tried to cancel my appointment, but you insisted on working as usual, and wouldn't even consider staying away from the Palace, although I pleaded with you to take a holiday."

"Julia drowned in the Atlantic, your Majesty," said Evans. "This is the Channel. The situation's entirely different. Besides, it was more than fifteen years ago now, and so much progress has been made in design that steam ships never sink after a collision these days."

"But we're on a yacht."

"Exactly," agreed Evans. "The *Gazelle* isn't a steam ship at all. That proves how safe we are."

"Oh, I'm not afraid of drowning," declared Eugénie. "I feel so sick that I'm sure to die at any moment, and I only hope that it's soon, very soon."

212

"We haven't come this far to be defeated by a few gusts of wind."

"You can't master the weather by will-power, Dr Evans," said Burgoyne the ineffectual.

At least it was not going to be a run-of-the-mill average sort of death, reflected Lady Burgoyne. To go down in a shipwreck, accompanied by the ex-Empress of France while she was escaping from a revolution with her dentist, ought to be good for several columns in all the newspapers. And how surprised everyone would be that the dull and conventional Burgoynes had managed to die in so dramatic a fashion.

"We won't be shipwrecked," declared Evans. "Why would I be chosen by destiny to rescue the Empress from cut-throat mobs, only for fate to drown us a couple of days later? It would be quite pointless."

"Oh, why didn't I just stay in Paris, and be guillotined in comfort?" wailed Eugénie.

"If the storm continues, we'll have to turn back," said Burgoyne the defeatist. "We've got no choice."

"The storm won't continue," Evans informed him. "This wind was quite obviously sent to stop the Empress's enemies following her, and now that it's served its purpose, things will ease."

"I wouldn't mind in the least, if every bloodthirsty mob in France captured me," declared Eugénie, "as long as they killed me this minute."

Evans always said afterwards that it was the Empress's fearless attitude to death that gave him the courage and determination to go on. Burgoyne had no chance of captaining his own yacht, for Evans had decided that they were to head for the British coast, and so to the British coast they would go, even if it took all day. The *Gazelle*, facing the wind, plunged and swayed in waves that rose higher than her

213

deck and then crashed down against the stateroom door. On several occasions, the Empress thought that the boat had overturned, but each time Eugénie was disappointed. To Madame Lebreton, the voyage became a nightmare that she knew must be a dream, but could not wake up from, because time had frozen, leaving the storm and the yacht as the only reality. Her past life had belonged to someone else, and there was no possibility of a future; there was nothing but the stateroom of the yacht, and a storm that would roar on for all eternity. She was not afraid, merely submissive, and the Burgoynes were equally passive, having given themselves up for dead hours previously.

Yet the *Gazelle*, buoyant as a cork, triumphantly survived onslaught after onslaught, as the hurricane raged on. Something of Evans's stubborn tenacity seemed to have been built into the yacht, and she rode out the highest of seas with the brisk confidence of one who knew her job. The crew, too busy for fear, struggled to keep her facing into the wind, so she tackled the gale herself, side-stepping waves and then bowing with the grace of a dancer.

Evans, sure of his destiny, remained as nonchalant as the *Gazelle*, even though afternoon had faded into evening. He suspected that Burgoyne had deliberately exaggerated the danger for his own cowardly ends, probably to curry favour with the French Republicans by returning the Empress to the clutches of the revolution for immediate execution. It would be a typically underhand British scheme, from a country that had long since descended to the depths of malevolence, as shown by the inexcusable affairs of both Mullin's Pond and the Emperor's hat, and a spot or two of squally rain was clearly going to be used as a paltry excuse by the perfidious Burgoyne to turn back to the French coast. But Evans was wrong, very wrong.

In the western approaches to the Channel, not far from the Isles of Scilly, another ship was in difficulties that night. A Royal Navy vessel, the *HMS Captain,* overturned at the height of the storm, and sank with the loss of everyone on board, more than five hundred men. For days afterwards, bodies were washed up on Bryher beach: bodies that included the ship's commander, Hugh Talbot Burgoyne.

Secure in the knowledge of his own more successful seamanship throughout the storm, John Burgoyne later spent many enjoyable hours explaining in detail, in great detail, all the mistakes his poor cousin Hugh made on that terrible night: mistakes that could so easily have been avoided, had poor Hugh been foresighted enough to seek the advice of somebody with superior navigational skills and a gallant yacht called the *Gazelle*. No doubt poor Hugh had done his best, and nobody was more devastated by grief than Cousin John, but poor Hugh should not have been quite so dismissive of what he had ridiculed as "toy boats." The *Gazelle* was no toy; the *Gazelle* was a heroine.

Not until well after midnight did the storm begin to subside, when the wind, at last realizing that it was unable to defy destiny, gave up the struggle against Evans, and meekly backed to the west. At six, on the morning of Thursday, September 8th, the *Gazelle* finally anchored off the Isle of Wight, twenty-three hours after leaving France. A cheerful Evans was on deck, chatting to the exhausted crew, and very generously refraining from a smug "I told you so" in the direction of the wilting Burgoyne.

"Sir John, you've redeemed your surname," announced Evans.

"I didn't realize that it needed redemption." However, Burgoyne knew precisely what was about to be discussed, because no American could discover his name without bringing up the topic of Saratoga Springs sooner or later.

"You must have heard of that incompetent General, the one whose name you're unfortunate enough to share, the General who was so roundly trounced by superior American tactics during our celebrated War of Independence."

"Yes, I've heard of him," Burgoyne agreed glumly.

"I guess it's pretty much of an embarrassment for you, being a soldier and all, having to walk around labelled with that name," said Evans, prepared to sympathize, even with a Britisher, after the *Gazelle*'s noble performance.

"Are you going ashore immediately?" asked Burgoyne, to steer the conversation away from any inquiries concerning ancestry. No lieutenant-colonel would care to be reminded of a surrendering forebear, and Burgoyne in particular preferred not to acknowledge his great-great-great-grandfather in front of an American with a grasp of history. "Perhaps you'd like some breakfast before you leave?"

"Oh, I had breakfast hours ago," replied Evans.

They bred their inspectors tough in the Sanitary Service, thought Poldray in awe.

****

At sunrise, the gentle sunrise after a storm, the Empress and Madame Lebreton, both amazed to find themselves still alive, were walking on the jetty at Ryde with Dr Evans.

"If the Imperial dynasty's ever re-established in France, it'll have to manage without me," Eugénie declared. "Never again will I venture out on that dreadful Channel."

"It'd be France's loss, your Majesty," said Evans. He had had little sleep for nights but, on that Isle of Wight morning, was sure that he could have climbed a mountain, had there been one in the vicinity.

"Find me a house in England, Dr Evans," Eugénie

ordered. "As far as I'm concerned, Great Britain's stuck with me, even if I live to be ninety."

Madame Lebreton supposed that she was in exile as well, but nothing seemed to matter very much because she had expected to be lying full fathom five beneath Channel waves that day, not strolling along Ryde pier, and the rest of her existence, long or short, felt like a bonus. Being alive was the important thing; the actual country she chanced to be alive in, a mere detail. The sea air was wonderful. Breathing was wonderful. The pale gold of sunlight flickering on water was wonderful. A gull's flight across the wide expanse of blue sky was wonderful. In fact, the whole of life was wonderful.

Evans led the way off the jetty and across the dawn-deserted road to the tall severity of the Pier Hotel, a fortress designed to vanquish England's climate. "This place might not be what your Majesty's accustomed to," he warned, as they went inside. "A British seaside hotel doesn't usually provide the most luxurious of accommodation."

"After surviving an inn without room service, I'm practically a democrat these days," said Eugénie, pleased to note that the lobby looked clean, with comfortable chairs and potted palms, but even a hovel would have been acceptable to her that morning, as long as it remained firmly rooted on dry land.

Humphrey Hurst had just come on duty at the reception desk. A thin, brown-haired, ambitious young man, he yearned for greater achievement than the life of a mere clerk. One day, a day hopefully in the not too distant future, he would be the hotel's under-manager, and that lofty rank might eventually lead on to the soaring heights of full executive power, should the head-managerial mantle come to rest on his shoulders. Therefore, he had no intention of allowing the hotel's elevated standards to ebb away, and three strangers off the street, with no attentive servants, no heavy luggage, and no fancy carriage equalled no class, and even worse, no money.

"My sisters and I want to book into your hotel for the day," began Evans. "We require your best rooms, a meal and —"

Hurst raised a silencing hand. "One moment, please," he said, knocking on the door of the manager's office behind the reception desk, before gliding inside.

"No luggage, no servants, no carriage," Hurst reported. "He says they're his sisters. They want a room for the day."

"In the Pier Hotel, Ryde? Never!" Horace Grainger had had fifteen hard years of gruelling experience with a public determined to besmirch the proud name of the haughty Pier Hotel and, smooth features as bland as his smooth fair hair, he emerged from the office, with a disdainful manner that was faithfully duplicated by his assistant.

"I'm so sorry," Grainger said, employing his silkiest voice, while he gazed in contempt at the disgraceful trio polluting the lobby. "We're full. Absolutely chock-a-block. Not a room vacant. The season, you know. Please leave at once."

Even brazen depravity did not usually laugh when rejected by the almighty manager of the Pier Hotel, Ryde, but the two women seemed greatly entertained. Rowdy as well as shameless, thought Grainger; he could always spot them. They lowered the tone of the place, just by breathing the hotel's respectable air, and he turned away after a final look of scorn that added to the women's amusement.

"These British!" fumed Evans, as he stamped his way out into the street. "Who does he think he is? Going around with those teeth in his head."

"I must remember my new station in life, and not aspire to stay at the Pier Hotel, Ryde, during the very height of the social season," said Eugénie. "Such delights are too much to hope for now."

"I've a good mind to go back, and inform him exactly who he's just turned away from his wretched establishment, only —"

"Only he wouldn't believe a word you said, Dr Evans," declared Madame Lebreton, still laughing.

"I don't want to stay here anyway," announced Eugénie, "not even to mix with the fashionable set in Ryde. We'll go straight to Hastings. My son could be there already, waiting for me."

"But you need to rest, your Majesty, after such a dreadful voyage. The journey might be too much for —"

"No, Dr Evans. I feel so much better that we can go to Hastings immediately." The ex-Empress of France could be imperial again, because the danger had ended, and therefore Dr Evans was relieved of his command. "Assuming the manager of the Marine Hotel permits me to stay there, of course. After all, the Hastings social season might very well be as exclusive as the one in Ryde."

Evans sighed dolefully, still dismayed by the mundane sound of a meeting place chosen for the French Imperial dynasty's grand reunion. Even the lowliest of manor houses would surely have been a step up from a provincial hotel, should a castle or palace be unobtainable. His wife had imagined ordinary people on ordinary holidays staying there, and Evans mentally added cantankerous invalids in bath chairs, elderly matriarchs, and retired civil servants to their number. Of course, the Emperor was impeccably correct in all his decisions, and if he had decreed that the Marine Hotel should be the Imperial assembly point, Evans would not deny the Marine Hotel its place in history. All the same, a Marine Hotel?

With a quick grasp of the geographic situation, Eugénie realized that she had a choice between enduring another voyage on the high seas or spending the remainder of her days as an Isle of Wight resident, and after a mere five minutes of dithering, she fearlessly agreed to risk her life on salt water once again, and they crossed by the steamer *Princess Alice* to Southsea.

"That's it," declared Eugénie, when she was able to take a renewed interest in living. "I refuse to board another boat ever again, and I doubt that I'll even consent to cross a bridge in future, should there chance to be a river underneath it."

From Southsea, a horse-drawn tramcar would take them to Portsmouth station, and at the tramway terminal, Eugenie found herself waiting in a queue, yet again anonymous amongst a crowd. In France such a lack of recognition hurt; in England, it was fun, and a tramcar even more of a novelty.

"But there are no private compartments."

"No, your Majesty," said Evans. "The passengers all sit together."

"So I see. Who introduces them to each other?"

"Nobody."

"Nobody?"

"It's a very egalitarian mode of transport," explained Madame Lebreton. "No first or second class tickets: everyone equal."

"And Britain isn't even a republic," marvelled Eugénie. "It's certainly been an experience, sharing the privations of the lower members of society. I feel quite intrepid, just like an explorer."

As a reward for an ex-empress's valour, the morning papers at Portsmouth railway station announced the arrival of the Prince Imperial and his tutor at the Marine Hotel, Hastings. At some stage during the fighting at Sedan, the Emperor Napoleon III, with all his usual astuteness, had finally come to the conclusion that he seemed to be losing a war, and as a result of his deliberations, he sent his son via Belgium to England and safety, despite the grave risk to the boy's palate of a diet that might consist primarily of boiled cabbage with watery potato. Eugénie was both delighted and relieved, and so was Evans, because the papers contained other good news. The manager of the Marine Hotel, in several interviews, described his establishment as imposing and luxurious, its spacious rooms and magnificent grounds a popular destination for the aristocracy, both foreign and domestic. His mind at rest, Evans realized how wrong, how very wrong, he had been to doubt, even for a split-second, the Emperor's judgment in such a vital matter.

12

Newhaven harbour front was crowded and windy, autumn showers blown away almost as soon as they began. Evans impatiently scanned passengers leaving the Dieppe ferry, but it took some time before he was able to locate his wife. The war and revolution in France meant that travellers had returned home early, and the more experienced of them hurried to disembark before all the seats in the boat train to London were claimed. Despite her telegram, Evans had started to think that Agnes must have missed the ferry, or perhaps been arrested by one of her detectives smart enough not to believe the story of a day-trip to Dieppe, when he spotted his wife at the top of the gangplank.

"I'm house-hunting," Evans informed Agnes, the moment she stepped onto the dock.

"Already? That's good. Have you found any possibilities?"

"Not so far. The British have no idea how to build houses, and they seem to be under the illusion that they reside in the tropics. Every place I've viewed has been far too cold and draughty for a lady to live in."

"We can't afford to be too choosy," said Mrs Evans, touched by the concern for her comfort. "I don't mind roughing it for a while, so wherever's best for your work is fine by me."

"Oh, not house-hunting for us. I haven't had the time," explained Evans, dismissing such a secondary matter. "The Empress has entrusted me with the task of finding the new Imperial residence: a temporary residence, naturally. As soon as the Emperor offers the Prussians peace terms, the French are bound to regain their sanity and stop all that nonsense about a republic."

"But what are we supposed to do in the meantime? Where

will we live?" demanded Mrs Evans, clutching her hat with one hand as they pushed their way through the crowd. "And where are we going now?"

"To the Marine Hotel, Hastings, of course. The Emperor chose it specially, remember, and the hotel's a popular destination for the European aristocracy. It said so in all the newspapers, after the manager condescended to give an exclusive interview to each of them. There don't seem to be any dukes or lords staying there at present for some reason, but that's unimportant because, as part of the Imperial entourage, we couldn't mingle with ordinary guests anyway. Oh, and we never speak to the press either. Never! When journalists pester you, don't tell them a thing. Simply refer them to me."

Mrs Evans had a horrible vision of herself being trapped inside the Marine Hotel, potted plants and endless cups of tea the only company for a prisoner unable to venture out into the street because of a journalistic phalanx who would charge after her, bellowing questions. Deauville had been bad enough, with those invisible detectives writing descriptions of her in their invisible notebooks, something that had become especially problematic after the first day, forcing Agnes to dither between sticking with her best dress or displaying a lesser variety to prove that she had an extensive wardrobe; but pursuit by reporters would be much worse, as their observations might be printed for everybody to read, not safely locked away in some secret file or other. "Have you had to hide to avoid journalists?" Mrs Evans asked apprehensively.

"Well, not so far," admitted Evans, "but it's bound to happen soon, when they realize who I am and what I've achieved. Though, of course, I'm out house-hunting such a lot that I probably missed them when they called. In fact, I've been so busy, I only found time to treat one patient so far. That was the hotel clerk: the previous hotel clerk, I should say, because he quit his job right after the first appointment with me. Still, there are plenty of other staff members left, and every last one of them with British mouths. A harrowing sight more often than not, but wherever I happen to be, I'm determined to live by the American Constitution: a constitution that guarantees servants the same inalienable right as aristocrats to keep their own teeth."

"It all sounds most democratic, Thomas, but where are we going to live, after you find a house for the Empress?" inquired Mrs Evans, who could be very persistent about unimportant details.

"We'll be somewhere near the Empress, naturally. Where else? How could I trust the Imperial teeth to a British dentist? I shudder in horror at the mere thought. Besides, I gave my word to the Emperor that I'd never desert the Empress, and now I'm solely responsible for the Prince Imperial as well."

"So we'll have to stay in Britain then?"

"Until the triumphant return of the Emperor to the Tuileries Palace."

Mrs Evans sighed, and mentally resigned herself to a lengthy sojourn on British soil. "Will we live in London or on the South Coast?"

"It'd be downright selfish to consider our own problems at a time like this," declared Evans. "Just think what the poor Emperor must be suffering: let down by his army, abandoned by his subjects, and now a prisoner-of-war in Prussia. He's so alone, so isolated, among those Germanic dentists. Dentists! None of them would ever make it through the first semester at Jefferson College, never mind get a Dental Diploma. The minute that the Empress and Prince Imperial are settled in their new residence, wherever it is, I'll leave at

224

once for Wilhelmshohe, to see the Emperor. How he must be missing me!"

"But what about our house?" Yet, even as she spoke, Mrs Evans knew that she had little chance of competing with the Napoleonic teeth.

"First things first," Evans said reprovingly.

****

However, both Empress and Prince Imperial found their teeth quite neglected during the next week, as Dr Evans embarked on a whirlwind tour of house-agents and property viewing. There was no question of buying a house, for naturally the Imperial family would return to the Tuileries Palace, as soon as the French got over their tantrum; therefore, Eugénie's stay in England would perhaps be a matter of weeks only: a few months at the most.

"I must live somewhere within reach of the theatres," the Empress had stipulated, thinking of Mayfair or St. James's and regretting that Queen Victoria did not have a more sympathetic nature. Anybody else would have been only too pleased to offer the use of the conveniently situated Buckingham Palace, but Victoria could be so selfish at times, especially when one considered all those other palaces and castles she could have moved herself into, nicely out of the way. But self, self, self: that was Victoria.

"Within reach of the London theatres," Evans repeated to the house-agents, who promptly assured him that anything south of Staffordshire gave almost instantaneous access to every London theatre without exception. Evans found himself in Devon, Oxfordshire, Rutland, Lincolnshire, Norfolk — but, alas, nothing met his standards for Imperial living. However, to a man of destiny, even house-agents are unnecessary.

"The Emperor stayed, once or twice, at a house called

Camden Place when he was young, and he said that Chislehurst is very handy for London, so you could try looking in Kent," the Empress had remarked, after rejecting an Evans possibility in Torquay. "Surrey or Hampshire might be suitable as well, if there's a railway station close by. You forget how egalitarian I am these days."

That afternoon, Dr and Mrs Evans made an apparently futile venture into Kent where the plumbing, or rather lack of plumbing, appalled the President of the American Sanitary Commission of Paris, who had been astounded to discover that such primitive conditions still existed in the latter part of the scientific nineteenth century.

"These British," Evans was saying as they approached Chislehurst in a cab. "They seem to expect the Empress of France to exist in squalor, absolute squalor! I wouldn't let a dog live in such conditions. I wouldn't let a pig live there. Why, Agnes, I wouldn't even let you live in that house."

To find herself treated with such consideration after so many years of marriage must have moved Mrs Evans deeply, for she spoke somewhat snappishly to control her emotion. "And where will you let me live, Thomas?"

But Evans was not listening. "Stop the cab! Stop at once!" He had a large, Georgian house within his sights, an elegantly graceful house standing in its own grounds, approached by a driveway lined with elms, cedars and beeches. A few minutes, and the Empress could be at Chislehurst station; twenty minutes later, she would arrive at Charing Cross, with all the theatres of London spread out before her. Evans was a rationalist, a man of science as well as destiny, who credited only what he could explain or see, and the plumbing inside the house was still an unknown quantity; even so, he had a distinct premonition of things to come.

"That house is the Empress's new home," Evans announced. After all, he could hire a good plumber, even if one had to be imported from the States, because judging by what he had seen of British houses, there was no such thing as a good plumber anywhere nearer than New York.

"But I don't think the house is to let," objected Mrs Evans, glancing at the name on the wrought iron gates. "Camden Place isn't on the agent's list."

"Camden Place!" gasped Evans. "The Emperor stayed here when he was a young man; the Empress herself mentioned the fact to me this very day. It's a sign, an omen."

"But, Thomas, you don't believe in signs or omens."

A mere detail, and Evans had no time for details at that auspicious moment.

Nathaniel Strode, owner of Camden Place, had just finished his afternoon tea, and was looking forward to a quiet time before dinner, not writing the letters that he ought to write and not reading the books that he ought to read. A pleasant-looking, plump man in his early fifties, with a nature that his mother had described as easy-going, and everybody else in the family called weak, Strode was to regret for many years the day that he agreed to see the President of the American Sanitary Commission; but, as he told anyone who would listen afterwards, he thought his visitor was something to do with the drains.

As Evans rapidly gave the specifics of his assignment, Strode attempted to explain that he had never planned to let his house and that he had no intention of renting it to evicted empresses in the future, because he rather liked his home. However, under cross-examination, he was forced to admit that he did indeed belong to a London club, although Strode protested that he had no particular wish to live there should his house be let to a tenant.

227

"Why pay out good money to belong to a club that you don't like?" demanded Evans.

"But I do like the Garrick."

"Excellent! You'll be perfectly happy there."

"But I don't want to live at the club."

"Then you really ought to think seriously about renting an apartment this fall, perhaps until Christmas," Evans advised, because, as rescuer of empresses, he was not about to be vanquished by one selfish Britisher, intent on remaining in his own home. "London can't compete with Philadelphia, New York and Paris, of course, but I'm sure any city must be livelier than Chislehurst. And it's only for a month or two, three at the most. Look on it as a holiday."

"But I don't want a holiday. Why can't the Empress rent an apartment?"

"She could hardly fit an entire Imperial entourage into an apartment," Evans pointed out, amused. "So it's all agreed? Splendid."

"No, nothing's agreed, and there's ghost, anyway. Three of them, in fact."

"Not in the nineteenth century."

"Nineteenth century or not, they insist on hanging around here. I don't take much notice of spectres myself. Live and let live, that's my motto, but the housekeeper's just left because of them. Apparently it wasn't so much the noise that upset her, as the furniture trundling about the rooms all by itself. She simply couldn't get used to it."

"But no doubt the Empress will. A lady who can tackle a revolution won't be fazed by mere superstition. Please don't hesitate to ask if you need help with your move.

"But I'm not moving anywhere," claimed Strode, still unaware of the force of destiny.

On September 20th, Evans had seen Camden Place. On

September 21st, he had the lease drawn up. On September 22nd, he presented the lease to Strode for signing. On September 23rd, Strode was moved out of the house. On September 24th, Empress Eugénie and the Prince Imperial were moved in. On September 25th, Strode sat in the Garrick Club, still trying to work out what had happened to him.

"Camden Place is adequate, I hope, your Majesty," said Evans, supremely confident that the house undoubtedly was, as he glanced around the large drawing-room, its wood-panelled walls pleasantly reflecting the mellow light from an autumnal garden.

"Quite adequate, thank you, Dr Evans. Almost luxurious in its way," replied Eugénie, agreeably surprised that democracy's limit could be stretched so far. "Only having twenty-three bedrooms is going to mean severe restrictions on the number of house guests I can accommodate, but I'm sure true friends won't mind putting up with such cramped conditions."

"The moment I inspected the plumbing system, your Majesty, I knew that destiny intended Camden Place to be the Imperial residence. Strode seems a fairly enlightened house owner, by British standards. Shame about the murders, of course, but every old house has these little stories, and it was nearly sixty years ago. Footmen are much more dependable now. We hardly ever hear of one bludgeoning his master and mistress to death with a poker these days."

"All the same, I've told Madame Lebreton to be very careful about the servants' references. I know coincidences are scientifically unproven, but that's no reason to take unnecessary chances."

"Very practical, your Majesty." His mind at peace where the Empress was concerned, Evans felt free to worry about

Napoleon again.

"July 27th was the Emperor's last appointment with me: a whole two months ago. Now there are only German so-called dentists to attend his Majesty, and the bitter cold of a Prussian winter ahead for those sensitive teeth."

"You must go to him, Dr Evans," urged Eugénie. "Cancel my appointment. The Prince Imperial wants you to go away as well. He's told me so many times: many, many times. The Emperor's need is greater than ours, and I'd like you to stay with him throughout the winter, throughout the spring — in fact, just stay with him; refuse to leave, whatever he says."

"But I can't desert you so recklessly, your Majesty."

"Indeed you can," declared Eugénie. "I insist you do exactly that."

"Such self-sacrifice," Evans informed Agnes that evening, when he returned to the room that they were renting in Chislehurst. "The Empress insists I go away for an indefinite time, without thought of her own teeth, and just when she most needs all the support she can get, after being forced to take refuge in a strange country, with few friends and even fewer acquaintances."

"Rather like us," Mrs Evans commented frostily. "Except we haven't got a house to live in, just a room, and I expect everything we left in Paris has been blown to bits by now."

"The Empress's situation precisely," agreed Evans. "And think how much more she had to lose. A lucky chance that she sent her jewellery to Britain with Princess Metternich in August."

"And equal luck that she made a couple of hefty deposits in a British bank account at the same time."

"Yes, splendid foresight. The Empress has learnt such a lot from the Emperor."

"At least it means that your salary should be paid."

"The Empress mentioned that very point to me herself, and she assured me I could have all the money I need to get to Prussia, but that's so like her Majesty. She's always thinking of others, and the Prince Imperial's exactly the same. Not fifteen years old, and yet he's prepared, indeed eager, to cancel all his dental appointments so that I'm free to leave the country. People say the modern child's selfish, but he actually suggested that I start for Prussia today rather than wait until tomorrow morning, so keen was he to send me on my way to —"

"Our apartment, Thomas: the one we haven't found. Before you go to Prussia, we must get something a little better than one room."

"Oh, I haven't time to bother about that now, Agnes. You'll find somewhere, I expect. Just make sure it's near the Empress. And I rely on you to telegraph me if any sort of problem arises. You mustn't hesitate; telegraph immediately, and don't try to economize with a few words. I'll want to know every detail of whatever the situation is. You won't forget, Agnes? Every single detail."

"Yes, I'll telegraph if something awful happens," promised Mrs Evans, appeased by his concern. "But don't worry about me. I'll be all right."

"You? Oh yes, of course you'll be fine. I meant telegraph if the Empress or Prince Imperial need me. Should either of them have the slightest toothache, the slightest discomfort, you must telegraph at once, and I'll race back. I'd travel day and night to protect them from British dentists, believe me."

Mrs Evans believed him.

13

To Evans's surprise, the war between France and Prussia still went on. He had been positive that the new Republican Government would crumble before the onslaught as, minus its Emperor, the country was leaderless in Evans's opinion; yet Paris had not surrendered at the first bombardment, and nor had the remnants of the French Army given up the fight.

Napoleon was just as surprised, and considerably annoyed. His capture should have demoralized the entire nation, and they had no right to manage without him, no right whatsoever. After all, he had selflessly seized absolute power on their behalf, and it was no picnic, being Emperor, because Imperial life was one of constant danger. Several times he had nearly tripped over his ceremonial sword, twice the corner of a flag belted him in the eye, and nobody would credit the hours he had put in, posing for portraits; but what did Napoleon get in return? A country that declared itself a republic the very second his back had been turned.

Wilhelmshohe Palace was called, by the Prussians if nobody else, the Versailles of the German States, and Napoleon had been given a luxuriously furnished suite of rooms, decorated with paintings and tapestries, but when one had become accustomed to the run of the Tuileries, to say nothing of the Elysée and St. Cloud, a mere suite was slumming it. And the Prussian King had been so very smug, just because he seemed to have won a war. It was the dregs of Napoleon's life, but he comforted himself with the thought that things could not possibly get any worse. He was wrong.

"Your Majesty!"

"Evans!"

Now he was cracking up under the strain and starting to hallucinate. Napoleon swore that he would cut down on the cigarettes and coffee, eat more vegetables, get some exercise, anything to stop such a horrifying vision from the past haunting his captivity. However, the situation was far worse than Napoleon feared, because he had not gone mad at all. It was no ineffectual *doppelganger*, who rushed into the room, but the real Evans in person.

"There's not the slightest need to worry about your teeth any more, sire. I won't leave your Majesty's side, not if we're held here for years to come, not if we're imprisoned together for decades. We'll never be separated again."

Even a hopelessly defeated Emperor can fight back, if he is desperate enough, and Napoleon rallied forces that he thought had deserted him for good. "Wherever you're staying, it's not here with me. I order you to leave at once."

Despite considering himself the Emperor's closest friend, Evans had not fully realized until then the true depths of generosity to be found in Napoleon's character. "You mean I mustn't neglect my Red Cross duties, while I'm in Prussia? But, sire, I can easily manage to fit them into the odd moments when your Majesty's negotiating the peace treaty with King Wilhelm. There are plenty of prisoner-of-war camps in the vicinity, crammed to the barbed wire fencing with your soldiers. I'll arrange for dental care, toothpowder, warm clothing and food to be sent to them, leaving the rest of my time entirely at your Imperial command."

"Then I command you to go away immediately."

"When I tell the French prisoners how concerned the Emperor is about their teeth, they'll be overcome," declared Evans.

"Yes, go to those French prisoners-of-war." And serve them right as well, thought Napoleon. Incompetent lot. Call themselves soldiers? All they did was lose battle after battle with a lack of care for their sovereign that bordered on treason, and it was pleasant to think that he had such an effective means of revenge. "They've just lost a war, Evans, so now is the time to look to the future, and I insist that their future must include teeth. I rely on you. No matter how much they protest, you must examine each soldier's mouth personally, because the Army dentists just aren't as thorough as you. No, Evans, it must be you who attends those soldiers. Treat them as you've treated me over the years, and I'll be content."

"The very second that my Red Cross work's done, I'll be back," Evans promised, greatly moved.

"No! You must return to the Empress, as soon as possible. I insist." A fine Regent she'd turned out to be, reflected Napoleon; couldn't hang onto Paris for more than five minutes. Eugénie deserved all the wonders of modern dentistry inflicted on her, and at length.

"But her Majesty insists that I stay with you, sire, and so does the Prince Imperial."

"They would! That reminds me, Evans, although I've no idea why it should, there's one thing you could do for me —"

"Yes, your Majesty?" Evans inquired, eager for his instructions as Napoleon paused to search and find the right words.

"There's a child, a boy aged seven, son of a young chambermaid at the Tuileries Palace —"

"Yes, sire?"

"When I heard of the chambermaid's plight, I felt sorry for the unfortunate girl, and so take an interest in her child —"

"Sire, give me the name and address. I'll be a guardian to the boy, and ensure his future by seeing that he has the finest of educations, even to the extent of sending him to Jefferson College should his abilities warrant it. When the newspapers hear of this matter, the whole world will marvel at your Majesty's unbounded charitableness toward a forlorn chambermaid."

"Oh, there's no need to make the details public," Napoleon said hastily.

To be in the presence of such greatness would have humbled Evans, except that he had nothing in his life to be humble about. He parted reluctantly from Napoleon, who bore the separation with a resilience bordering on glee, and then Evans sped to the prisoner-of-war camps, where men, far from home and knowing that their country was being destroyed, found that those painful thoughts evaporated to nothingness, whenever Dr Evans was around to show them what real pain was like.

Yet, even in their agony, the men thought only of comrades, and urged Dr Evans to visit other camps: any other camps. From Emperor to the lowliest private soldier, all shared the same determination that others, not themselves, should be on the receiving end of Dr Evans's skill, proving that Napoleon III, although isolated and under guard, was still able to lead the French Army in spirit.

****

A provisional Government of National Defence was formed in Paris the same day that Léon Gambetta stood on a chair in the Chamber of Deputies and announced the birth of a new republic. The youngest Deputy had even more exciting news to tell his aunt, when he hurried home that night; he had been appointed Minister of the Interior in the Emergency Cabinet, and as the war was quite definitely taking place in the French interior, Gambetta found himself in charge of the day-to-day running of it. There were more guns to find, as well as enough Army recruits to fire them, supplies to be organized, train timetables to co-ordinate, and reproofs to hurl at the head of any unpatriotic bureaucrat who expected to spend the evenings with his family. Inspiring circulars had to be composed about the vital importance of civilian resistance and, as soon as Gambetta's fiery words blazed into print, they were sent post-haste to all Prefects whose Departments unfortunately chanced to be in the direct path of the Prussian advance on Paris. There also a daily refusal to declaim at the Provisional Cabinet, concerning the suggestion that he remove himself and his headquarters to the safety of Tours.

"You're refusing to go?" said Gambetta's aunt, looking at her nephew in astonishment. "For heaven's sake, Léon, why?"

"I have to refuse. I can't possibly leave Paris, just when the Prussians are about to arrive and shell us all to oblivion."

"It seems rather a good time to leave, if you ask me," observed Jenny Messabie, who often thought that Léon, although undoubtedly clever, would have benefited had a little commonsense been added to his many talents. Jenny was in her forties, dark-haired and rake-thin, despite the culinary brilliance that had led to her nephew's ever-increasing portliness. It surprised her family that Jenny remained single, for she was still attractive, an efficient housekeeper, an agreeable companion and, even more importantly, possessed a little money of her own. When she had been younger, proposals of marriage were a regular occurrence, but Jenny was particular, and no offer had come from any man whose conversation she thought she could endure for fifty or so years.

"I can't abandon Paris," declared Gambetta. "I won't abandon Paris. My constituents in Belleville have to stay here. What would they say if I left?"

"That they wished they had the chance to get out as well.

Besides, how will you be able to organize the war effort, now that the city's practically surrounded? The Prussians are sure to cut the telegraph wires, Léon. It's certainly the first thing I'd do, in their place. How are you going to communicate with the Army and the rest of France?"

"Pigeon post?" Gambetta suggested tentatively.

However, the Minister of the Interior was a firm believer in democracy, and democracy prevailed. With all the Cabinet members more afraid of looking like cowards on the run than of Prussian shells, a vote was held to choose the sacrificial victim required to head the Government-in-exile: a doomed martyr, whose post-war political career would probably never recover from the fact that he had done his bit by fleeing to the safe haven of Tours. Because Gambetta was intelligent, young, energetic and popular with the electorate, as well as being a fluent speaker, the other politicians prudently decided to increase their own prospects of Prime Ministerial, or even Presidential, office by dispatching him to the provinces and future obscurity. As far as his colleagues were concerned, Léon Gambetta was to drift skywards to anonymity.

****

It was eleven o'clock on the morning of Friday October 7th 1870, and by the heights of Montmartre, a huge hot-air balloon, striped in pale blue and white, was being inflated above an extremely fragile-looking basket.

"The wind's exactly right," Félix Trichet said cheerfully. He was a young and enthusiastic aeronautist, confident that mankind's future journeys would all take place overhead. In fifty years time, he predicted, air-travel would be regarded a normal part of everyday life, as the skies filled with more and more balloons, just like his. He was very certain and very stout, making Gambetta suspect that, between the two of them, there was not going to be much room to spare inside the diminutive basket. "We'll be in Amiens in no time."

"Amiens!" repeated Gambetta in surprise. "I'm going to Tours."

"Yes, but the wind's going to Amiens, unless it changes its mind, of course. That's part of the fun of ballooning. You never know where you'll end up."

"But I have to end up in Tours."

"You will, I expect: eventually," said Trichet. "You'll probably find a train or something in Amiens, if you're in a hurry."

"I am. I have to save France."

"Then I suppose we'd best start quite soon."

"Very soon, if I'm going to the wrong place," agreed Gambetta, awkwardly clambering into the basket, and realizing that he had been right; there was little space for either of them when forced into such close proximity. "How long will it take us to get to Amiens?"

"Oh, as long as it takes," replied Trichet. "But don't worry; the war isn't going to run away."

"I know," said Gambetta, gloomily reflecting that he would be the one who had run away in the opinion of Parisian voters.

"Good camouflage," commented his aunt, indicating the blue and white stripes of the balloon. "With any luck, the Prussian snipers might mistake you for the sky, so let's hope it doesn't cloud over until you're safely beyond enemy lines. Now, Léon, here are some sandwiches for the journey. Fortunately, I added a few biscuits, as it seems you'll be longer getting to Tours than I anticipated. There's some cheese as well, and several chestnut pastries with fruit —"

"Marvellous!" said Trichet. "I'm starving already, and the siege has only just begun."

238

Mademoiselle Messabie stepped back and waved, as calmly as if her nephew were leaving for an ordinary day in his office, while the balloon left the ground with a lurch, and began to rise above Montmartre, drifting through the cold air toward the Prussian lines. Gambetta clung to the side of the basket, looked down, and then hastily averted his gaze to the tricolour tied to one of the ropes. "What happens if they shoot the balloon?"

"We go down quicker than we came up," said Trichet, laughing merrily. "But it won't happen because we're far too high for their rifles."

A sudden searing pain made Gambetta gasp, and he clutched his left hand to his chest.

"Well, we should be too high for their rifles in a minute," amended Trichet. "Sorry, I forgot to mention keeping away from the edge of the basket, though that was just a lucky shot. He was really aiming at the balloon, not you."

However, the thought failed to encourage Gambetta, as he moodily wrapped his hand in a scarf.

****

Throughout the bitter winter of 1870-1871, Evans pursued the French Army from prisoner-of-war camps to hospitals, with a few battlefield visits along the way, in his determination to fulfil the duty entrusted to him by the Emperor. Coming from a background where glorious tales were still daily told of the handful of farmers and shopkeepers who had defeated the haughty might of Great Britain, Evans began to understand the Republican Government's stubborn insistence on continuing a war that seemed hopeless to most people, and unfortunately those people included General Bourbaki, commander of the Army of the Loire.

Bourbaki was in his mid-fifties, but felt more like a rapidly ageing centenarian, and he could no longer cope with Léon Gambetta's lengthy telegrams from Tours ordering him to march, to challenge, to confront, to attack, to fight and to defeat the Prussians immediately. At Gambetta's age, doubtless one could charge all over the place in balloons and trains, making rousing speeches and dictating the sort of telegrams that Racine might have sent when in particularly loquacious mood, but the novelty of such active service had definitely worn off by Bourbaki's time of life. Gambetta, safely restored to the ground with a war wound that he trusted would leave a dramatic scar, was all aflame with patriotism, and did not appear to understand that lesser men needed regular meals, sleep, warm clothing, waterproof boots, and an adequate supply of ammunition to keep their underlings in the mood to face shells and bullets.

Bourbaki had not realized when he became a General that he would be hungry, frozen to the marrow, forced to continue wearing his summer uniform in winter, and live in an unheated farmhouse in January. He had imagined that life at the top would be akin to retirement with the advantage of full pay, while nothing more strenuous than delivering a few ceremonial toasts at mess dinners would tax his declining years. How could he possibly have foreseen that a war would come along to take all the fun out of military life? And it was definitely not fun to be blamed for everything by everybody. Gambetta blamed him for not defeating the Prussians single-handedly through sheer will-power; the newspapers blamed him for every French casualty, as though he had gone out of his way to shoot each one personally; the railway people blamed him for wrecking their timetables, as he tried to move his Army into position, and his men blamed him for the freezing weather. If one more thing went wrong, Bourbaki told himself, just one more thing, he would simply give up altogether.

"I'm sorry, General, but the work can't be put off," decreed Evans. "I told you last summer that it would have to be done sooner or later, and now I must insist. A few days, no more: a week at the most, and I'll be finished. For the moment, at least. Present pain is future gain, as we say in the States."

"But I've got an army to command. I can't have my mouth rearranged as well," protested Bourbaki. The General felt totally inadequate. He had failed in every conceivable way, and was rightly despised for having let his country down. The additional threat of dental torture had come as the final blow, and Bourbaki knew that it was time to seek an exit strategy. Fresh ammunition supplies were not getting through, and he only had one bullet remaining in his revolver, but one bullet would be enough.

"I'll see you first thing tomorrow," Evans said as he left, his tone clearly indicating that he would tolerate no feeble excuse for non-attendance at their rendezvous. "First thing, General. Don't forget."

Bourbaki sat down at the farmhouse table, wrote a letter of resignation addressed to Gambetta, and then went into the bare room where the glacial cold of the nights had denied him sleep. He perched on the edge of the bed, picked up his revolver, aimed it at his head, and squeezed the trigger. Bourbaki knew that his luck was really out, when he missed the target.

****

By January 1871, the people in besieged Paris were starving, and there was no fuel left in the city. The Republic's Provisional Government knew that the end was near, and sent their Foreign Minister to negotiate an Armistice with the German Chancellor, Otto von Bismarck, who had

241

commandeered the Rothschild estate at Ferrières, just outside Paris. It was all right, as chateaux go, but the Chancellor looked forward to his occupation of the Tuileries Palace, so centrally placed, and convenient for any shops that might remain after the Prussian bombardment of the city. Bismarck was at the high-point of his career and knew it because, only days previously, he had succeeded in achieving his lifelong dream of persuading the lesser German States to unify with Prussia and form the Second Reich, a scheme unopposed by the recruits to his new Germany, after the 1870 example of what the Prussian Army could do to any country it considered an adversary.

Bismarck, every inch the sternly cropped-haired Iron Chancellor, glared at the wilting French Foreign Minister who slunk into the ex-Rothschild dining-room and sat meekly on an ex-Rothschild chair at the far end of the ex-Rothschild table. Behind him stood the rest of the French delegation, their anger and resentment all too apparent.

"These are my demands," announced Bismarck. They were actually Prussia's demands, but it came to the same thing. "All of them quite straightforward. Now that we Prussians have gone to the trouble of liberating Alsace and Lorraine from French occupation, both provinces are to remain part of the new united Germany. You'll pay a war indemnity of fifty million francs, though we'll take it in marks and pfennigs, and until we get our hands on the dosh, the German Army will remain in France, entirely supported by you French, naturally. It's not that I don't trust the new Republic; oh no, don't think that for a moment, but the other German States insist that it's better to be safe than sorry when it comes to cash, and I don't like to upset them, because I consider it my duty to let them feel as though they have a voice in our unified Germany. However, as soon as

France has coughed up, and it shouldn't take you more than ten years or so, I'll reconsider the rôle of the Army of Occupation. As I was saying only the other day to the King— I mean the Kaiser, of course. Such an evocative title Wilhelm's chosen to lead our new Germany. I hear Wagner's thrilled to bits with it. Anyway, as I was saying to the —" Bismarck's chatty reminiscences stopped abruptly, and he stared in astonishment at the French Foreign Minister, who had started to weep uncontrollably.

"You're destroying my country, destroying France, destroying our Republic," he managed to gasp out between his sobs. Jules Favre, the emotional lawyer turned Deputy, had been appointed the equally emotional Minister of Foreign Affairs in the Provisional Government, and sending him to negotiate with the Prussians was the only revenge left to the French. "You're destroying my native land."

"Yes, that's right," agreed Bismarck. "You lost the war," He prided himself on playing by the rules, as long as the rules suited him, and the rules were quite clear. You lose a war, you pay up. No welching. No weeping either.

However, the Minister seemed quite unable to grasp what was expected of him, and went on sobbing, his head in his hands. The French delegation filled the gap with casual conversation amongst themselves, but the Prussians, who had no idea whatsoever of the etiquette involved when a Government official was in floods of tears, merely stood around and looked awkward.

"Well, those are my terms. Take them or leave them," said Bismarck at last. He was not accustomed to being upstaged, and did not care to prolong the experience. "I could always order the Parisian bombardment to start again, if you prefer. Alfred Krupp himself has assured me that we've got no shortages of either armaments or ammunition."

"But you'll destroy my city," wailed Favre.

"Precisely," said Bismarck, pleased to note that the Minister was at last talking sense. "Or you could accept the terms of my Armistice. I leave the choice entirely to you."

"But either way, my country's ruined! Ruined!"

"Good. We've reached agreement on one point. Now we can make some progress," declared Bismarck with satisfaction, but to his bafflement, the Minister reached for yet another handkerchief. "Look, I'm being really lenient here. My wife, my very own wife, urged me to be firm, and slaughter the whole French population right down to the youngest baby. 'That should keep the peace in Europe,' she said. Always so thorough, my wife, so practical, and yet I've decided to be magnanimous, even if it does lead to a certain disharmony in the home."

"But my country!" cried Favre, "My poor, poor country!"

"Poor? Oh yes, almost certainly. But only after the indemnity's been paid in full," Bismarck replied reassuringly.

****

The Armistice was signed in Paris at the end of January 1871, much to the fury of Léon Gambetta in Tours, who informed his colleagues in vehement telegram after telegram that the war had just been on the point of turning in France's favour. Evans was half-way up an Alp in Switzerland at the time, where the remnants of the French Army had retreated in a vain attempt to avoid him, and only the news that Napoleon had been freed by the Germans, and was on his way to England, could persuade the Imperial Dentist that his duty lay elsewhere.

"Your Majesty!" exclaimed Evans, as he hurried into the Camden Place drawing-room. "You should have let me know what was happening, and I could have accompanied you every step of the way from Prussia to Britain. I wouldn't have left your side for a split-second."

"I'm sure you wouldn't have." However, the idea did not rally Napoleon's spirits because, if anything, he looked even more depressed. "But don't let me delay you, Evans. I'm sure the Red Cross can find something or other to keep you occupied."

"The moment General Clinchant saw me coming up the Alp towards him, he insisted that I go to Britain immediately. He said the thought of me, in close attendance on the Emperor, was the only thing that could bring him any comfort, after all your Majesty had done for France. The General also said that if I vowed never to leave the Imperial family again, the entire French Army would rejoice with him, as they pictured me taking scrupulous care of your Majesty's teeth."

The instant he regained power, Napoleon promised himself that Clinchant would be reduced to the ranks, and then shot for treason. "I insist you return at once to Clinchant, Evans, and remain there until you've examined every tooth in his head. Twice."

"But, sire, my Red Cross work's finished, and your soldiers are returning to their homes." Evans paused for effect, happy in the knowledge that he had saved the best news for last. "I'm now free to devote myself entirely to your Imperial Majesty's service."

"But your other patients —" Napoleon protested.

"They can wait. Your Majesty's teeth have priority, so I've decided to clear the next fortnight —"

"Fortnight!" The shock was severe, and Napoleon not a well man.

****

Evans ran into the drawing-room before Eugénie had time

245

to pretend that she was not at home, or to hide the magazine held in her hands. "I cancelled my appointment, Dr Evans. Didn't you get my message? I can't possibly leave the Emperor's side while he's so ill: not even for a single moment."

"As soon as I heard the dreadful news, I rushed here at once. Is his Majesty any better?"

"I believe so. The doctors told me that Napoleon's condition improved a little overnight," reported Eugénie, with a casualness that an outsider might have mistaken for indifference.

"That's wonderful! So there is hope?"

"I suppose so. His heart's very weak, but the doctors seem confident that he'll survive this attack."

"Excellent!"

"However, I still can't possibly see you today," added Eugénie. "My appointment will have to wait: quite a long while, in fact."

"Nothing matters, except that the Emperor's been spared to us. And we can always fit your Majesty's appointment in while he's sleeping. We've much to be thankful for."

"Especially as the attack stopped him talking about Sedan the whole of yesterday. I wouldn't mind if he varied the battlefield occasionally, but it's always Sedan."

"Is the Emperor allowed visitors yet?" Evans asked, hardly daring to hope for such a privilege. "Perhaps I might see his Majesty, just for a few minutes, to remind him of happier days, when he and I were together so often."

"That should take his mind right off Sedan," commented Eugénie.

****

Of course, the whole thing had been Marshal MacMahon's

fault, Napoleon decided. Yes, MacMahon was definitely the one to blame. If he had not been fool enough to get shot at that precise moment, the battle of Sedan might have ended very differently. After all, Napoleon himself had managed to come through the entire war without so much as a scratch, and the least MacMahon could have done was to make a similar effort. But no, the Marshal insisted on lying there, doing absolutely nothing, just because he had a bullet in him. Some people have no consideration for others, and MacMahon failed even to apologize. Not a single word. He just lay there on his back, gasping for breath in that irritatingly theatrical manner, as though his Emperor mattered less than the dust on the ground to him, and apparently not caring a whit that the Imperial dynasty might be about to come to an abrupt end at any second. Totally self-centred, MacMahon. But Napoleon had always had his doubts concerning that particular Marshal. What genuinely loyal Frenchman would go around answering to a surname like MacMahon?

The door opened, and Eugénie, the so-called Regent who had gadded off to the seaside, blithely leaving Paris in the hands of the Republicans, came in. "You have a visitor," she announced cheerfully.

"Your Majesty! I'm rejoiced to see you looking so well. My congratulations on your splendid recovery, sire."

"Evans!" gasped Napoleon. It was the last straw, after a mountain of straws. "No! Not Evans!"

"Indeed it is, and here to assure you, sire, that your teeth will have my constant attention, now that your Majesty's better," declared Evans. "It'll be just like the old days, only this time we can have hours and hours together because there'll be no interruptions, no affairs of state to disturb us, no distractions at all. Day after day, I'll be here from early morning until late in the eve — your Majesty? Is something

247

wrong?"

"He seems to be turning blue," remarked Eugénie.

****

The Emperor's funeral service was held in St. Mary's church, one of the very few Imperial funeral services to take place in Chislehurst, Kent. The venue was only half a mile from Camden Place, but the Empress decided not to attend.

"I'm quite worn out, what with the arrangements and invitations and trying to get hold of some flowers," Eugénie told Evans. "January's the most awkward month for a funeral; rather thoughtless of the Emperor to choose it. And I really must write to Queen Victoria and thank her for the sarcophagus. Such an original Christmas present, and yet, as things turned out, so practical."

"The service might have been too much of an ordeal for your Majesty to bear," said Evans. "The cataclysmic grief would surely have proved overwhelming."

"Possibly, and I still have to decide which jewellery I should be wearing now. I've never liked jet; it always looks so depressing. Anyway, I wouldn't want Victoria to think that I was copying her."

"After such a loss, your Majesty's fortitude is awe-inspiring. The whole world will miss Napoleon III, but we who knew the man can never recover from our grief. The absence of one so kind, so considerate — why, even a lowly servant was not beneath the Emperor's notice. His Majesty had so much concern for the welfare of an unfortunate chambermaid that I was asked to become a guardian to her child."

"Oh yes, Napoleon's son."

"I wasn't referring to the Prince Imperial, your Majesty, but to the plight of a hapless young chambermaid. The boy in question is her son."

"And Napoleon's as well," Eugénie said absently. "I think rubies often look quite mournful, don't you?"

"But the child can't be the Emperor's son," Evans pointed out gently, fearing that sorrow had affected Eugénie's mind. "The boy's half the age of the Prince Imperial."

"French husbands," said Eugénie, with an indifference that startled Evans. "My sister warned me what would happen if I married a Frenchman. Yes, rubies, I think."

Had his source been anybody else, Evans would have dismissed the account of the child's parentage as slander, because he was unable to imagine a man lucky enough to call the beautiful Eugénie his wife being tempted by another woman, even if an unsuspecting Emperor had fallen victim to the wiles of a seductive chambermaid. Nor could Evans imagine Agnes quite so tolerant of an erring husband's foibles. Despite his closeness to the Imperial couple and his years of residence in Europe, it was clear to Evans that he still had much to learn about life.

****

The Prince Imperial, now the Emperor Napoleon IV according to both his mother and Dr Evans, went to the funeral dressed in a Woolwich Military Academy uniform. At his age, it was a brave decision to tackle so unpleasant a duty without his mother's support, but the boy seemed to have an almost reckless courage, for to go to a British Military Academy in the nineteenth century with the surname Bonaparte, and so shortly after his father had led one of the most disastrous campaigns in the history of warfare, showed audacity to the point of foolhardiness.

Eight black horses pulled the carriage containing the coffin on a slow journey from Camden Place to the church, and it would have been such an inconvenient time for the

249

adolescent Pretender to the French Imperial throne to develop toothache that Evans insisted on walking beside the young Napoleon IV in the cortège. Like father, like son: the boy protested, but Evans was firm.

As guardian to the new Emperor's teeth, Evans tried to look to the future on that desolate winter's day, but it seemed as if the best part of his life were over, and although he might not have been the official chief mourner, no one grieved for the late Emperor more sincerely than Evans. It was an elaborate service by Chislehurst standards, but definitely not the State Funeral in Notre Dame Cathedral that Napoleon III had imagined for himself, and there was only an audience of Kentish labourers and servants to gawp at the sight of Bonaparte princes and exiled French courtiers, led by the Imperial Dentist resplendently clad in his gold-embroidered Court uniform, ambling down an English lane in the wake of the black-wreathed carriage.

Throughout the interment, Evans recalled his twenty years at the very centre of European power, the closest friend and adviser of the late Emperor: almost one of the family, Evans told himself. The great adventure of his life, snatching an empress from the clutches of a bloodthirsty mob, also moved further into the past with every hour; but, of course, there would be exciting times ahead, especially on the day when the youthful Napoleon IV returned to France in triumph, with his gleaming mouthful of teeth, to lead the French back to glory, and that hope alone gave Evans courage to face the future on the bleak, cold day of the Chislehurst Imperial funeral, as he stood at the open grave, occasional flakes of snow drifting from a leaden sky onto the black coats of the mourners. It was fortunate that prophesy could not be counted among his many skills, or Evans would have found the day more than he could bear.

14

After the end of the Franco-Prussian War, and when wholesale slaughter had solved the problem of yet more civil insurrection in Paris, Dr and Mrs Evans decided to return to France to see if anything could be salvaged from their old life. Perhaps the two rooms they rented in Chislehurst might expand to include three, or even four, should they recover a few of their former possessions, but hopes were not high, and dashed completely when they arrived in the city that had been home for so many years.

The once bustling Paris they remembered was subdued and seemed almost depopulated, as they walked out of the railway station in the autumn of 1871. The few remaining carriages made their way cautiously around shell craters and the débris of destroyed buildings, while shops, although open for trade, had windows boarded up, awaiting repairs.

"Nobody's done a thing, not a thing, about the damage," said Evans in astonishment. "It's like a ghost town. Why, if we were in the States, the entire city would have been rebuilt by this time. They've had months, and yet they haven't even bothered to clear the rubble from the streets."

"I suppose tidying up might not seem that important, after you've been starved and shelled," suggested Mrs Evans. "Besides, there aren't that many people around to undertake the work. When the Prussians defeat a nation, they appear to do it very emphatically."

"All the same, you'd think someone could have wielded a broom or a shovel at the very least."

Paris needed more than a broom and shovel. The houses left standing were often windowless, and occasionally roofless as well; railway bridges had been reduced to heaps of wood and brick; trees lay on pavements, while telegraph wire draped itself like string around twisted and bent lamp-posts. The aftermath of the Prussian storm was more than just physical damage; the Parisian spirit had been left completely unable to tackle normal life again.

Mrs Evans had written to their servants, hardly expecting a reply from the devastated city because, after the tales of death and destruction that she had read in the British newspapers, it seemed impossible that anyone at all could have survived the bombardment, then the starvation of the siege with its epidemics of cholera and smallpox, before the final brutality of the Commune uprising, when French political extremists went out of their way to kill each other, as though the Prussians had not done a thorough enough job. "But Cook sounded quite cheerful in her letter. Do you suppose that she's gone off her head with the strain? Things can't possibly be fine. Thomas, the poor woman's been starved and shelled into madness; I'm sure of it. She's probably raving by now."

"We'll soon find out," Evans replied grimly. He was ready for any horror, as Jefferson College turned out the complete dentist, and his training had included practical tuition on the various techniques of overpowering people who suddenly become violent.

Their cab reached the corner of the Avenue that Evans was determined to continue calling *de l'Impératrice*, no matter how many times the Republican authorities decreed that it was now named Avenue du Bois de Boulogne, and he sighed nostalgically. "The last time I came around this corner, I was in my carriage with Crane, and had no idea that I was about to find the Empress of France waiting for me inside my house."

"I don't think I can bear to look," said Mrs Evans, preparing herself for the sight of rubble heaps strewn the length of the

252

avenue, while their deranged cook camped out in the shell crater that had once been a garden. "I'd like to remember our home as it was, not as a hole in the ground."

"Nothing can take our memories from us." Evans resolved to accept the house's fate with philosophical detachment, but what he and his wife actually saw was a perfection that seemed to belong to another city entirely, a city that had no connection with the Paris they had just travelled through. A peaceful road stretched before them, not a single tile or brick or tree out of place, each house standing precisely where it had stood before the war. As though sensing the home of a man of destiny, the Prussian shells had had the consideration to fall on lesser streets, and leave everything in the avenue exactly where it was when Evans had departed with the Empress a year earlier. Even the American flag still fluttered contentedly on its pole in the garden.

"But the house is still here!" exclaimed Mrs Evans, as their cab stopped. "Everything's still here. Cook was right."

"We haven't seen the inside yet," Evans reminded his wife.

Miraculously, however, the Franco-Prussian War and the subsequent carnage of the Paris Commune had bypassed the interior, just as deftly as it had the avenue; ornaments were in place, pictures remained on walls, vases held flowers from the garden, the dining-room table stood ready for the next meal, and the drawing-room fire was lit.

"It's as if the ladies and I had only just gone out of the door this minute," said Evans. "I'm astonished!"

But not as astonished as Clothilde the cook. She had failed to appreciate the casual sophistication of American wives, who were apparently undaunted by the knowledge that the moment they were safely out of the way in Deauville, their husbands entertained lady patients overnight, and then went jaunting off with them into the unknown. And people said that French wives were complacent, Clothilde thought in awe.

Not only was the house in perfect order, so too were the stables, complete with the Evans landau and horses, back from their own wartime adventures, as became the carriage and team of a man who had established his place in history.

After Dr Evans and his mysterious party drove off in the newly-hired brougham to their unidentified destination, Célestin, the coachman left behind in Mantes, had done some thinking while the horses rested. He came to the conclusion that he was not all that keen on the idea of rushing back to Paris to be blown to bits by Prussian shells, and as Dr Evans had told him to take his time returning to the city, Célestin very sensibly decided to go the long way home. The diversion took him and the landau to his cousin's house in Tours, where he resolved to give the horses an even longer rest and do a little more thinking until the war situation improved.

Célestin's cousin was the caretaker of an infant school: a school commandeered for use by the Ministry of the Interior, despite the difficulty of persuading grown men to sit on such minute chairs and work at desks that they were unable to force their legs under. After Léon Gambetta had dashingly dropped from the skies above Amiens in his balloon, and then hurried less dramatically by train to Tours, he found a convenient landau complete with horses and driver doing nothing in particular at the school caretaker's lodge, and promptly requisitioned vehicle, animals and human. For the duration of the war, the Imperial Dentist's carriage, which had taken the Empress of France out of Paris to safety, became the carriage of the man who stood on a chair in the Chamber of Deputies and announced that Louis-Napoleon Bonaparte had been deposed as Emperor.

Gambetta ran a twenty-four hour day, tearing out from the infant school to view battlefields, inspect training camps, attend Army recruitment drives, deliver some of his more stirring speeches, and hassle General Bourbaki with demands for greater effort. Dictating lengthy telegrams at furious speed to his assistant *en route*, Gambetta hustled Célestin from place to place, never once doubting his ability to defeat the Prussians through sheer will-power, and giving Célestin the uneasy feeling that Dr Evans had managed to take over another man's identity. He was not the only one who thought so.

"It's odd, but your horses act as though they've known me for years," Gambetta remarked, after receiving a welcome the first time he encountered the Evans equipage. The horses, like the majority of the French nation, had embraced republicanism without a backward glance.

Gambetta was a man who did not forget favours, and he recalled with gratitude the generosity of the American who had so freely donated his carriage and team to the Republican war effort. When he discovered that this American was the same American who had pursued the entire French Army to enforce Red Cross dental care on the soldiers, whether they wanted it or not, Gambetta decided to nominate so democratic a dentist for the Legion of Honour. By that time, Gambetta was barely on speaking terms with his Deputy colleagues, having resigned from the Cabinet in a tantrum when he found out that they had inconsiderately made peace with the Prussians behind his back and were refusing to let him fight his war to the finish; but Dr Evans was obviously a man who felt as strongly about the Republic as Gambetta himself did, and to insist that such a man be honoured would shame the spineless Cabinet, who had caved in to Prussian bullies merely because of a few temporary blips.

"You might be a little less belligerent, Léon, if you'd done some of the starving and freezing that we did in Paris, and been shelled into the bargain," Aunt Jenny suggested.

"I was quite prepared to starve for the Republic," Gambetta declared indignantly. "Although, as things turned out, I didn't actually have to. But it could get quite chilly at times in Touraine, I can tell you. And once, the train I was in had to backtrack because of Prussians on the line."

"Most inconvenient, I'm sure."

"And at least you had decent-sized chairs in Paris. We were more or less on the floor," Gambetta added, eager that his aunt should realize the full extent of his wartime suffering. "You wouldn't believe the chairs in Tours. I can't think how the poor infants manage. I'd have been permanently doubled up like a jack-knife by now, if I hadn't had the American dentist's carriage to escape into, and I'm certain my back won't ever be the same again, although the doctor that Evans recommended is very good. Edward Crane went to Jefferson College as well. It's the American equivalent of the Sorbonne, Evans told me, only with a higher academic standard. Crane worked tirelessly for the French throughout the war, just like Evans. Which is more than can be said for certain members of the Government of National Defence. I've decided to nominate Dr Crane for the Legion of Honour too. Evans said I really ought to."

"Well, it's one way to keep in with both your dentist and doctor," Jenny Messabie commented.

****

As a loyal member of the ex-Imperial Court, Evans felt that he must accept the Republican Government's award. "I'm positive it's what the Emperor would have told me to do," he explained to Mrs Evans. "After all, it's really an honour for Jefferson College dentistry, represented by me, and my duty as an American is to accept. If I refuse, it might damage relations between the States and France, and I don't want to be the cause of a diplomatic incident. It'd distress the President so."

"Which President?" asked Mrs Evans. "Theirs or ours?"

"Both," declared Evans. Besides, life in post-war France was so drab, he felt that a bit of red ribbon would brighten things up nicely. "I've told Crane to accept as well."

Evans took celebrity status in his stride, but Crane had been amazed to find himself fêted in the unaccustomed rôle of official hero, embraced by dignitaries and praised in columns of newsprint. "It's not so much an honour as a mistake," he said after the ceremony, as they lingered in the hallway of the Elysée Palace, once as familiar to Evans as the hallway of his own home.

"What mistake?" asked Evans.

"Well, the Republicans can't possibly know everything that we did during the war; it stands to reason."

"But obviously the Republicans know, because that's why they've let us into the Legion of Honour. The French are very keen on the Red Cross."

"I meant the Empress. I'm sure the Republicans can't know about our part in her escape."

"Of course they do," declared Evans. "It's quite clear that I must have been the person who saved her Majesty from the revolution. Who else would the Empress Eugénie have turned to for help but her Imperial Dentist?"

"And yet the Republican Government's still prepared to give us an award?" Crane looked doubtful, but Evans's rôle as leader was too well-established for any of his opinions to be seriously challenged.

"We saved her Majesty's life, and that's exactly what the Red Cross was founded to do: save lives."

"Well, yes —" Crane agreed, even more doubtfully. "But it was an imperial life we saved, and this is the Republic we saved it from."

"The Red Cross is above politics."

"But politicians aren't."

"That's their problem. This is an excellent start to your career in Paris, Crane, particularly with the ceremony being reported in all the newspapers. You'll have patients hammering on the door to consult you, especially after they read that you graduated from Jefferson College."

"And I thought the French were going to guillotine me," Crane said, marvelling at his change of fortune.

"Nonsense," stated Evans. "I never had the slightest intention of letting anybody guillotine us."

"Well done!" said Gambetta, hurrying up to shake their hands. "We've all been talking about you, and your exceptional achievements."

"Oh, it was no more than any other American dentist or doctor would have done," Evans declared nonchalantly; however, strict truth compelled him to add, "Although fate did select me to be the actual dentist at hand, but of course, I do have the Jefferson College Dental Diploma."

"Ah, yes, that celebrated college," said Gambetta. "American democratic education at its finest, turning out men of culture, wisdom and determination. I hear you even went half-way up the Alps at one point."

"That was some months after we'd crossed North-West France to get to the *Hotel du Casino* in Deauville. My wife always stays there, when she isn't at the Marine Hotel, Hastings, of course: excellent establishments, both of them, with a first-rate clientele."

"Splendid. I must recommend them to my aunt," said Gambetta, who, now that he was in his second year as a Deputy, had sensibly learned to ignore the incomprehensible talk of non-politicians. "To think that we in Paris are lucky enough to have two graduates of the renowned Jefferson College in our midst, and all the advances of modern medical treatment to alleviate our slightest pain. Talking of which, I'm afraid I'll have to cancel my appointment with you, Dr Evans, as I'm going on a speaking tour in the south. And I'm leaving immediately."

It was the last time that Evans would visit the Elysée Palace, and he felt reluctant to walk out of the front door that symbolized the strides he had made for the status of his profession in Europe. The other guests had gone, but Evans delayed his departure until the last possible moment, sharing his memories of the Emperor and Empress with the obliging Crane: memories that were to become an increasingly important element of Evans's future.

****

After the glorious days of Imperial society were snatched from him, Evans felt that life had turned to dust and ashes. The extraordinary dentist, now forced to live among ordinary people, found his weeks drab, and not just professionally. Domesticity had become predictably and monotonously dull because of a problem that would not go away: Agnes. Still attractive, with teeth that were a glowing tribute to her husband's skill, Agnes was a thrifty housekeeper who had offered loyal support, even during the dark days of the tradesman's entrance; she was also a welcoming hostess, a spirited champion of causes and an enthusiastic charity worker. In only one area could Agnes be faulted: no Evans heir. When history books were written about the Second French Empire and the giant strides made by nineteenth century dentistry, the name of Thomas W Evans was going to live on, but in the physical world, there would be no proud descendants to carry on his mission to humanity. Agnes had failed him, although not a single reproach ever escaped Evans's teeth, but she should have realized without being told that people who shirked their duty could no longer be respected.

A surplus nephew was dispatched from Philadelphia to Paris by an elder brother, in the hope that the young man would prove a suitable partner in, and eventual inheritor of, the lucrative dental practice; but most unfortunately, John was prone to levity, and inclined to tease patients who were already at a particularly low ebb and not altogether in the mood for jokes. Agnes had laughed merrily at the tale of the banker's wallet and the pliers, and she urged Thomas not to return a disinherited John, but Evans remained sternly tight-lipped. Agnes's acceptance of people as they were, and not as her husband would prefer them to be, had started to annoy Evans, and he was not the dentist to lower his standards, even when the magic had gone from life and there seemed no alternative to the drearily mundane existence ahead of him, while he waited for a chambermaid's son to grow up and take an interest in teeth.

Then a possible solace presented itself, or rather herself, one evening at the theatre. A pretty actress in her early twenties, auburn hair like the Empress Eugénie, beautiful teeth like the Empress Eugénie, spectacular figure like the Empress Eugénie, but unlike the Empress Eugénie, Marie Laurent was accessible to Evans. The Emperor had blazed a trail with his chambermaid, and the temptation to follow the Imperial track overwhelmed Evans. Paris won and

Philadelphia lost, as his once strict Puritanism wavered feebly and then departed forever, when Marie Laurent chose to smile at him. He sent her flowers, he sent her jewellery, he became her dentist, and she became his mistress. An impoverished, unprotected actress was prepared to do a lot for free dental care, and the wild oats that Evans had never sown as a young man flourished into a luxuriant harvest on the afternoon of his fiftieth birthday, after which Marie announced that she would change her name to Méry in honour of Evans's American pronunciation.

It was not the first time that Méry Laurent had changed her name. At the age of fifteen, Anne-Rose Louviot married a young shopkeeper called Jean-Gabriel Laurent in their home town of Nancy, but the excitement of romance died abruptly in the reality of provincial trade, especially after her husband made the mistake of being declared bankrupt, and the bride fled to Paris, where Anne-Rose became Marie and made her stage début aged sixteen. It was a short career that owed everything to beauty and nothing to thespian skill, but Méry's looks enabled her to branch out as an artist's model: the auburn-haired woman in so many of Edouard Manet's paintings. She might not have been a hundred per cent faithful to Evans, but as he was no longer a hundred per cent faithful to Agnes, he had little right to complain, especially as Méry herself was a substitute: the closest he would ever get to seducing Eugénie. Evans could pretend to be unaware of Méry's infidelities and she could have some security in her life. It seemed a fair exchange.

****

"I'm so thankful that I was able to be with the Emperor at the end," Evans told his wife yet again, as they ate breakfast one morning. "My name was the very last word he ever uttered, and it's such a consolation to know that I made his final moments on earth such happy ones."

"He knew that you'd never leave him," said Mrs Evans. "He was certain you'd be right there with him, no matter what."

"Yes, he knew that nothing but death could separate us," agreed Evans, but then he sighed. "How can the Empress go on now? Not only the Emperor dead, but their son as well. My only comfort is that they both took their own teeth to the grave with them."

"Eugénie's got plenty of courage."

"She's astonishing!" declared Evans. "Why, after the Emperor died, she seemed positively cheerful: out to dinner and the theatre in no time."

"Yes, she bore her grief remarkably well. Everybody commented on her fortitude. I've heard that Queen Victoria got a bit annoyed, and took it as personal criticism."

"But the loss of an only child will test Eugénie's courage severely." Evans sighed again, before anger took over: the futile anger that demanded reasons for a meaningless death. "What right did the British have to let the boy go to Africa and face the Zulus alone?"

"Not exactly alone. He did have a whole army with him." Mrs Evans still persisted in being fair, even to the British, and it was another trait that had long irritated her husband, especially as Méry Laurent went out of her way to agree with whatever opinion he chose to air.

"What use was that Army when he got ambushed? The British just galloped off to save themselves. Not a single one of them had enough fellow-feeling to fall off his horse, the way the young Emperor did, and be slaughtered alongside him."

"Well, at least they went back for the body, though I

suppose that was leaving it a bit late."

"Don't even try to excuse their selfishness."

The ex-Empress Eugénie had been persuaded by her son, after months of pleading, to allow him to go on a visit to Africa as an observer of the Zulu War, in which his companions from the Woolwich Military Academy were serving. Thrown from his horse during an ambush, the young Bonaparte had the distinction of being the first Napoleon to die in a war, albeit a war in which he was not a combatant; but the pointless death of the young Emperor-in-exile was also the death of Dr Evans's brilliant future, and he had difficulty in coping with the end of a magnificent dream.

"They were always jealous of the Prince Imperial; the whole British nation was bright green with envy," Evans continued bitterly. "Look at Queen Victoria's useless son. I'm told he cracks walnut shells open with his teeth, when he isn't crunching barley-sugar and chocolate caramels. He won't have a tooth in his head by the time he's forty. What sort of a king will he make then?"

"The British don't appear too concerned with the sort of monarchs they have, so I shouldn't think a toothless sovereign will faze them. Their kings don't even have to be British, and often they're completely mad as well."

Evans gave another sigh, and wearily stood up. "It's time I left to see my next patient, I suppose. An abscess to be drained, but my heart just won't be in it today."

There was no denying the reality; mouths came and mouths went, but even the most intriguing sight within could not compete with past glories. Evans often shared reminiscences with Edward Crane, and one summer they took a slow carriage journey together over the one-time escape route, to remind Evans of minor details for the memoirs that he knew the world expected from him, yet his present could not compete with his past. There was still the Empress Eugénie, of course; there would always be the Empress Eugénie, but the days of palaces and courtiers had gone, and it was fortunate that Evans should be such a staunch democrat, because he would have to make do with a distinctly bourgeois dental practice from then on.

Evans's life became divided between his patients in Paris and Eugénie at Chislehurst, she of course having priority, even over the fascinating Méry Laurent. Whenever Madame Lebreton, the Empress and Evans were together, poor General Lebreton never had a hope of relating his own war experiences, because he was doomed to near-silence as long as the Evans visit lasted.

"Do you remember the fearsome mob at Evreux?"

"What about that green and yellow carriage with the fly-by-night whiffletree?"

"And that dreadful Channel crossing!"

As a General, dramatically handsome in his Imperial uniform among drabber civilians, Lebreton was unfamiliar with the rôle of listener, and inclined to assume that his opinion was essential to the liveliness of any conversation, but the other three had a tendency to forget his presence altogether with their interminable "Do you remember—?" He might be in charge of the Imperial household at Chislehurst, but even Lebreton was unable to keep the talk flowing along in respectful military fashion, with the order of precedence clearly defined, and occasionally he had the disturbing impression that his dentist regarded him, in a kindly but patronizing way, as an outsider.

The Empress was not as fortunate as Evans, because she could never return to her former home whatever happened. The Tuileries Palace, untouched by the Prussian bombardment, had been burnt to a shell only a few months after the war by the French themselves, as they attempted yet another revolution through sheer force of habit, when the radicals of the Paris Commune had made a vain attempt to seize control of the city from the Republican Government; and so Eugénie remained at Camden Place, and Nathaniel Strode, the owner of the house, remained at the Garrick Club in London. Not until eleven years later, after the Prince Imperial's death, did the ex-Empress accept that she was never going to return to France, and finally bought herself an English home: the Farnborough Hill estate in Hampshire.

Evans sometimes felt that his life had become little more than an aftermath, even though he was still one of the most advanced and daring thinkers in his profession, as he frequently assured himself; but without the radiance of the Imperial Court and the challenge of the Emperor's teeth, France would stay dull and everyday to him, despite the charms of Méry Laurent. The great days, the golden days, were over even before Kent's County Coroner had asked Evans to identify, from dental records, the returned body of the Zulu-ambushed Napoleon IV. Ordinary men with ordinary mouths held power, and no worthy Bonaparte successor arose to challenge the mediocrity and restore Evans to his rightful place. Yet, when the Imperial Dentist reflected on his life of success and achievement, he found it impossible to remain utterly despondent for long. He was one of the men who had made a place for themselves in history, and he knew that when nineteenth century France was mentioned, his name would live on — Dr Thomas Wiltberger Evans, the man who had rescued an empress from riot and revolution, and perhaps saved the French people from committing a terrible act of brutality. Nothing could take that away from him.

Years earlier, when a very young man in Philadelphia,

Evans visited a house that, being an American, he thought of as old, because it had been built more than half a century earlier, not long after the War of Independence. The people who lived in the house, he had forgotten; the reason he went there also escaped his memory, but he clearly recalled the garden, where an urn-shaped white sundial stood on a square block of granite that had a couplet attributed to Dryden carved around its base.

Not heaven itself upon the past has power;

But what has been has been, and I have had my hour.

Those words stayed in his mind, unlike the people of the house, almost as if Evans had realized that the lines would one day become important to him; almost as if, when he wrote them, the poet must somehow have had foreknowledge of the triumphs of the Dentist Imperial. For Evans knew that he was one of the men celebrated by poets, one of the men who changed history, one of the men whose deeds would be admired for centuries to come. The hour of the American Dentist had been an hour of glory, and that glory was destined to make him immortal.

References

The Memoirs of Dr Thomas W Evans — Recollections of the Second French Empire
edited by Dr Edward A Crane.
Fisher Unwin. London 1906

The Life of the Empress Eugénie. Robert Sencourt
Ernest Benn Ltd. London 1931

Gambetta and the Foundation of the Third Republic. Harold Stannard M.A.
Methuen & Co. Ltd. London 1921

The Fall of Paris — The Siege and the Commune 1870-1.
Alistair Horne
Macmillan and Co. Ltd. London 1965

Paris, Ses organes, Ses Fonctions Et Ses Vie. Maxime du Camp.
Hachette et Cie. Paris 1875.

Le Second Empire. Armand Dayot.
Flammarion. Paris. 1900.

Le Second Empire. Octave Aubry.
Librairie Artheme Fayard. Paris. 1938.

Napoleon III. J F McMillan.
Longman. London. 1991.

Napoleon III A Life. Fenton Bresler.
Carroll & Graf Publishers. 1999.

XIXe Siècle. Albert Malet. Pierre Grillet.
Hachette et Cie. Paris. 1917.

The Franco-Prussian War. Michael Howard.
Rupert Hart-Davies Ltd. 1961.

Battle Cry Of Freedom The Civil War Era. James M
McPherson
Penguin. 2001.

American Colonies. Alan Taylor
Allen Lane The Penguin Press 2001

Edouard Manet Rebel In A Frock Coat. Beth Archer
Brombert.
University of Chicago. 1997.

Women And Children Last. Alexander Crosby Brown.
The Anthoenson Press. 1954.

Life and Letters of George Perkins Marsh. Volume 1.
Caroline Crane Marsh.
C. Scribner & Sons. 1888.